ASAO MONOGRAPH SERIES

Clowning
AS CRITICAL PRACTICE

Performance Humor in the South Pacific

William E. Mitchell, Editor

8/27/5
For Bill & Beverly —
Some exotic clowning — while not always conventionally funny, may intellectually amuse you —
Bill

UNIVERSITY OF PITTSBURGH PRESS
Pittsburgh and London

ASAO Monograph No. 13
Published by the University of Pittsburgh Press, Pittsburgh, Pa. 15260
Copyright © 1992, Association for Social Anthropology in Oceania
All rights reserved
Eurospan, London
Manufactured in the United States of America
Printed on acid-free paper

Clowning as critical practice : performance humor in the South Pacific
  / William E. Mitchell, editor.
      p.   cm. — (An Association for Social Anthropology in Oceania
  monograph ; no. 13)
    Includes bibliographical references and index.
    ISBN 0-8229-3734-4. — ISBN 0-8229-5487-7 (pbk.)
    1. Papuans—Humor. 2. Clowning—Papua New Guinea. 3. Philosophy,
  Papuan. 4. Sex role—Papua New Guinea. 5. Papuans—Social
  conditions. 6. Papua New Guinea—Social life and customs.
  I. Mitchell, William E.   II. Series: ASAO monograph ; no. 13.
  DU740.42.C595   1992
  306.4'81—dc20   92-50195
                                                                       CIP

A CIP catalogue record for this book is available from the British Library

Contents

Preface   vii

Introduction: Mother Folly in the Islands   3
William E. Mitchell

"Dance When I Die!": Context and Role in the
Clowning of Murik Women   58
Kathleen Barlow

Exaggeration and Reversal: Clowning Among the Lusi-Kaliai   88
David R. Counts and Dorothy A. Counts

Clowning with Food: Mortuary Humor and Social
Reproduction Among the North Mekeo   104
Mark S. Mosko

Reflections of an Anthropologist Who Mistook Her
Husband for a Yam: Female Comedy on Tubetube   130
Martha Macintyre

Horrific Humor and Festal Farce: Carnival
Clowning in Wape Society   145
William E. Mitchell

When She Reigns Supreme: Clowning and
Culture in Rotuman Weddings   167
Vilsoni Hereniko

Where the Spirits Laugh Last: Comic Theater in Samoa   192
Caroline Sinavaiana

Notes on Contributors   220
Index   223

CULTURE INDEX

1 WAPE
2 MURIK
3 NORTH MEKEO
4 LUSI-KALIAI
5 TUBETUBE
6 ROTUMA
7 SAMOA

CULTURE LOCATOR MAP

Preface

As a child, I was frightened of circus clowns. I still am. But my deepest response towards them is envy. Their license to break the rules, to behave outrageously, to mock others, and to be vain or vulgar without shame, still captivates me. A man raised in the midwestern Bible Belt has a special reason to be jealous of clowns.

When I went to Papua New Guinea to do fieldwork in the Torricelli mountains, clowns were the farthest thing from my mind. However, while still a newcomer to Wape society, I attended a large curing festival where I witnessed performances I could only call clowning. I was intrigued and puzzled. Types of behavior one takes for granted at home can become startlingly strange in an exotic setting. On returning home, I was convinced that other Oceania ethnographers like myself had clowning data they might be encouraged to examine. At the 1988 and 1989 annual meetings of the Association for Social Anthropology in Oceania, a small group of us prepared papers on clowning in South Pacific island societies where we had fieldwork experience. We revised these papers in light of our discussions, and this volume is the result of our efforts.

Contemporary humanists and social and behavioral scientists who write about humor and clowning generally bypass the few scattered references to South Pacific clowns. A primary intent of the group's work was to assemble new data on South Pacific clowning in the hope that, by calling attention to the region's clowning traditions, we might bring these into the mainstream of the world's clowning and humor literature. As these papers show, circus clowns and the Pueblo Indians do not have a corner on humorous antics. By focusing on the practice of clowning in the South Pacific, this volume reveals new dimensions of clowning and offers to Oceania specialists new cultural perspectives on the region.

While editing these papers for publication, I began to explore the myriad problems they generated in my own thoughts about clowning and the anthropological enterprise. The introduction for the book that emerged from my reading and musings is a wide-ranging review of some of the intellectual traditions and theoretical problems related to humor in which clowning is historically ensconced. In this review I take a variety of intellectual stances, including, for example, a universal approach to locate the "essence of humor," and a relativistic stance to appreciate the "aesthetics of a joke." In writing the introduction, the innovative work of anthropologists Edwin Bruner, Don Handelman, and Victor Turner, sociologist Anton Zijderveld, philosopher John Morreall, and psychologist Paul McGhee especially stimulated my thinking.

Because clowning is not a serious concern to most anthropologists, I have tried to show the methodological importance of studying clowns. As the title of the book indicates, clowning is a *critical* practice; critical both in the sense of its censorious pronouncements about others and in the sense of its ability to initiate change at a decisive juncture in human affairs. In either case, the work of the clown is avowedly political. The clown is passionately opinionated about the human condition and, via parody and burlesque, breaks the frames of proper behavior to instruct, criticize, and transform. Whether the clowning performance is a critique of others' actions, appearances, and beliefs or is initiated to effect a cultural transformation, the clown is a political force who commands recognition.

The term *performance humor* locates clowning as purposeful histrionic action to elicit laughter. While speech plays a strategic role in some forms of clowning, it usually does not dominate, as it does in more linguistically oriented forms of humor such as telling jokes and witty repartee. In clowning, it is behavioral absurdity, often broad and exaggerated, that generates the laughter.

These essays on clowning cover five Melanesian societies of Papua New Guinea: the North Mekeo (Gulf Province), Tubetube islanders (Milne Bay Province), the Lusi-Kaliai (West New Britain Province), the Murik Lakes people (East Sepik Province), and the Wape (Sandaun Province); and two Polynesian societies: Samoa and the Rotuman islanders of Fiji. Each chapter treats a single society, with a focus on specific aspects of clowning; none pretends to be definitive in locating a society's clowning forms. Regardless of the authors' individual theoretical perspectives, they are agreed that

Preface

clowning is never simply comic relief, a superficial explanation that Handelman (1981:367) noted "may well be the most shallow way of approaching this subject, not only culturally but also cognitively." The essays here amply demonstrate that Oceania clowning is a profound and complex phenomenon.

Like most human practices, clowning is embedded in a thick cultural matrix. Multiple factors like gender, cultural setting, age, kinship, and intentionality, among others, shape a personal view of what is funny. Consequently, a clowning performance may be reacted to differently by various observers. What may appear funny to one observer may appear inane, threatening, or cruel to another. As Lee Siegel (1987:251) has noted in his study of the comic in Sanskrit literature, "Folly is relative." What is funny in Peoria may not get a laugh in Talahassee. The problem of appreciating a particular humorous event in Oceania may become even more problematical when the cultural backgrounds of performers and their audience are drastically dissimilar. Indeed, some of the contributors did not always appreciate the indigenous humor in the clowning they witnessed.

A related caveat is that, although the book is about clowning, this is not a humorous book. These essays were not written with the intent to be amusing or to entertain any more than a collection of anthropological papers on cross-cousin marriage or gender antagonism would be. Our concern is a scholarly one: to provide a descriptive analysis of the practice of clowning in societies we have studied firsthand.

The volume's international group of contributors—Kathleen Barlow, David and Dorothy Counts, Vilsoni Hereniko, Martha Macintyre, Mark Mosko, and Caroline Sinavaiana—hail variously from Australia, Canada, Fiji, Samoa, and the United States. I wish to thank each of them for their good humor and excellent cooperation throughout this project. The editorial committee of the Association for Social Anthropology in Oceania Monograph Series, Lamont Lindstrom, Joycelyn Linnekin, and Nancy McDowell, as well as a University of Pittsburgh Press anonymous reviewer, read the entire manuscript and offered thoughtful comments. I am grateful to Thomas O. Beidelman, Gillian Feeley-Harnick, and Rena Lederman for their helpful comments on the introduction and to Annette B. Weiner, who discussed her comments with me on numerous drafts. Others who offered assistance in a variety of ways include Robert Gordon, William Haviland, Geoff Mandel, Marjory Power,

Rosita Rios, David Rodgers, Richard Scaglion, and Andrew Strathern. The book was copy-edited by Ms. Jane McGarry and Ms. Kathy McLaughlin supervised its overall editing and production. To all of the above, I extend my thanks for their expertise, encouragement, and generous support.

This book is dedicated to the clowns who appear within its pages. Their antics, sometimes with shocking intensity, forced each of us to confront the cultural significance of humor in the study and representation of island life.

William E. Mitchell

Clowning
AS CRITICAL PRACTICE

INTRODUCTION:
MOTHER FOLLY IN THE ISLANDS
William E. Mitchell

> All the acts of the drama of world history were performed before a chorus of the laughing people. Without hearing this chorus we cannot understand the drama as a whole.
> *Mikhail Bakhtin,* Rabelais and His World

> Haven't you ever heard the healing power of laughter?
> *Jack Nicholson as the Joker in* Batman

THE SEPIK RIVER, one must admit, is an extravagant place. The mosquitoes are ubiquitous and voracious, the great houses and ceremonial masks are artistically magnificent, and the ritual clowning performances are as outrageous as any in the world. As a graduate student I read Bateson's account of the Iatmul mother's brothers' *naven* clowning, which honors an achievement by their sister's child. Costumed in tattered and dirty women's dress, the men, now "mothers," hobbled decrepitly about the village using canoe paddles for canes, stumbled and fell, and then "demonstrated their femaleness by assuming on the ground grotesque attitudes with their legs widespread." The village children responded to this ribald performance "with screams of laughter," and I had gained an unforgettable image of a ritual farce that is both deeply serious and deeply funny (Bateson 1958:12). Such contradictory juxtapositions of humor and gravity (cf. Handelman 1981:366) — silliness, if you will, in the service of serious ends — is characteristic of ritual clowning. As Steward (1931:198) notes in his pioneering paper on the ceremonial buffoon, "the clown is seldom purely a comedian."

When I went to the sprawling Sepik Basin for my own fieldwork, I settled with the Wape in the Torricelli foothills and discovered they too had occasions for clowning that, while different from

3

the Iatmul, were vivid in practice and ethnographically challenging. The other contributors to this book on clowning performances also were challenged and intrigued by the *humor*—a term I gloss for all that is comical and funny—of their South Pacific hosts.[1] Using fieldwork data from the islands of New Guinea, Tubetube, New Britain, Rotuma, and Samoa, they have written essays, the first to be collected together on Oceanic humor, that convey the breadth and intensity, and the pathos and joy, of the laughter they have heard.

Historically, the anthropological study of clowning is almost exclusively devoted to the study of the *sacred* ritual clown. But the essays in this volume also present data on clowning in other socially significant contexts such as, secular ritual performances, theatrical performances, and the spontaneous high jinks of just horsing around. This augmentation in the practice of clowning pushes us beyond the narrow literature of the sacred ritual clown to examine clowning within a larger intellectual arena that, in turn, suggests new questions of historical and theoretical importance, not the least of which is the place of clowning in gender studies and political practice. If by rummaging in Mother Folly's comedic grab bag I seem at times to stray far from the South Pacific, my intent is to expand the conventional anthropological approach to clowning so as to understand better the practice of clowning in Oceania as it informs these chapters.[2]

This will necessitate a critical examination of the phenomena of humor and laughter—issues of great antiquity in Western thought—in which clowning is embedded. A related task is to explore the controversial nature of contemporary anthropology, including the postmodern stance, as it impacts the study of humor generally and of clowning more specifically. My goal, then, is to situate the practice of clowning—which is but one, representational type of humor—within an expanded intellectual and historical frame. This enables me to comment on the cultural construction of folly, to confront the nature of humor itself and the various approaches to its study in anthropology and the other social sciences and humanities, and to locate as practice the forms of Oceanic clowning presented in these chapters. By viewing the clown within this enlarged arena of contrasting ideas, the performances of Oceanic clowns presented in these pages also assume deeper meanings with theoretical relevance to the areas of play, ritual, performance, emotion, and gender.

Of special import for a theory of clowning practice is the

Introduction

potential of clowning as a political act. Playing the fool to comment critically on life, the clown interrupts social discourse with a performance that may range from gentle chiding to cold ridicule. As these essays demonstrate, clowning thrives as a multivariant form of political intervention.

Taking Humor Seriously

A human baby, from its very first breath, can cry. Our capacity to express pain precedes that for pleasure; only later can we smile and, even later, laugh. This gift for laughter, this sometime ability to circumvent the tragedies of life and perceive and appreciate nonsense in a cognitive world culturally constructed on sense and reason, is one of the greatest rewards for being human. To chuckle, to chortle, to titter, to snigger, to giggle, to guffaw, is to be exuberantly alive and human.[3] While other primate species also are said to laugh, none do it as often, as contagiously, and in such rapacious variety as the human species.[4] We are truly the laughing animal — *homo ridens*.

Not all laughter, however, is a response to humor. It also may be induced by tickling, hysteria, the disease *kuru*, or drugs like cannabis and nitrous oxide. The polite, ingratiating laughter of strangers being introduced to one another is not humorous, nor is much of the laughter of preschool children's play groups.[5] As a physical activity, the eruptive, jerky, generally inchoate, and sometimes uncontrollable nature of laughter is, except for crying and sexual orgasm, quite unlike any other human behavior.[6] Just how and when one laughs is partially shaped by situation, culture, class, personality, and gender. For a few, however, laughter — any laughter — is decidedly vulgar and base. Lord Chesterfield, although a noted wit, could proudly write his son that "since I had full use of my reason, nobody has ever heard me laugh," adding that laughter is excited by "low buffoonery" and that "people of sense and breeding" should show themselves above this form of merriment (1901: 57–58).

One of the ironies of humor is that to appreciate something as purposeless as nonsense and silliness, it takes a creature of marked cognitive complexity who can recognize differences in classes of objects and actions. Without the sophisticated sense of rational order that humans alone possess, it is impossible to perceive the kinds of disorder and incongruity we identify as humorous. These ideas of order and classification are encoded in language and speech. It is not until toddlers can classify things that they are able to create their own verbal humor, by, for example, misnaming objects and events or, (once they learn the differences between naughty and nice and clean and dirty) flaunting taboo words and actions, which American parents and teachers call bathroom humor.

Anthropology prides itself on being the most inclusive science inquiring into the nature of human existence. In spite of Malinowski's (1966:vii) jocular remark that "anthropology is the science of the sense of humor," a recent cross-cultural study of humor notes that field-workers seldom consider humor a "central subject of study" (Alford 1981:151). Neither Malinowski nor most other anthropologists have treated humor and comedy as a privileged area of inquiry and theory. Only two general books on humor, Piddington's (1933) and Apte's (1985) — with a 50-year gap between them — have been written by anthropologists.[7] In many ethnographic accounts, humorous acts are completely ignored, or, when they do appear, it is as an epiphenomenon in a passing reference.

It is not, however, that the field-worker is blind to the comedic or is primarily interested in the tragic and violent aspects of human existence; more than any other scientific discipline, anthropology examines in detail the commonplace actions of everyday life. The quotidian experience is the stuff of ethnography that fills fieldworkers' notebooks. But where in their publications is the horseplay, the clowning, the fun so inherent in the human condition? Are people really as humorless as their ethnographers' portray them? While many anthropologists have a delightful sense of the ridiculous — a fact deftly revealed in their autobiographical accounts about *doing* fieldwork — it is ironic that they "have generally ignored the topic of humor in their research" (Apte 1985:9).[8] The problem is not so much that a people's comic interludes and what they mean are deliberately screened from entering the notebook, but that in the act of writing ethnography the fun is generally left out.

There are several reasons for the neglect of the comedic in most ethnographic writing. Science is serious; it studies serious phenomena in a serious way. While the arts can be playful, science is not. At least this is the stereotypical view of the scientific enterprise shared by most scientists and by the public. Anthropology, as a fledgling nineteenth-century discipline, modeled itself on the prestigious natural sciences by adopting a positivist approach. Anthropology was, first, naturalistic and descriptive; then, in the twentieth-century as data accumulated and a more varied sense of problems evolved, it took a functionalist stance.

But whether the anthropologist simply described a society or attempted to show how it functioned, the invented organizing rubrics—kinship, politics, religion, subsistence, and so on—did not include humor as a category that stood alone. With few exceptions (for example, Hill's interesting 1943 paper on Navaho humor), humor and comedy were taken seriously only when they fell under one of the major rubrics for constructing ethnographic representation. Early descriptions of the scatological antics of Zuni Indian clowns (e.g., Fewkes 1891; Stevenson 1904) were reported as religious ritual because of the clowns' ceremonial status. Also, without the functionalists' abiding interest in kinship and social structure, the vast literature on joking relationships pioneered by Radcliffe-Brown (1940) and others never would have existed.

While anthropology generally has not found humor, in and of itself, to be a riveting area of inquiry, other fields have been more appreciative of its intrinsic importance in human affairs. Philosophy's interest, because of its own antiquity and concern with all things human, is particularly ancient. Its historic concern is with the phenomenological identification of the essential nature or essence of humor. Plato, Aristotle, Hobbes, Schopenhauer, and Bergson, among others, have written critically and influentially on humor and laughter.

The field of literary criticism has created an even larger literature on the comedic, with a special interest in analyzing the genres of tragedy and comedy as related, but essentially different, ways of dramatizing the human experience. Although anthropologists have hesitated to examine humor cross-culturally, the novelist and critic Meredith (1906) undauntingly compares the sense of comedy in several different European countries. Literary critics, however, have been intrigued with distinguishing forms of humor, including, for example, parody, farce, burlesque, irony, satire, and caricature, and their exegeses on these topics are immense.[9]

Psychoanalysis, a much more recent field of inquiry, has treated humor with utmost seriousness from the beginning. With its binary focus on the clinical and theoretical, psychoanalytical writings continue to build on Freud's theories (1960, 1928) to explore the meaning and psychodynamics of humor in the everyday lives of both the mundane and the mad.[10] It also was Freud's widely publicized and controversial theories on humor and the unconscious, as well as his international reputation as a serious and highly unconventional thinker, that helped prepare the ground for the study of humor as a reputable scholarly endeavor in the social sciences.[11]

Psychology was the first social science to develop a serious interest in humor per se as a legitimate and important area of research. Around the middle of this century, psychologists began to take both an empirical and a theoretical interest in the definition and explication of humor and laughter—work that was, and is, largely experimental in design.[12] They have dealt with a wide variety of problems, from the origin and development of children's humor to gender differences in humorous displays, and, unlike the other social sciences, their use of terms is relatively precise if somewhat jargonistic. They also have been the most insistent on demonstrating that laughter is not always correlated with humor, a point discussed later.

Folklorists long have had an active interest in collecting and reporting popular oral traditions in which humor is frequently a central concern. Trickster stories, for example, have been collected and compared from many parts of the world, as have riddles, tongue twisters, and humorous songs. Folklorists also have a dedicated interest in the collection of jokes, including joke crazes that sweep across continents as well as the ubiquitous ethnic slur jokes that seem a staple of most societies.[13] A more recent interest is in the individual as a communicator of humor (Oring 1984).

If anthropology was slow to recognize the place of humor in human affairs, sociology was even more reluctant. Classical sociologists, with the exception of a brief discussion of derisive laughter and the superiority of the self by Mead (1934:206–207), generally ignore the role of the comedic. However, the "human relations" emphasis of Mayo (1933) and his students in their pioneering 1927–1932 studies at the Western Electric Company's Hawthorne Works in Chicago, could not ignore the importance of humor in the informal organization of workers on the job. These studies, especially Roethlisberger and Dickson's (1939) description of the famous Bank Wiring Observation Room group, clearly document the significance of nonrational aspects in informal organizational behavior, such as horse play, ridicule, and joke telling. Stemming from this early work, the examination of humor within the small group in terms of tension management and as a way to interpret and control social relationships is an important sociological concern.[14] Other current sociological interests in humor range from its use as a norm enforcer in the control of deviance to the study of ethnic, racial, and religious stereotypes in the inevitable jokes about the stupid outsider.[15]

Anthropology and Folly in the Postmodern Era

Several current and overlapping developments in the practice of American anthropology indicate that the discipline's research constraints around fun and folly—even the conceptual constraints around anthropology itself—are loosening, and loosening fast. In the period after World War II, the American version of anthropology as a quadripartite enterprise comprising ethnology, archeology, linguistics, and physical anthropology was thought to be falling apart. Not since then has anthropology appeared so threatened as a discipline. Although all of the subfields of anthropology have been affected by postmodern criticism, ethnology has been the most severely jolted.

To those who have embraced the postmodern turn in anthropology, the established paradigms of functionalism and structuralism appear constrictingly contrived, while earlier versions of interpretivism seem antagonistically elegant. For some, the solution is to abandon all established paradigms and proceed with imaginative eclectiveness (Marcus and Fischer 1986). Regardless of whether or not one agrees with the deconstructing stance of postmodernism, its irreverent approach to accepted theory and data is helping to liberate humor from the restricting analytical conventions that have prevented its fuller representation in anthropological research and writing. In postmodern anthropology, genres are inverted, boundaries are collapsed, truth is relativized, sacred concepts are trivialized, and once discrete phenomena are jostled and teasingly stroked.

Farce, as Sorell (1972:90) notes, thrives in an atmosphere of improvisation, and today anthropology itself is sometimes a comedy performance.[16] One of the more amusing ironies of anthropological postmodernism is that the more strongly it espouses, for example, polyphonic discourse and multiple cultural horizons, the more shrill, univocal, and self-righteously declamatory its discourse. When Tyler appropriates the stigmatizing language of psychiatry to characterize his lagging colleagues, one can only step back, smile, and watch the fun.[17] At the same time, the proper and sententious are rushing in, clumsy and cross as finger-wagging white-faced clowns, to set right the intellectual mayhem created by the audacious and irreverent postmodern harlequins. A lot of good people who thought they knew what anthropology stood for are as nonplussed as if their pockets had been picked in their own classrooms. It's carnival time in anthropology!

Now, while confusion reigns, is the time for those with new anthropological agendas to set them forth. During carnival, anything is possible. Bruner characterizes the 1980s as "an 'opening up' of anthropology," a time when "the spontaneity, improvisation, and innovation inherent in social practice" is taken account of, a time that is "skeptical of fixed meanings and resolved endings" and that "recognizes the inconsistency and ambiguity of social life" (1984: 13).[18] If not quite a definition of humor, Bruner's characterization certainly denotes a social environment in which comedy thrives. While the opening or loosening up of anthropology has continued into the 1990s, several areas of study intimately related to humor, comedy, and the clown are enoying critical and popular growth. Performance studies and the anthropologies of play and of emotion are stretching, and sometimes replacing, the frames of an older anthropology.

Play, Performance, and Emotion

Play, as a form of pleasure, is a special concern of the young in many species. But regardless of the age of the player, the pleasure is in the process, the activity itself. The distinctive features in human play, depending on the activity, are repetition, exaggeration, inversion, and make-believe (Lancy 1980:472–73). These characteristics are closely related to humor; indeed, humor and laughter are a frequent aspect of play, a microevent within a larger one.

While the study of play goes back at least to Victorian times—Gross's (1898) pioneering work is usually mentioned—the attention given to performance is more recent. The interest in performance is multimedia, multidisciplinary, and multicultural; as McNamara and Schechner observe, "performance is no longer easy to define or locate: the concept and structure has spread all over the place" (1982:4). Anthropologists and others using an anthropological perspective who write on performance theory—for example, Turner (1977), Kapferer (1983), MacAloon (1984), Schechner (1985) and Barba and Savarese (1991)—would probably agree that "cul-

Introduction

tures are performed" (Bruner 1984:25), even if they may not agree on a definition of performance itself.

The most common theme in performance studies by anthropologists is a concern with process, experience, and practice in contradistinction to structure and stasis. In focusing on cultural performances—that is, humans or animals acting, wittingly or unwittingly, for the gaze of others—the action is engaged with the life around it. Clowning, by definition, is always a performance. It is this performatory aspect of clowning as a culturally constituted humorous and expressive event that is stressed in the following chapters.

The emotions, the active expressions of animals and humans, have long fascinated both writers and scientists. Darwin's famous 1872 monograph, *The Expression of the Emotions in Man and Animals*, assumes the problem is primarily a biological one and emphasizes the universality of the emotions among humans. Ekman (1980), on the basis of his "neuro-cultural" approach to emotion, identifies surprise, happiness, anger, fear, sadness, and disgust as universal emotions, applicable to all people regardless of culture, and expressed with the same distinctive pattern of facial muscle movements. But, as Ekman and others also observe, emotions are expressed with the entire body, not just the face, so there are individual as well as cultural differences in the overall physical patterns of expressiveness as various parts of the body are brought into play. A further complication is that Ekman's biologically identified emotions are not necessarily isometric to a language's affective lexemes. As Wierzbicka notes, "different systems of emotion terms are likely to reflect different ways of conceptualizing emotion" (1986:593).

For a long time most anthropologists dismissed the emotions as a field of study because of mistrust in Freudian theory or, given the emotions' strong biological base, because they assumed there was general behavioral and lexical uniformity. In other words, there seemed too little that was subect to cultural analysis to bother studying emotions. But as Lutz and White (1986) indicate, the anthropology of emotion is today a vigorous area of study. Anthropologists who study and write about the relation of emotion and culture situate the problem in a variety of ways, ranging from cultural studies of a few key emotion words (Rosaldo 1980) to the relation of emotion and concepts of the self (Potter 1988).[19] But regardless of the approach, most bypass the more joyous aspects of human expression. The Pacific Islander anthropologist and novelist

Hau'ofa is especially critical of the generally derisive and distorted images that ethnographies present of Melanesians, noting that "we have neglected to portray them as rounded human beings who love as well as hate, who laugh joyously as well as quarrel, who are peaceful as well as warlike, and who are generous and kindly as well as mean and calculating." (1975:287)

Unlike Darwin, who paid close attention to laughter, the anthropological interest in emotion is primarily in those experiences and terms that indicate pain, not pleasure, or, to use a theatrical metaphor, tragedy, not comedy. This emphasis on the problematic aspects of emotion is unfortunate. For the benefit of the human species—whose grip on happiness, according to most anthropological studies, is precarious at best—it could be instructive to dedicate more research energy to apprehending the cultural phenomenon of joy and the ways it is culturally constructed and perpetuated or destroyed. This is not a plea for a vacuous anthropology of feel-goodism but the voicing of a concern about a formidable lacuna in emotion studies that is reflected in the lopsided way many ethnographies are constructed. Joy and happiness, however transitory, are far more complicated subjects than generally assumed, with many modes of approach. One sure route is that of humor, especially as expressed in the broad and sometimes vulgar antics of harlequins, fools, and clowns. Focusing on a part of the world whose anthropological fame is more known for its fierceness than fun, these essays on Oceanic clowning document that humor and laughter, as salient dimensions of human emotion, are worthy of critical study and interpretation.

The Essence of Humor

This book is about humor as cultural performance or, more specifically, about clowning as a kind of performance that amuses. But *amuses* is a broad term; while one observer may only smile wryly at a funny incident, another may laugh uproariously.[20] How behavior is evaluated and judged, as anthropologists have been pointing out for most of this century, depends on the reference point of the evaluator. Regardless of the extent of amusement displayed, a curious onlooker might inquire about the necessary conditions that stimulated the two humorous responses. Why is it that some things are funny? Philosophers, especially, have been intrigued by such questions and have written extensively, primarily from a phenomenological per-

Introduction   13

spective, on the essential nature of humor and laughter and their relationship.

What, then, is humor.[21] Is humor culture-specific, or are there certain necessary conditions for the expression of humor in all cultures? While philosophers do not phrase the question in cultural terms, they imply the universality of the causes for humor by seeking its "essence" or typical characteristics (Clark 1987:140).

We can enter this special world of the comedic by identifying some of the humorous things that make people laugh: clumsiness, puns and word play, grotesqueness, nonsense, stupidity, unusual dress or behavior, taboo breaking,[22] exaggerated imitation, non-threatening surprise, and embarrassment.[23] While not a complete list, it at least outlines the domain of the sources of humorous laughter. Monro, in his classic 1951 work, identifies three fundamental types of theory to explain the psychosocial origins of humor: superiority theories, relief theories, and incongruity theories.[24] I will take a brief look at each, quite aware that none explains all instances of humorous laughter.

Although today few scholars deride the nature of comedy, humor was not always kindly thought of by philosophers and intellectuals. One Western tradition, beginning at least with Plato and echoed, as we have seen, by Lord Chesterfield, regards humor as one of the meaner and more self-serving aspects of humanity. One laughs at those who are in some way inferior. Because there is malice in such laughter, it should be avoided. Plato's *Republic* sets forth a scheme for an ideal state wherein the "guardian" leaders should "not be given to laughter" to the extent that even Homer's accounts of the gods' laughing should be expunged from their reading (1937:864–65). Aristotle, also on moral grounds, takes a critical view of laughter because comedy "is an imitation of men worse than the average, (1941:1459).[25] Jourbet, writing in the sixteenth century, sententiously declares that laughter is "an empty and foolish joyousness" aroused by "ugliness and impropriety" (1980:44).

This ancient *superiority* theory that laughter is an expression of superiority over others was given its most formidable and influential reading in Hobbes's *Leviathan*. In a famous phrase he wrote, "sudden glory is the passion which maketh those grimaces called laughter" (Hobbes 1967:45). He is speaking of the glory of superiority an individual feels when another looks foolish and, by comparison, "applauds themselves." Even the humblest person can laugh with superiority as he watches on the evening news his president stumble unhurt down the airliner's steps. Most of us do laugh when we see someone make a fool of herself—unless it is someone with whom we are closely identified; then we, too, experience embarrassment—but there are many instances of humor where no feelings of superiority over another person are involved.[26]

The *relief* theory had its first extensive presentation by the prolific Victorian thinker and writer, Spencer, although it was prefigured by Aristotle's comment about comedy as catharsis. Spencer's essay, "On the Physiology of Laughter," claims that our emotions take the form of "nervous energy" that is released in a variety of ways (1891:452–66). One way is when we express a particular emotion and then, realizing it is inappropriate, laugh; for example, when a woman becomes frightened on hearing the kitchen door open only to find her daughter home early from school. Her laughter, according to Spencer, is simply a dissipation of energy built up by fear.[27] This mechanistic theory of laughter is similar to Freud's view of laughter as the release of excess psychic energy that is normally used to suppress forbidden feelings and thoughts.

While these two theories have enjoyed considerable acclaim at one time or another and offer an explanation for some kinds of humorous laughter, the *incongruity* theory receives the most recognition today because of its wider explanatory power. Kant, Kierkegaard, Schopenhauer, and others set forth various versions of this theory, involving the recognition of an incongruity, contradiction, or discontinuity of one kind or another as the source of laughter.[28] A basic assumption of the theory is that people live more or less orderly lives and usually know what to expect and how to interpret it. When an event occurs that subverts these expectations, the response is a laugh. Thus, when two New Guinea men with whom I was walking in the forest heard me exclaim "ouch!" when a branch whipped my face, they laughed; "ouch," they explained, is a sound crocodiles make, not men. The incongruous animal sound coming from their human companion both surprised and amused them, just as it would me if they had been struck and said "meow!" Then it was my turn to laugh, not because I had said "ouch!" but because they had misconstrued its Western meaning.

Recently Morreall offered a single explanation for humorous laughter and nonhumorous laughter resulting from embarrassment and tickling that combines aspects of all three theories (1987:128–38). First, all laughter situations, according to Morreall, involve a *sudden* change in the individual's psychological state, which in "incongruous" laughter is primarily cognitive and in "relief" and "superior" laughter is primarily affective. "To laugh," Morreall claims, "we must be caught offguard by the change so that we cannot smoothly adjust to what we are experiencing" (133). The second aspect of his theory is that the sudden change in the individual's psychological state must be a pleasant one, like the mother discovering the kitchen door was opened by her daughter and not a thief. "Enoying self-glory, being amused by some incongruity, releasing pent-up nervous energy—all these feel good, and can cause us to laugh" (133). However, there are instances of laughter that are not precipitated by a sudden change in psychological state. For example, old friends can recall, without being caught off guard, some former disastrous situation that, in retrospect, is amusing. Family jokes are of this order; everyone knows them in detail but laughs when they are retold.

The Cultural Construction of Folly

Folly is an old-fashioned, multivalent word whose meanings lie between *silly* and *colossal mistake*. Today it is rarely used in ordinary speech, but in academe, it is still a term favored by humanist scholars of humor. Folly—human foolishness—may be stupid or crazy and ofttimes funny. The cultural construction of folly, of course, is dependent upon a society's ideas about what constitutes earnestness, seriousness, responsibility, and dignity. To reverse these traits is to create folly—the work of the fool.

As a human archetype, the fool is a universal character that jigs and stumbles through place and time, weaving her or his nuttiness firmly into the cultural warp. Wherever humans have wandered, the fool, a perennial transcultural type, is found performing, an entertaining oddity to her audience. The fool's appearance sets up a social tension of ambivalence; the boundaries of propriety blur, fantasy and reality oscillate, and one's cognitive control over the environment recedes. As Welsford notes, "the Fool by his mere presence dissolves events, evades issues, and throws doubt on the finality of fact" (1966:324). If we surrender, it is fun and temporarily liberating; if we balk, the fool has bested us and we retreat, vaguely ashamed and annoyed. Since Homo sapiens' modest beginnings 200,000 years ago, human communication has ramified and intensified, carrying the fool into new formats and genres—until, today, Hollywood's newest comedian or Washington's latest bumbling politician is part of the humorous vocabulary of the world.

Celebrated in films, television, newsprint, and literature, the fool never was more pervasive in human affairs than in our postmodern world.

Fools: Natural and Artificial

A distinction frequently made by historians and literary critics is between *natural* and *artificial* fools, a folk construction dating back to the twelfth century (Welsford 1966:119). In 1608, the veteran London actor, Robert Armin expressed it this way:

> Natural fooles are prone to selfe conceipt:
> Fooles artificiall, with their wits lay wayte
> To make themselues fooles, liking the disguise,
> To feede their owne mindes, and the gazers eyes
> (Collier 1842:12).

The natural fool—"half-witted simpletons or mentally deranged psychotics" (Zijderveld 1982:35) who, devoid of ordinary reason, flouts community custom—is probably as old as humanity itself.[29] No group, small or large, can ignore the woman or man who trashes social conventions. Whether half-witted, mad, or stubbornly perverse, the fool, pathetic, frightening, wise, and funny by turn, commands attention. A fool by nature, he seems congenitally unable to follow the rules. With an inherent bent toward subverting conventional reason, he creates images of incongruity that startle and, depending upon the degree of one's sensitivity to the fool's predicament, amuse.

For thousands of years natural fools—when they survived—were tolerated creatures, not fully human but still a vivid presence in the everyday lives of villagers and townspeople. In medieval times, natural fools without family or unattached to a sponsor fended for themselves. If their behavior became too troublesome to others, they were temporarily jailed or driven from town to wander in the countryside. Given the times, they were treated quite humanely by their medieval contemporaries, contrary to unsubstantiated views (Zijderveld 1982:3).[30] However, with the political ascendancy of bourgeois notions of normal behavior in early-modern times, beginning in the seventeenth century there was a consistent move across Europe to remove the natural fool from public life. Stigmatized as indigent and irresponsible undesirables, they were incarcerated, along with the poor and the criminal, as an underclass best removed from sight.

Introduction

Even as natural fools began to disappear from the streets of Europe, their presence in the villages of Oceania remained relatively untouched by Western exploration and colonization. Just as in European societies, the island societies of the South Pacific made little or no distinction between the retarded and the crazy individual, as the behavior of both was often patently foolish. After the South Pacific islands came under colonial domination, violently mad men and women were sometimes removed by the colonial authorities at the villagers' request, while other communities were just as likely to continue their toleration.[31]

The natural fool is still a fairly common person in village Oceania and, depending upon the society, is tolerated to various degrees. Just as the mad were a source of amusement to those who visited the eighteenth-century European madhouses on a Sunday afternoon, so are the natural fools of village Oceania frequently objects of amusement and mockery, especially to the young.[32] Most anthropologists are privy to such situations, but, as they are generally offensive to the mores of a twentieth-century Westerner and tangential to their research problem, they are rarely reported.

The significance of the natural fool in the cultural construction of folly is as a negative reflection of humanity, a troublesomely alive inversion that may be perverse, capricious, playful, illogical, and silly. It is this inverted perspective of the natural fool that the *artificial* fool exploits, intellectually and behaviorally, to mock and tease her targets. A skilled performer and manipulator of humor, the artificial fool only acts the fool to serve his or others' ends. By pretending to be a fool, he playacts a strategic role in society's sacral and secular performances of folly.

The Middle Ages mark the efflorescence of the fool in European popular culture. The notorious Feast of Fools, in which those of lesser ecclesiastic status burlesqued the mass, was not finally supressed by church authorities until the sixteenth century. There were also the revels of carnival season, professional court fools, and, on the Continent, the young men of the secular Joyous Societies who played the fool on the streets and in satirical playlets, in which Mother Folly and her cast critically commented on contemporary life.[33]

Historical documentation shows that the court fools of Europe were mostly male artificial fools.[34] Some were deformed, their anomalous appearance an obvious sign of their being both objects and originators of humor.[35] One historical finding reveals that the court fool is a feature of highly stratified societies with absolute rulers. The earliest known court fool was a member of Pharaoh

Dadkeri-Assi's court in Egypt's Fifth Dynasty (Towsen 1976:24). In medieval and Renaissance Europe, where sovereigns set the fashions, not only did kings have their court fools, but others of means, including lords, high churchmen, rich merchants, city governments, monasteries, and even the keepers of taverns and brothels, might keep a fool or two. Although outside of Europe the data are not as complete, court fools served rulers of the Middle East, Africa, India, China, and Japan.[36] The lavish court of Montezuma II also had jesters, jugglers, and tumblers, two of whom were sent to Pope Clement VII by Cortez.[37]

The court fool remained a familiar figure throughout the Renaissance and into the seventeenth century. Philip IV's Spanish jesters, soberly immortalized by Velasquez, today cast an ironic eye on the Prado's tourist hordes. However, by the eighteenth century and the fall of the absolute monarchies, the court fool had mostly disappeared in Europe. Important exceptions were Russia, where the traditional court fool remained in vogue, and the German courts, where the buffoon-philosopher or learned fool—men of genuine erudition—played the fool, often more mocked than mocking.[38] In the courts of some Muslim potentates, the court fool survived into the twentieth century. Welsford (1966:194) reports that in the mid-1930s in what is today northern Nigeria, the Emir of Katsina's court jester performed "a spirited rendering of Felix the Cat, in a fancy-dress costume."

There is evidence that the powerful rulers of Polynesia's stratified societies also had jesters among their retinues when first contacted by the West. Although no one has researched the problem in depth, even a rudimentary search of the early Western postcontact literature indicates that jesters did exist in some Polynesian societies. For example, the Englishman Turner, who spent nineteen years in Polynesia, comments that the "court buffoons" of important chiefs furnished amusement at various festivals and meetings, "who, by oddity in dress, gait, or gesture, or by lascivious jokes, tried to excite laughter" (1884:126).

Clowning as Critical Practice

The Western lexicon for artificial fools is an extensive one: buffoon, trickster, clown, humorist, prankster, harlequin, droll, comedian, comic, joker, mime, and mummer all refer to individuals who, one way or another, evoke laughter. But, not surprisingly,

Introduction

there is no consensus on the semantic differentiation or overlap of these terms.

The English word *fool* first appears in the thirteenth century, and its meaning in ordinary speech and studies of folly was similar until modern times. While the term has changed little in academe, in everyday parlance it has lost Erasmus's humanistic gloss and today is a word of insulting and dismissive contempt (cf. *Oxford English Dictionary*; Billington 1984:97). An example of a fool in the modern sense of the term is the overbearing and opportunistic information officer described in the Counts's chapter in this volume, who is held in contempt by villagers because of his stupidity and tactlessness. Surreptitiously mocked, ridiculed, and gulled because of his insensitivity and position of power, he also provides his hosts with considerable amusement during his unwelcome stay. A contemptible fool, he is also an unwitting clown.

The word *clown* is of later vintage than *fool*, having come into use in the last half of the sixteenth century. Of all the English terms referring to artificial fools, it seems best suited to designate the performers described in this book. Clown is a term that travels easily through time and across cultures, but, most importantly, its semantic connotations are more positive than pejorative, and its scholarly usage in anthropology is well established.

Clowning, the practice that informs these essays, refers to a public performance characterized variously by burlesque, buffoonery, nonsense, and irony. As a performance genre, clowning is practiced and appreciated throughout the world. Whether in a Russian circus, a Samoan wedding, a Japanese monkey act, a Balinese temple play, a New Guinea mortuary feast, a Greek TV sitcom, or one's own kitchen, clowning's overdrawn sense of the ridiculous is a form of expressive behavior that can excite both laughter and fear and whose ancient roots lie in our common humanity.

By breaking or challenging frames of sensible conduct and thought, the clown deconstructs order. With her tricks of inversion, contradiction, and exaggeration, she creates mayhem by dismantling cognitive coherence and continuity. In doing so, she takes a critical stance. For the anthropologist, this is the heuristic significance of studying clowning: the clown—a highly opinionated moralist—points baldly, if sometimes opportunistically, to the prickly issues of everyday life and beyond. As such, clowning is criticism. Although clowns are not kings in terms of political clout, depending upon the extent of a clown's wit and courage, as well as the circumstances, the clown may momentarily ravage the status quo; at the very least, her subversive scars linger. Even a Bread and Puppet Resurrection Circus clown cavorting on a Vermont summer meadow can sabotage one's received ideas about the benevolent powers of government.

Although much clowning is critical, it is far from rebellious. As many of the Oceanic examples in the following chapters demonstrate, clowning may use its considerable expressive powers to conserve established cultural values. Clowning as a prevalent force in cultural reproduction is an underappreciated phenomenon that I will return to later.

Most scholars, including the contributors to this volume, write on clowning in a specific time and place. The few interpretive transcultural or historical studies that exist are concerned primarily with fools and clowns in either Western (e.g., Billington 1984; Willeford 1969) or non-Western societies (e.g., Handelman 1981; Makarius 1970); few analysts concern themselves with the sweep of clowns in both types of societies. An important exception is Zijderveld's closely documented 1982 sociological study of folly and the rise and fall of the European court fool, which includes a chapter on artificial fools in non-Western societies.[39] Citing material from the traditional non-Western societies of Nootka, Zuni, Tibet, and Tokugawa, Japan, Zijderveld finds some strong resemblances to the fools and folly of Western European society. But he is especially rueful regarding the wane of ceremonial or ritual clowning among the American Indian in response to modernity. Zijderveld would undoubtedly agree with anthropologist Apte that "as societies change, so should humor" (1985:263).

Unlike the court fool, who endured for only a few hundred years because his fate was tied to that of the absolute rulers of the Middle Ages and Renaissance, the ritual clown dates back to prehistoric religious practices and is tied, not to an all-powerful potentate, but to a powerful magical world. But the spread of colonialism across the planet brought the ideas of modern reason, science, and the ritually sanitized religions of Christianity and Islam into collision with ancient beliefs. The socioeconomic impact of colonialism, abetted by hegemonic humor, (to be discussed later) and political force, has conspired toward the diminution or disappearance of the practice of ritual clowning in many parts of the world. While this is also true for Oceania, traditional ritual clowning, although threat-

Introduction

ened by change, remains a comic force in the lives of many, as the essays in this collection indicate.

This persistence is especially true for Papua New Guinea. Because most of Papua New Guinea was brought under Western control much later than other parts of Oceania, ritual clowning is still performed in some societies.[40] One of the more complete accounts of Melanesian sacral ritual clowning is in Gell's 1975 account of the Ida "fertility" ceremony among the Umeda villagers in Sandaun Province of Papua New Guinea. The characterization of these costumed clowns, who with various masked heroes complete the cast of the Ida ceremonial, include transvestism, mock aggression, and buffoonery.[41]

I have mentioned the presence of court jesters in some Polynesian societies, but the eighteenth-century explorers' reports of theatrical performances of humor in Polynesia also indicate that there was a widely distributed clowning tradition involving pageants and satirical sketches.[42] In some parts of Polynesia, aspects of this clowning tradition have survived Western contact. Shore (1982:259–60) writes about Samoan clowns dancing crazily in juxtaposition to the graceful dancing of young women of high status, and Sinavaiana's chapter in this volume shows that the Samoan tradition of comedy sketches has continued to flourish not only on the islands but that Samoan immigrants have transported it to their communities in New Zealand and the United States.

Comedy also was an important part of the famous *arioi* society of Tahiti and other Society Islands. Members included men and women of high status who traveled throughout the islands giving performances. Early Western observers were especially impressed with the satirical plays that lampooned the behavior of youthful nonconformists or oppressive elders. Because of the *arioi* society's practice of promiscuity, infanticide, and sexually suggestive comic dances, they were the scourge of the missionaries, and their activities were soon suppressed. Captain Bligh describes three male dancers clowning with their genitalia at a public entertainment:

> They suddenly took off what clothing they had about their hips and appeared quite naked. . . . for the whole business now became the power and capability of distorting the penis and testicles, making at the same time wanton and lascivious motions. The person who was ready to begin had his penis swelled and distorted out into an erection. . . . The second brought his stones to the head of his

penis ... stretching them at the same time very violently until they were near a foot in length.... The third person was more horrible than the other two, for with both hands seizing the extremity of the scrotum, he pulled out with such force that the penis went in totally out of sight and the scrotum became shockingly distended. In this manner they danced about the ring for a few minutes when I desired them to desist and the Heivah ended. It however afforded much laughter among the spectators. (1937:II:35)

Although the early explorers and sailors to Tonga do not report clowning performances comparable to the one that failed to amuse Bligh, they do report watching brief comedy skits, but there is no mention of the more elaborate satirical plays as seen in Tahiti.[43] According to Hau'ofa (1988), comedy skits are still important on Tonga and, as in Samoa, are performed as part of variety concerts to raise money for community projects.

Hegemonic Humor

Humor, obviously, is not always motivated by compassionate fun; when derisive, it can be used as a power ploy. Mocking laughter—even when expressed gently—is a political act of ridicule against a person whose actions are rebuked. Everyone has experienced being the butt of a humiliating joke and bearing the taunting laughter of disapproval.

Bergson's (1911) influential essay on the meaning of the comic, while in the tradition of the *superiority* view, does not emphasize the laughing person's superiority feelings but stresses that the function of such laughter is to humiliate those who are insensitive to the uniqueness in experience and who perceive the new as the old. We laugh at their mechanical inflexibility as a way to help free them. Bergson's hegemonic humor is that of a beneficent reformer, but for others it can be deeply rancorous.

When Ridicule Reigns

Sweet (1989:72) and others write about the power of the Pueblo ritual clown to humiliate and the audience's delight in "seeing an outsider or one of their own made the fool." This dark, manipulative side of humor that worried Plato has been embraced with gusto by both profane and pious individuals. Pascal, the seventeenth-century French scientist and religious philosopher, took umbrage when the Jesuits charged him with "turning sacred things into ridicule" and, in, a stinging reply, insisted "that ridicule is, in some cases, a very appropriate means of reclaiming men from their errors." To clinch his argument he cites St. Augustine's observation that "the wise laugh at the foolish, because they are wise, not after their own wisdom, but after that divine wisdom which shall laugh at the death of the wicked" (1941:469–70).

Who is wise, and whether their laughter is malicious or beneficent, are relative questions. In Wape clowning, what sentiment, one wonders, lies behind the young men's theatrical skits that mock women? Or, in the colonialist South Pacific, Western government officials, missionaries, and entrepreneurs considered themselves both wise and politically powerful and so could, when they wished, employ ridicule and laughter as simple yet effective weapons to enforce change in local customs. As the pioneering Chinese anthropologist Xiaotong experienced in jeering humiliations from China's Red Guard, ridicule is a powerful and effective psychological force (Pasternak 1988). While we read with outrage, not amusement, about his public humiliations, to his Red Guard captors he was an ideological enemy and therefore a fitting object of humorous derision. Similarly, many of the Russian court fools were men of social standing "degraded into that position for having in some way offended the Czar" (Welsford 1966:186).

Davis (1971) has written of the charivaris of sixteenth-century France carried out by young village husbands against those who they feel have violated the community's mores, especially in regard to premarital and marital behavior. Coming at night in grotesque masks, they approach the offender's home making a terrific racket, beating on pots and pans, blowing horns, and ringing bells. Depending upon the offense, they continue until the victim pays a fine, is paraded through the village riding backward on a donkey, or is ducked into water. The charivari is a great practical joke but has a serious intent to punish and instruct through ridicule.

The roast, an American institution, is a carnivalesque form of hegemonic humor typified by a temporary reversal of power. A person of high status, often a celebrity or politician, watches as he is mocked and made fun of — usually good naturedly but with a telling effect on his composure — throughout an evening while millions may be watching the performance on television. Levy (1973:139) describes how Tahitian children are sometimes bitterly teased and mocked if they cross-dress. Whether an individual is humiliatingly forced to clown by his critics (forced clowning) or they clown to ridicule and mock him (voluntary clowning), hegemonic humor is always politically inspired. Its intent is to influence or control another by putting him in his place, or, more radically, to effect a marked behavioral change. In Barlow's chapter, Murik Lakes women aren't falling off house ladders just to get a laugh but to criticize a relative's awkwardness.[44]

Handelman and Kapferer indicate that individuals who wish to joke "must receive a 'license to joke' from the persons toward whom their activity is directed" (1972:484). They also assume that the joking is an "enjoyment" shared by all the participants. This is not, however, usually the case with hegemonic humor. Here, the butt of the joke is either forced to act or look like a fool or must witness his behavior burlesqued by a clown. In either case, the targets of ridicule and those close to them may not be amused.

Folly's Two Faces

Although forced and voluntary clowning as forms of hegemonic humor are probably practiced in all human societies, what does vary is the relation of the clown's performance to prevalent cultural values. A hegemonic clowning performance may be subversive or conservative; the former when it ridicules culturally accepted practices, persons, and ideas, the latter when it ridicules the culturally unacceptable. Both are representations of clowning as critical practice.

It is a truism that societies tend to reproduce themselves more often than they subvert themselves and that sacral ritual clowning, as Mosko pointedly shows in his essay, is a recognized strategy in cultural reproduction. Because of these factors, Oceanic clowning, as described in this book, is more culturally conservative than subversive. As an abettor of cultural reproduction, clowning is generally assumed to support established cultural values when it (1) ridicules and parodies deviations from the norm, (2) is tolerated by the powerful as "rituals of license" in tight temporal frames (the hoary safety valve theory)[45] and (3) acts as a catalyst in the transformation of status at a critical social juncture such as weddings or the end of mourning.

If we accept the "rituals of license" functionalist explanation of subversive clowning as strengthening the status quo as it appears to be subverted, then clowning as a sometime subversive activity is explained away. However, even ignoring the occasional subversive clowning performance that does subvert authority, the functionalist explanation is not as conclusive as it appears. In emphasizing a systemic level of analysis, it overlooks the importance of person and memory. As I argue later, in reference to carnival clowning as a repository of the heretical, episodic clowning that lampoons established values may persist in the memory as images of difference that continue to challenge the known and the now. In this way, remembered images of the subversive clown are kept alive as impossible possibilities that can affect the future. Subversive clowning that mockingly berates the empowered is not necessarily a futile exercise but may be a social harbinger of creative change.[46] Although the kings and nobles of France resolutely contained the practice of subversive public clowning, it persisted as a potent symbol of discontent until its culmination in the Revolution.

By this I am not implying that subversive clowning alone can create revolutions in the social order. Its power is in mockingly chipping away at the culture, acting as a political accessory to temporal social transformation. While subversive clowning alone cannot transform a society, it does have the power to transform or modify the actions of an authority figure who may, for example, embarrassed by a mocking performance of his oppressive demeanor, alter his parodied behavior.

Not all clowning is hegemonic in the sense of attempting to exert an influence over protagonists. Nevertheless, the majority of the clowning described in these essays demonstrates that Oceanic clowning is not so much a socially neutral act of silliness as one that, while silly, expresses approbation. These are political clowns, in the widest possible sense, whose critical commentary on persons or community practices varies extensively in form and whose intent (more often than not) is culturally conservative rather than subversive.

The Aesthetics of a Joke

Humor and laughter are complex phenomena; not everyone always gets the joke. There are *New Yorker* cartoons I will never understand, and inside witticisms will continue to slip by me while others titter. Humor, like beauty, is in the perception of the beholder. The experience is there, but to be amused by it I must read it in an amusing way. So to me, Xiaotong's humiliations were barbarous; to his Red Guard captors, they were self-righteously amusing. Although the subfield *humor hermeneutics* is yet to be invented, the potential is more real than risible. Some experiences are almost universally humorous; Chaplin's early, broadly acted films amuse all ages all over the world, and a circus clown's "biggest laugh getter is a kick in the pants" (Ballantine 1982:260). Other humorous experiences are more culturally and experientially circumscribed; if you aren't an Iatmul villager or a Scarsdale Little Leaguer, you probably will not get the joke. Finally, there is the humor that is inherently personal: a fantasy skit I play in my mind makes me grin from ear to ear, or I laugh when, standing in a multimirrored disco, I suddenly see that the person looking at me is myself.

There is, then, an aesthetics of humor, a pleasure in perceiving or remembering ambivalent disjunctures, an enjoyment of the sudden transformation from perplexity (or not knowing) to amused insight. The pleasure is in seeing our ordered world suddenly disordered—if only for a fleeting instant, as with a witty remark, or for minutes or more by a farcical performance. Our laughter, itself physiologically convulsive and chaotic, is an audible metaphor for the cognitive disorder we are enjoying. As an unmediated response, humorous laughter is a time-out or out-of-time covering response for savoring the disruptive event until cognitive order and speech returns. It is a rather strange pleasure with a touch of thrill—even ecstasy at times—that is spontaneous and, even when anticipated, unmannered.[47] That the object of our pleasure may be grotesque or repulsive, as it sometimes is, does not necessarily diminish the aesthetic pleasure.[48] Hegemonic clowning, crude practical jokes, and delight in the scatological are no less funny and pleasing to some than witty repartee, satire, and musical or visual puns may be to others.

It is this pleasure that humor gives that makes the comedic in everyday life so personally rewarding.[49] There is a seductive sensuousness in humor, sometimes languid and suggestive, sometimes sharp and salty, or sometimes even twisted and horrific. Regardless of the type of humor, attention is focused on some disjunction in life: a word with two conflicting meanings, a gesture that can be read in opposite ways, an object grotesquely out of context. It is the little surprises of verbal wit, the obscene joke, the unanticipated solution to a cognitive dilemma, suddenly seeing the ordinary in an exotic way—or the exotic in an ordinary way—that keeps the mind lubricated, intrigued, and alert.[50] A delight of Lévi Strauss's structuralism is its transformative resolutions of set-up polarities that are not unlike the delight in grasping the idea that resolves the contra-

Introduction

dictory sides of a joke. What does it matter how true or contrived it might be; we are talking about cognitive fun.

Because there is a great range of what is construed as funny as well as marked differences in how individuals like their humor, the construction of an aesthetics of humor—which we popularly call a *sense of humor*—varies considerably. For instance, not everyone will think *Wet Dream* emblazoned across a boat's stern is funny or that listening to jokes is a comic high. If one doesn't immediately grasp the punch line and burst into a knowing laugh, one may be perceived as slow or humorless. Sharing a sense of humor is a much underrated factor in establishing social bonds. Most people choose, often unconsciously, individuals who share their sense of humor for companionship. The comedic, while it may be enjoyed alone, is usually funnier when it is shared with those who laugh as you do.

It should not, then, surprise us that many of the clowning events in Oceanic societies described in this volume may not seem funny. Humor as a psychosocial act is one of the most culturally relative of human actions. What we laugh at is a matter of taste and subject to evolving personal evaluation and interpretation. As one's cultural values change, so does one's sense of humor. The problem of humorous communication is further compounded when the clowning event, as in these essays, is set in an exotic society and discussed in scholarly rhetoric. Unlike translations of humorous folktales and stories that recreate the story verbatim (e.g., Siegel 1987), these essays on clowning do not recreate the event but only report on it. It is like explaining a joke; insight so labored usually does not incite laughter. As the English critic Hazlitt observed long ago, "You cannot force people to laugh: you cannot give a reason why they should laugh: they must laugh of themselves, or not at all" (1819:11).

Ordering Disorder

Some practices invite analytical ordering and seem to grow in social importance and scholarly esteem even as they are taken apart. But when clowning is subjected to analysis, its symbolic and affective power tends to shrivel and its humor drivels away. It is the ultimate clowning irony; the fun dissolves as you study it. Still, there are far drearier things to study than fools, and even analyzing the folly cannot completely annihilate the rambunctious intent of a clown.

Most of the clowning performances in this book are *formal*, in the sense that they are scripted by design or custom. While the details of a formal performance may be inventive, the status and role of the performer are normatively prescribed. This is true for both sacral and secular *ritual* clowning as well as for *theatrical* clowning. In contrast, *informal* clowning is more open and spontaneous, depending not so much upon customary scripts as upon the peculiar exigencies of the situation to shape the wit of the performance.[51]

These clowning genres—informal, ritual and theatrical—suggested by our data on Oceanic clowning are offered as heuristic constructions to facilitate analysis and discussion. In practice, the boundaries among them are porous and leaky, so if a particular clowning performance flows from one genre into another, fine; for it belongs there too. Clowning delights in orderliness only to confound it.

Informal Clowning

It seems probable that clowning always has been a part of the human behavioral repertoire. The captious imitation of others is an omnipresent human practice. Because informal clowning is commonplace and, unlike formal clowning, not clearly delineated by ritual or theatrical frames, it appears unimportant to both layperson and scholar and is thus easily minimized or forgotten. In terms of research findings, it is the least studied and understood form of clowning.

Two of these essays, the Counts's and Macintyre's, describe performances of informal clowning. Both present vivid descriptions that catch something of the spontaneity that is the essence of informal humor, humor that is shaped by the quirky contingencies of human interaction rather than by a ritual or theatrical script. Informal clowning is an open process, a syntagmatic progression of creative acts, dramatically framed from within the performance rather than from without, and driven by the interaction between the clown and his participating observers. Unlike a satirical skit, a funny storytelling, or the performance of a tightly scripted sacred clown, informal clowning plays with the evanescent present, fortuitously grasping aspects of the immediate situation to clown. For Macintyre's women friends on Tubetube, her voluntary celibacy in the field was an improbable and incongruous situation for a woman unaccompanied by her husband and free to take lovers. This supposed foolishness amused her friends and provided the material for some friendly clowning at her expense.

Introduction

Informal clowning is often of very brief duration, a matter of seconds or, if the mood is relaxed and the clowning clever and reinforced with laughter, considerably longer. In the small face-to-face communities of Oceania, a joke theme, as in Macintyre's example, may provide the basis for clowning for weeks at a time. The Counts describe an impromptu clown who, wearing a split-open white volleyball over his head, suddenly would appear from the vicinity of the men's house to strut up and down the village terrorizing the children and regaling the adults with laughter. Over a period of months, various men and women clowned with the volleyball mask until the performance, like a joke told too many times, lost its ability to startle and amuse.

While the spontaneity of informal clowning enlivens the social senses and punctuates the ordinary, the individual who plays the fool too frequently risks stigmatization as a marginal person. To clown is to behave without dignity, and someone who constructs an exclusively raffish and comic persona, while often popular with her peers, is rarely entrusted with high political status. The class clown in a New York high school or his equivalent in a New Guinea village may be rewarded with laughs but not the class presidency or village headship. The complete clown, in Zucker's words, "has accepted the twofold role of breaking all taboos and receiving all the punishments for it" (1969:82).

Ritual Clowning

The situation, however, is quite different for those who clown within a ritual or theatrical frame. Here the performance is formalized and the person as actor is more than himself. The Mekeo relatives described by Mosko who eat themselves sick to the amusement of their grieving kin are clowning within a ritual frame that prescribes their ridiculous behavior; they are no more personally responsible for their public gluttony than a movie actor gorging himself in a film. There is also a transformative public purpose in their clowning: to mark the end of mourning and return the aggrieved to everyday life.

In contrast to informal clowning, ritual clowning has received extensive anthropological attention as both practice and theory. To most analysts, ritual clowning means *sacred*, *sacral* or *ceremonial* clowning (e.g., Handelman 1981; Hieb 1972a; and Makarius 1970), but following Leach (1966), I widen the usage of ritual to include secular performances as well. The identifying aspect of ritual clowning, sacral or secular—other than its capacity for being funny—is its symbolic aspect; its efficacy is more than entertainment. The potency of ritual clowning in comparison to informal clowning is in its metamessages, often submerged in ambiguity but nonetheless communicated in practice.

Thus ritual clowning, as in the Mekeo example, usually juxtaposes hilarity and gravity. While relatives grieve over a death, their affinal kin begin a ritual performance of disgusting hilarity that will dissolve grief into laughter and return the aggrieved to everyday life. Because of the transformative nature of the ritual clown's performance, she cannot, as Handelman (1981:364) insightfully observes, be wholly comic. Her work is to generate laughter for a reason, a reason far beyond the superficial one of comic relief. As the Counts note in their essay, although ritual clowns are fun, they also address serious business.

Like a spinning, two-sided mirror, the ritual clown's performance is a bedazzling act that transcends its inherent contradiction. The ritual clown is a performing oxymoron of the seriocomic; his secret is in his dissembling, concealing in laughter the service of earnest work. As these essays show, the teleological laughter generated by his antics can transform the participants by, for example, moving them across awkward cultural seams, chastising their behavior, or flashing a glint of a chaotic social cosmos only dimly perceived.

The classic distinction between sacred and secular marks the difference between ritual clowning that is performed in magical and religious circumstances and that enacted without reference to transcendental powers. As we might predict, this distinction in Oceania is not always a sharp one. Although Mekeo clowning occurs around the subject of death, the clowning appears not to be as instrumentally oriented toward the spirit world as it is toward getting on with the responsibilities of village life. Similarly, Macintyre tells us that on Tubetube, the end of mourning is signaled by an accomplished raconteur relating satirical stories using slapstick and parody to regale the grimy and hungry mourners. Breaking into laughter, they are soon physically and emotionally transformed from marginal mourners into gracious hosts. Barlow's account of mourning among the Murik Lakes people is another example of mortuary clowning that seems to be neither clearly sacral nor secular. When a father's sister dies, her brother's daughters, who are also her joking partners, come to her house and, kicking her bier and striking at it with hatchets, goad her to rise and dance with

Introduction 31

them, a performance that brings whoops of laughter from the assembled mourners.

A straightforward example of sacral ritual clowning is my report on a curing festival where a Wape woman's parents break the taboo against adult nudity by dancing naked with their sacredly masked son-in-law. It is a performance that echoes from half a world away the dancing of pueblo scatological clowns with sacred rain gods. Hereniko speculates that the female clown, who presides as the comically imperious mistress of ceremonies at Rotuman weddings, traditionally had sacred powers that gave her the license to be a bossy buffoon whose word, however ridiculous, the celebrants, chiefs included, obeyed. Today, however, her performance is more secular than sacred, being backed not by the spirits per se, but by wedding customs that are gradually changing in accommodation to introduced Western practices and ideas. Less ambiguous examples of secular ritual clowning are the performances of the voluntary clowns at Rotuman weddings. These clowns are usually older women who delight in playing the fool but, unlike the woman clown who "rules" the proceedings, they have no official status.

Anthropological thinking about joking relationships—in my terms a form of secular ritual clowning—has been primarily in terms of kinship (albeit taboo breaking), not comedy. Barlow's essay, while cognizant of the kinship implications of her data, emphasizes the nature of the comedic performances among Murik Lakes women. In performances etched with hegemonic humor, women tease their joking partners into conformity by mocking their social transgressions. An even harsher form of hegemonic humor is described by Macintyre regarding the charivari custom of clowning insults directed against island miscreants.

Mosko's discussion of mortuary clowning among the Mekeo is of special interest as he challenges Apte's (1985:30–66; 152–61) theoretical distinction between joking relations and ritual clowning. In terms of the Mekeo data, it is not whether the interactions are dyadic among the former and multiple among the latter that is significant, but that in both forms it is the affinal versus cognatic nature of the relationships among the participants that is operative. For Mosko, however, the concern is not to what extent indigenous forms of humor conform to anthropological categories, but the place they have in the indigenous system of cultural symbols and relationships. As Mosko demonstrates, Mekeo mortuary humor not only is a transformer of social relations, but helps reproduce the total sociocultural system.

Theatrical Clowning

I use the term *theatrical clowning* in a broad sense to refer to clowning that is guided by a plot, however tight or loose, and usually rehearsed before the act is performed. Included in this clowning genre are, for example, stand-up comedians, mimes, farceurs, and circus and street clowns. While living with the Wape, one of the things that first surprised me were the miniature mimed skits performed by young men, sometimes cross-dressed, at Niyel-curing festivals. The skits, only tangentially related to the curing rituals, are roving side shows that amuse by commenting satirically, if sometimes darkly, on Wape society.

Theorists on the origin of Western theatrical comedy often find its roots in the Dionysian ritual revels that antedated Greece's sixth century B.C. archaic comedy (Cornford 1961; Lever 1956). These revels culminated in fifth-century B.C. Old Comedy, with Aristophanes its most hilariously vulgar surviving playwright. In Oceania, the data suggest that, similarly, ritual clowning is a developmental precursor to the theatrical forms of comedy that early explorers to Polynesia witnessed and that have continued to evolve. Dancing, singing, playing instruments, and clowning within an amusement frame whose intent is more openly pleasurable than is ritual clowning's are characteristic of theatrical performances. With their miming skits, the Melanesian Wape have the beginning of a theater of the absurd.

Sinavaiana's essay on Polynesian Samoa documents a much more complex form of indigenous farcical theater. Although Wape miming is much less sophisticated than the Samoan skits in the development of character and plot, their very simplicity gives them the poetic force of Japanese haiku. *Minimalist clowning,* we might call it, with an air of silent bemusement; it appeals more to the intellect than the hearty farce of a Samoan skit, which intends to break you up laughing.

The broad and ribald slapstick comedy of Samoan skits is reminiscent of the folk theater traditions of the famous commedia dell'arte that originated in Italy and whose troupes were a common sight in Europe from the sixteenth to the eighteenth centuries. The slapstick style of theater characteristic of commedia dell'arte, Samoan skits, and early Greek comedy is probably the oldest form of theater and has been called, variously, low comedy, popular comedy, buffo, farce, and vulgar comedy (Caputi 1978). Because the comparative and historical literature on Oceania theater remains slight,

Introduction

detailed comparisons between Western and Oceania theatrical traditions are not yet possible. Nevertheless, the evidence indicates that the ritual and theatrical comedic forms of Oceania, although roughly analogous to those in the West, are indigenous inventions long antedating contact with Western colonialism. "Clowns," as Towsen emphasizes, "can and do emerge spontaneously out of their own native cultures, in the process reinventing ancient forms of comedy" (1976:64).

This discussion of clowning genres suggest a hypothesis for an evolving practice of clowning. The ability to play critically with symbols via movement, voice, and props (informal clowning) appears to have developed early in hominid development. With clowning established as a critical practice, it was extended via the invention of the repetitive cultural forms of secular and sacral ritual clowning to further comment on community life. Although we find evidence of rudimentary forms of theatrical clowning in egalitarian societies like the Wape, it is only in politically more complex societies like hierarchical Polynesia that the framing of clowning as a theatrical performance with preconceived plots assumes importance.

Gender and the Fool

One of the challenging findings revealed by the present essays is the extent to which women are involved in clowning, an activity that among Westerners is more frequently popularly associated with men. This stereotype of clowning as predominantly male is supported by the ethnographic record but, as Apte (1985:73–74) points out, this may be more an artifact of the discounting of women's activities by researchers than a faithful record of women and comedy. There certainly are societies where women, vis-à-vis men, are expected to be modest and retiring, but who knows what comedic antics are expressed when they are alone? Then there are those societies where women's clowning is recognized; for example, Parsons reports that Hopi women perform a burlesque of the men's war dance and that their obscene humor is "quite up to the men's" (Parsons and Beals 1934:493). The material in these essays indicates that in the South Pacific Mother Folly is also a practiced performer. Island women not only may clown informally when they are together, but in assuming the status of socially prominent ritual or theatrical clowns, they are empowered to confront gender distinctions, chastise the errant, parody the privileged, and act as transformative agents.

For many societies, we will never know women's true measure as creators and collaborators of comedy, just as we do not always know their contribution to other cultural features. But these essays should alert and help sensitize field-workers to the diversity and cultural importance of female clowning. Here we see women clowning in a variety of informal, ritual, and theatrical settings. We see women, for example, cross-dressed and parodying men, ordering chiefs to stand in the sun, teasing the chaste ethnologist, mocking errant kin, and speaking out boldly in front of mixed audiences. We see women making a spectacle of themselves, reproducing their society as they also subvert those aspects they find faulty. Although in each society the circumstances of female clowning are somewhat different, taken collectively, the presence of female clowns helps us to appreciate the diverse nature of clowning as critical practice. A neglected aspect of gender studies, female clowning also enhances our understanding of the multiple facets of women's social and political roles.

The Significance of Oceanic Clowning

As suggested in this introduction and documented in the following essays, the cultural and methodological significance of Oceanic clowning is multiple. First, these essays demonstrate the cultural importance of clowning in the South Pacific and the wide range of clowning that is employed. Not only do we learn about different types of clowning practices as they are embedded in the sociocultural matrixes that give them meaning, but the chapters run the gamut of clowning, from informal antics to more formalized ritual and theatrical performances, thereby recording Oceania's rich variety of the comic.

Second, by focusing on clowning as a laughter-inducing event, these essays offer a fuller and deeper account of the islanders' humanity by turning ethnographic attention to indigenous forms of humor, an arena of island life that is seldom considered. If the reader finds some of the accounts less than funny, it only gives added emphasis to the plasticity of human expressiveness and the myriad ways humor is culturally constructed. Third, by focusing on Oceanic clowning, the essays advance our understanding of cultural processes in a region long famous for its anthropological research. Individually, the studies offer ethnographic and theoretical points

Introduction

that augment and intensify our understanding of the relationships among clowning, community, and culture.

Fourth, the variety and importance of women clowns in these pages correct the previous ethnographic impression that clowning in Oceania is primarily a male prerogative. As the following essays vividly show, Oceanic women also are comedians. Island women clown in a wide variety of contexts and styles, commenting, often boldly and publicly, on events and individuals around them. Appreciating these women as clowns and recognizing the critical power of their humorous histrionics only dramatizes the absence of the female clown in gender studies and points to anthropology's continued tendency to view women in terms that diminish their behavioral and symbolic complexity.

Fifth and last, while the practice of clowning is not necessarily political — there is nothing inherently political about ten little circus clowns exiting from a miniature car — much of its intent is hegemonic. These accounts of Oceanic clowning compellingly demonstrate that clowning is seldom empty nonsense but is nonsense in service of a political end. The outrageous antics of a clown usually encode a critical message to her observers, including the ethnographer. The heuristic significance of studying clowning is that it unerringly directs the ethnographer's attention to contested views of social life and cultural belief. The troupe of unfamiliar clowns who inhabit this book provides a sustained look at the ways clowning is culturally constructed as critical practice in Oceanic society.

The Postmodern Imagination, Humor, and the Clown

Although this book has no pretensions to postmodern voice or intent, humor — that most ironic form of human expression — does, and thereby it deserves a hearing. There are a variety of ways to approach postmodernism; I view it as a way of imagining the world. It is not, as sometimes claimed, a jejeune and nihilistic response to sense, experience, and knowledge, but an open and creative response representing an amplification of spirit, not a loss of verve.[52] For the anthropologist, the postmodern imagination is culturally situated in human acts of thinking, feeling, and performance that go far beyond the narrow concerns of a textual critique of ethnographic writing, as revealing as this may be.

Postmodernism's features of flow, fragmentation, juxtaposition, ambiguity, contingency, relativeness, and irony[53] are heralded as the hallmarks of a new form of human consciousness that is gradually overtaking the planet's developed societies. It is a transformation rooted in the history of humankind and the interplay of those conceptual and physical environments constructed by human thought and muscle. This transformation to a more pluralistic, even contradictory, view of reality as difference is itself both paradoxical and ironic: human beings do not relish disorder. Like other organisms, they are wired to make sense of their environment and their experiences within it. Not to do so may threaten their existence.

An older and enduring irony of the modern world is that the cultural constructions of religion and science, in some ways so far apart, both propose worlds of order. Both explore and revel in the unknown, and both seek to convert it to domestic compliance. Much of human history is the confrontation of these formidable intellectual foes, each in its way—religion rationally and intuitively, science rationally and experimentally—advancing the cause of order over chaos. Religion remains a convenient and often rewarding way to explain or rationalize that which is deeply puzzling. If one will believe, there are clear answers. The scientific enterprise's less ancient approach has overwhelmed the world with its cool method and clever devices. Even in the developing nations, governments, if not necessarily the citizenry, are dedicated to its pursuit. But science's search for universal rhythms and its declamations on order are often at variance with personal experience which perceives a world shaken by nonsense, capriciousness, and ambiguity.

Instead of repairing these cognitive breaches with more science or more religion, what is striking about the postmodern imagination is that it surrenders to the ambiguity in human experience and, if not necessarily opting for nonsense, acknowledges its epistemological place in a phenomenological world. The postmodern imagination accepts disorder and difference as an inevitable constituent of experience, a sobering acknowledgment of the impermanence and ambiguity of phenomena, including the self.[54] In other words, Nietzsche was right—God is dead—and the metanarratives that pander to our own intrinsic sense of order and goodness are dissolved, even as science's search for universals and order is relativized by its paradigms.

The human imagination has groped its way from magic to religion to science, but it is not a linear progression; all three approaches for interpreting experience continue to exist side by side in even the most technologically advanced nations. What does

Introduction

change, and emphatically so, is their relative frequency and force as interpretations. In a much younger world in which cultural ideas could convincingly explain all, ritual clowning was a tiny lexical comment indexing a tear in a society's metanarratives of completeness, continuity, commensurability, and cosmic certainty. The postmodern imagination widens the tear to a gaping hole; just to be alive is a jest.

The social importance of all forms of ritual clowning has faded as totalizing cosmologies and epistemologies were abandoned and the sense and place of the mysterious shifted. In most of the Western world, informal and theatrical clowning long have been the dominant metaphors for disorder and the principle venues for celebrating the irrational nature of the world. While ritual clowning is often in the service of cultural reproduction, informal and theatrical clowning may be subversive, attacking with wit and ridicule established cultural truths. The party joker—even the TV clown who sells hamburgers—reminds us that behind the surface of a surmised cultural order lie discontinuities. Lowie's (in)famous characterization of "civilization" or culture as "a thing of shreds and patches," although strongly denied by his colleagues and later repudiated by him, is a very postmodern perspective (1920:441). Cultures are not tidy and seamless garments with an absence of dangling threads, rips, and patches, but are more like the motley dress of Bateson's Iautmul clowns.

Throughout human history, the clown has symbolized nonsense in a more or less culturally cognized, orderly world. As a universal phenomenon, the clown's power for revealing the quirky nature of the human imagination is her play with sense and order. But her nonsense, as repeatedly shown in this book, is politically focused. Violating the conventions of polite behavior, she attracts attention with antics that instruct, criticize, and transform. These Oceanic clowns remind us that in all societies reason and order are not constants but fluctuating attributes of thinking. However and wherever folly is manifested, it testifies to the durability, even necessity, of the artificial fool—the clown—whose critical capers celebrate the ambiguities within our culturally constructed worlds.

NOTES

1. Humor's current meaning as a general term for anything funny—a meaning Schopenhauer sharply criticized—is now accepted by many

modern theorists. "This means," as Martin explains, "setting aside the narrow usage in which humor is contrasted with wit (which is more intellectual and relies on verbal ingenuity), sarcasm (which is more derisive), satire (which aims to discredit vices and follies), slapstick (typically based on boisterous action), and farce (generated by one-dimensional characters and improbable situations)" (1987:173). It is possible, in a rough way, to distinguish conceptually between action humor (e.g., clowning and practical jokes) and narrative humor (e.g., punning and telling jokes and funny stories), but in the actual practice of humor, action and narrative, as in farce, are usually combined in varying ways. Only the mime completely eschews speech in a comic performance.

2. Around 1500, on the cusp between the Middle Ages and the Renaissance, "the fashion of interpreting human nature in terms of folly was near its greatest currency" (Swain 1932:102). In literature, folly was usually characterized as a woman attended by various fools representing different foibles of humankind. In earlier personifications, she tended to be treated in a somewhat derisive manner, but the great Dutch scholar Erasmus (1466?–1536), a herald of the Renaissance humanist spirit, created a Mother Folly whose eloquent soliloquy, *Praise of Folly* (1971), made allowances for the weaknesses inherent in human nature. Western writers have continued to use her name to symbolize the foolishness of men and women.

3. Laughter terms, like all language, are culturally loaded. In American society, gender encoding declares it is not manly for a man to giggle or womanly for a woman to guffaw. De Sousa also comments that "laughter is a great revealer of character," doubting that one would want her daughter to marry a man whose characteristic laughter is a "cackle" or a "snicker" (1987:229).

4. Both Darwin (1965:206) and Lawick-Goodall (1971:273), among others, note the ability for laughter in apes. For a summary of the evidence for humor and laughter in signing apes, see McGhee (1979:104–23).

5. For further data on the laughter and humor of preschool children, see McGhee (1979).

6. The physiological similarities of laughing and crying have been recognized and puzzled over by many writers. For example, Kern tells us that the poet Baudelaire, who considered "all laughter in essence satanic . . . believed nevertheless that neither laughter nor tears would have been conceivable before the Fall, since both involve ugly physiognomic convulsions incongruent with paradise and its harmony" (1980:3). For a more penetrating analysis, see Plessner (1970), who finds that both laughing and crying constitute a kind of momentary breakdown or disorganization. What appears not to have been observed, however, is the similarity of both laughing and sobbing to the out-of-time convulsive spasms of the sexual orgasm, which also may result in the suspension of sustained and coherent speech.

Introduction

7. Apte's admirable book surveys the literature and analyzes humor within a holistic and comparative anthropological framework emphasizing its links to sociocultural systems. Two other book length studies, but ethnographically focused, are by Bricker (1973) and Radin (1956). Among some of the earlier ethnographic articles dealing explicitly with humor are Bowman (1937) and Hill (1943) on the Navaho.

8. While the ethnographer's fieldwork bible, *Notes and Queries on Anthropology*, has four pages on the collection of "string figures" it has none on humor, with the exception of a brief paragraph on the "joking relationship" (1951). The *Annual Review of Anthropology* has never published an essay on the anthropology of humor, nor is this topic discussed in current introductory anthropology texts. Perhaps the most telling evidence regarding the exclusion of humor from the traditional anthropological paradigm is that the anthropologist Piddington (1933) wrote an important psychological study of humor, yet makes no mention of humor or laughter in his 1952 two-volume encyclopedic textbook on social anthropology.

9. See, for example, Charney (1978), Merchant (1972), Olson (1968), Pirandello (1960), Shershow (1986), and Sorell (1972).

10. For recent psychoanalytically oriented studies of humor, see Chasseguet-Smirgel (1988) and Poland (1990). Also see Sands (1984) for a critique of the growing literature on the use of humor in psychotherapy and Saper (1988) for a critique of the aphorism that "laughter is the best medicine."

11. See Berger (1987) for a multi-disciplinary publication on humor, with short papers from the fields of psychoanalysis, psychiatry, anthropology, psychology, folklore, communications, linguistics, and others. Also see McGhee and Goldstein (1983).

12. For a range of psychological studies on humor and laughter, see Chapman and Foot (1976) and Goldstein and McGhee (1972). On children's humor see Wolfenstein's pioneering 1954 study and McGhee's 1979 review of the literature.

13. For trickster stories, see Abrahams (1985:177–218) and Thompson (1973:53–77); for ethnic slur jokes, see Davies (1990).

14. Two recent studies are Holdaway's (1988:106–22) on police work and Linstead's (1988:123–48) on a factory bakery. For an analysis of joking in the workplace based on Caplow's triad theory, see Dwyer (1991:1–19).

15. Zijderveld (1983) has written an interesting review article on the sociology of humor indicating the extent to which anthropology has been an influence, which is critiqued by Davies (1984). Also see Powell and Paton's "first broad attempt to collate a representative sample of current work in the sociology of humour" (1988:xxi).

16. In a different context, Chambers (1989:589) emphasizes the similarities between comedy—especially eighteenth-century literary satire—and modern ethnography in terms of their reliance on the "literary

modes of exaggeration, exceptionality, reversal, and practice," which suggests to him that they have a "similar critical intent."

17. Here is Tyler; "Anthropologists are victims of a kind of mental illness that arises from the sense of guilt generated by pretending to do what they know cannot be done. This is the crisis of contemporary anthropology. It is a crisis of discourse, a crisis of poetics, and that is why we turn to poetry, to find there some solution to the dilemmas created by a mode of discourse whose master trope and ideology condemn us forever to failure, hypocrisy, and neurosis" (1984:335).

18. One of the more appealing features of the postmodern position is its eschewing of analytical closure and bounded systematics that says, "we've got it all together." The philosopher Irwin Edman, in apologizing to his readers that his book was not a "systematic work," comments that "some day, if I can overcome a sense of humor and a sense of doubt, I shall try to write such a systematic tome as professional philosophers require, or as is expected of a professional thinker by the general public," adding, however, that "in the most systematic work of thought, something is left out, something does not fit in, namely the miscellaneous facts of the world" (1947:274). No postmodernist could say it better.

19. The Western concept of *emotion* as a research focus has not gone unchallenged. For example, in her study of Balinese experience, Wikan believes that "it is only by facing the full consequences of a view that the Anglo-Saxon, emotion-thought split might be a myth that theory building will proceed fruitfully" (1990:138).

20. While the term *amusing* is often used interchangeably with *funny*, it also can refer to experiences that are primarily entertaining but devoid of humor, such as solving a simple crossword puzzle. To complicate the picture, *funny* also can mean something odd. In everyday parlance these are sometimes distinguished as *funny ha-ha* and *funny peculiar*. See McGhee for an insightful discussion of English terms related to the umbrella term *humor*, including absurd, incongruous, ridiculous, ludicrous, funny, amusing, and mirthful (1979:6–8).

21. The term *humor* comes to us from the Greeks, especially Hippocrates' theory that pain and disease are caused by an imbalance of the four humors: blood, phlegm, black bile, and yellow bile. Galen revised the theory, adding four basic temperaments that reflect the humors. In one form or another, the humors remained important in medicine until Virchow's work on cellular pathology in the nineteenth century. They also had an impact on literature, especially in Jonson's popular satirical plays *Every Man in His Humor* and *Every Man out of His Humour*, featuring "humour" characters typified by a single obsession or peculiarity who became objects of laughter. See *Columbia Encyclopedia*, 4th ed., s.v. "humor," and see Siegel (1973).

22. I wish to take exception with Alford's assertion that "In all cultures some subjects are considered too serious for humorous treatment

Introduction 41

(1981:153). On the contrary, it is violation of the most taboo subjects that sometimes provides the most extreme laughter. The English essayist and critic, Hazlitt recognized that "we laugh the more at any restraint upon this impulse" so that the occasion when "there is something that we ought to look grave at, is almost always a signal for laughing outright: we can hardly keep our countenance at a sermon, a funeral, or a wedding" (1819:12). As children my sister and I, bored to distraction by solemn and interminable Methodist sermons, surreptitiously poked each other and then, on the brink of hysterical laughter, were forced to bite our cheeks to contain our merriment.

23. Embarrassment needs a qualification. Embarrassed individuals may laugh only to cover their discomposure, seeing nothing funny about their humiliation, or they may laugh because they are genuinely amused by the embarrassing situation they are in (cf. Ekman 1980:101). For more extensive discussions of embarrassment, see Goffman (1956), Morreall (1983), and Plessner (1970).

24. In the following discussion, I also am indebted to Milner (1972) and, especially, Morreall's (1983, 1987) thorough yet imaginative approach to humor. Also see Keith-Spiegel (1972), whose typology, while essentially similar, has some interesting differences.

25. Aristotle's *Poetics II*, containing his more extensive views on comedy, is lost and, through the ages, has been the subject of much debate and conjecture. For a recent hypothetical reconstruction based on the controversial Tractatus Coislinianus, see Janko (1984).

26. Feinberg (1978) makes a challenging if not completely convincing case that all humor is the result of "playful aggression," including "nonsense" humor, which he interprets as "aggression against logic and order," and "word play," "aggression against conformity."

27. Fright itself is usually not conducive to humor. When one is terrified, laughter is rare. When the Nissan Atoll grand sorcerer ludicrously wags his painted penis at the initiate, his other hand is poised with a club to bash the youth if he smiles (Nachman 1982).

28. Also see Santayana's (1896) critique of the incongruity theory; he believes that humans, as rational beings, dislike incongruity or absurdity in any form but endure it because it is stimulating. For specific references to the philosophically important incongruity theories, see Morreall (1987), and for an anthropologist's related theory in terms of "figure-ground" reversals, see Bateson (1953) and his colleague Fry's (1963) additional comments.

29. For a brief yet penetrating biography of a modern natural fool, see Zijerveld (1982:vii–ix, 163–69).

30. Foucault (1973:8) reports that the practice of handing over troublesome fools to river boatmen for transport to the next city—hence Sebastian Brant's famous fifteenth century *Narrenschiff* (translated into English as *The Ship of Foles of the Worlde*) was not just a literary invention

but actually existed. Zijderveld's (1982:77) archival research, however, finds no evidence for Foucault's assertion.

31. In the Wape village of Taute, my 1970–1972 field site, "crazy" individuals were tolerated within the village, but if they became dangerously homicidal they were exiled by the villagers to live in garden houses in the forest.

32. Clarke (1973), for example, explicitly interprets "wild-man" behavior in the New Guinea Highlands as "theatre."

33. See, for example, Billington (1984), Swain (1932), and Zijderveld (1982).

34. For scholarly studies of the medieval and renaissance fools of Europe, see, for example, Billington (1984), Swain (1932), Welsford (1966), and Zijderveld (1982). Also see Towsen's (1976) more popularly written historical survey of fools and folly with an emphasis on modern clowns; Doran's (1966) account of specific court fools is a mine of detailed data, but it is generally undocumented and oftentimes prejudiced; Willeford's (1969) interpretative essays on the fool in both life and literature include a number of old and intriguing illustrations; Swortzel's (1978) popular and sweeping account of the fool in Western society from antiquity to now includes chapters on clowning in the modern theater, circus, films, and television. For a study of the contemporary church and the fool, see Cox (1969). There is also an extensive literature on court fools in German, French, and Italian.

35. O'Connor (1978), who explores the humorous characterization of physical deformity in Renaissance chivalric romances, notes that physical ugliness and deformity is an old butt of Western laughter. In polite society today, this form of humorous ridicule is taboo, although its popularity in street culture continues unabated.

36. References to non-Western court fools appear in passing in Rosenthal (1956), Schulman (1985), Swortzell (1978:121–36), and Zijderveld (1982:131–55).

37. For an eyewitness account of the jesters in Montezuma's court, see Diaz (1967:227–30); also see Prescott (1873:123). For a drawing from the *Codex Florentino* of Montezuma's musicians and jesters, see Vaillant (1941: plate 39). As an indication of just how prevalent court fools were in the sixteenth century, according to Prescott (1873:119), Cortez, a man on the warpath against the Aztecs, traveled in Mexico with his own fool.

38. See Welsford (1966:189–95) and Doran (1966:322–51) for descriptions of the sometimes pathetic learned fool in the German courts.

39. Towsen (1976) has a short chapter, "Asian Theater Clowns," and Swortzell (1978) includes a brief chapter on the clowns of India, China, Japan, and Southeast Asia but cites no sources. For a description of the clown types of the Szechuan theater, see Kalvodova (1965).

40. Melanesian clowning, of course, is not limited to Papua New

Introduction 43

Guinea; see, for example, Hereniko's comments on Fijian clowning in this volume.

41. Gell's basic interpretation of the clown's performances as comic relief is challenged as inadequate by Werbner (1989:176), who believes "that the clowns are the heroes turned topsy-turvy in a perverse way."

42. Hereniko's draft of his review of the clowning literature on Polynesia and Melanesia has been very helpful (personal communication with author). He notes that much of the documentation is by missionaries or expatriates, is highly subjective, anecdotal, and "very uneven, with the most information on Tahiti, Samoa and Papua New Guinea and nothing (as far as I can discover) on islands such as the Solomon Islands, New Caledonia, Niue, Tuvalu, Kiribati, and most of Micronesia." However, further to the west, in Indonesia, there is a rich and ancient tradition of theatrical clowning with origins that predate Hindu and Muslim influences. See, for example, Boon (1984), Jenkins (1980), and Peacock (1967).

43. For summaries of references to the precontact literature, including theatrical performances for the Society Islands, see Ferndon (1981); for Tonga, see Ferndon (1987). Also see Oliver (1974).

44. The line between McGhee's (1979:79–82) "tendentious humor" and my "hegemonic humor" is blurred, but generally the former is a simple expression of negativism while the latter is used to exert control over another.

45. Gluckman (1955:131–32) introduced the concept "rituals of license," but also see his more extensive discussion of the related concept of "rituals of rebellion" (Gluckman 1945). His functionalist argument is that the periodic rebellions in some African states did not weaken them but strengthened the political system. Thus, fighting might result in a new ruler but no change in the structure of the system. Hence, there were rebels, but no revolutionaries.

46. Connerton, influenced by Bakhtin, characterizes the popular Renaissance festivals including carnival as "anticipatory representations," emphasizing that the hierarchical inversions should be read, not as a "covert means of reaffirming hierarchy" but as "a mechanism of social liberation" (1989:50). Nelson takes the opposite position, commenting that, "where festivity is concerned, the safety-valve theory still seems more plausible than the theory of creative change" (1990:174). My position, like Turner's (1982), is that it is not an either-or situation. Both explanations are theoretically plausible but are meaningful only in terms of specific cases.

47. Obviously, there is no pleasure in hollow, false, or forced laughter. Quite the opposite; such laughter usually denotes frustration or confusion. In these situations we laugh because we think we must—for example, when we disapprove of the humor displayed but don't want to make a

point of it or, not grasping what is funny, laugh rather than call attention to our being out of it.

48. *Black humor* is a nihilist humor of the absurd, bizarre, and grotesque (cf. David 1967, Feinberg 1978, Friedman 1965, and Schultz 1973). Gallows humor and *Schadenfreude* are variant forms of black humor. As a significant twentieth-century comedic genre practiced in all of the arts and literature, black humor is sometimes more shocking than funny to bourgeois sensibilities. For a very insightful reflexive account of malicious laughter and anthropological fieldwork, see Nachman (1986). The grotesque has a rich critical theory of its own; see, for example, Harpham (1982) and Kayser (1981).

49. For recent discussions of the aesthetics of humor see Martin (1987) and especially Morreall (1983, 1987), but also see Kallen (1911) and Martin (1905).

50. Bachelard, for example, with delightful imagination, shows the humorous power—and profundity—of inversions in the perspective of size, especially in respect to "miniaturizing the world" (1964:148–92).

51. See Handelman and Kapferer (1972) for their distinction between two types of joking frames, "setting-specific" and "category-routinized," which are broadly related to my distinction between informal and formal clowning.

52. The initial gloss of postmodernism was in terms of cultural decline and exhaustion, for example, Toynbee (1954), Howe (1970), and Newman (1985), while others such as Hassan (1987), Lyotard (1984), and Fiedler (1971)—and I would add Tyler (1987)—see postmodernism as "a positive birth from the fallen giant of modernism" that signifies not fatigue, but "freedom and self-assertion" (Connor 1989:65–66). See Rose (1991) for a recent authoritative review of the various meanings of *postmodern* and related terms. For examples of the burgeoning literature expressing criticism of anthropological postmodernism, see, for example, Murphy (1990), Roth (1989), and Sangren (1988).

53. Wilde distinguishes between *disjunctive irony*, related to modernism, and *suspensive irony*, related to postmodernism. While both forms of irony "confronts a world that appears inherently disconnected and fragmented," disjunctive irony seeks to "control" the disconnections, while suspensive irony, "with its yet more radical vision of multiplicity, randomness, contingency, and even absurdity, abandons the quest for paradise altogether—the world in all its disorder is simply (or not so simply) accepted" (1987:10).

54. The positive acceptance of disorder is not, however, a *de nouveau* postmodern novelty but is prefigured in the work of, for example, Weber, Marx, and Simmel. There is also the problem that disorder itself is a relative phenomenon (cf. Gleick 1987). To me, my colleague's office is a domain of random chaos, but it is one in which he functions effectively.

Introduction

REFERENCES

Abrahams, Roger D., ed.
    1985   *Afro-American Folktales: Stories from Black Traditions in the New World*. New York: Random House.

Alford, Finnegan, and Richard Alford
    1981   A Holo-Cultural Study of Humor. *Ethos* 9:149–64.

Apte, Mahadev L.
    1985   *Humor and Laughter: An Anthropological Approach*. Ithaca: Cornell University Press.

Aristotle
    1941   *The Basic Works of Aristotle*. New York: Random House.

Bachelard, Gaston
    1969   *The Poetics of Space*. Boston: Beacon Press (Fr. orig. 1958).

Bakhtin, Mikhail
    1984   *Rabelais and His World*. Bloomington: Indiana University Press (Rus. orig. 1965).

Ballantine, Bill
    1982   *Clown Alley*. Boston: Little, Brown.

Barba, Eugenio and Nicola Savarese, eds.
    1991   *A Dictionary of Theatre Anthropology: The Secret Art of the Performance*. London and New York: Routledge.

Bateson, Gregory
    1953   The Position of Humor in Human Communication. In *Cybernetics*. (Transactions of the 9th Conference), ed. Heinz von Foerster, pp. 1–47, New York: Josiah Macy, Jr., Foundation.
    1958   *Naven: A Survey of the Problems Suggested by a Composite Picture of the Culture of a New Guinea Tribe Drawn from Three Points of View*. 2nd ed. Stanford: Stanford University Press.

Berger, Arthur A., ed.
    1987   Special Issue: Humor, the Psyche and Society. *American Behavioral Scientist* 30(3).

Bergson, Henri
    1911   *Laughter: An Essay on the Meaning of the Comic*. New York: Macmillan (Fr. orig. 1900).

Billington, Sandra
    1984   *A Social History of the Fool*. New York: St. Martin's Press.

Bligh, William
    1937   *The Log of the* Bounty, *Being Lieutenant William Bligh's Log of the Proceedings of His Majesty's Armed Vessel* Bounty *in a Voyage to the South Seas, to Take the Breadfruit from the Society Islands to the West Indies*. Vol. 1. London: Golden Cockerel Press.

Boon, James, A.
    1984   Folly, Bali, and Anthropology, or Satire Across Cultures. In *Text, Play and Story: The Construction and Reconstruction of Self and Society.* ed. Edward M. Bruner, pp 156–77, Prospect Heights, Ill.: Waveland Press.

Bowman, Henry A.
    1937   The Humor of Primitive Peoples. In *Studies in the Science of Society,* ed. George Peter Murdock, pp. 69–83. New Haven: Yale University Press.

Bricker, Victoria Reifler
    1973   *Ritual Humor in Highland Chiapas.* Austin: University of Texas Press.

Bruner, Edward M. ed.
    1984   *Text, Play, and Story: The Construction and Reconstruction of Self and Society.* Prospect Heights, Ill.: Waveland Press.

Caputi, Anthony
    1978   *Buffo: The Genius of Vulgar Comedy.* Detroit: Wayne State University Press.

Chambers, Erve
    1989   Thalia's Revenge: Ethnography and Theory of Comedy. *American Anthropologist* 91:589–98.

Chapman, A. J., and H. C. Foot, eds.
    1976   *Humour and Laughter: Theory, Research, and Applications.* London: Wiley.

Charney, Maurice, ed.
    1978   *Comedy: New Perspectives.* Vol. 1. New York: New York Literary Forum.

Chasseguet-Smirgel, J.
    1988   The Triumph of Humor. In *Fantasy, Myth and Reality: Essays in Honor of Jacob A. Arlow,* ed. H. P. Blum et al., pp. 197–213. Madison, Conn.: International Universities Press.

Chesterfield, Lord
    1901   *Letters to His Son.* Vol. 1. Washington: M. Walter Dunne (orig. 1774).

Clark, Michael
    1987   Humor and Incongruity. In *The Philosophy of Laughter and Humor,* ed. John Morreall. Albany: State University of New York Press.

Clarke, William C.
    1973   Temporary Madness as Theatre: Wild-Man Behaviour in New Guinea. *Oceania* 43:198–214.

Introduction

Collier, J. P., ed.
    1842   *Fools and Jesters: With a Reprint of Robert Armin's Nests of Ninnies.* London: Shakespeare Society.

Committee of the Royal Anthropological Institute of Great Britain and Ireland
    1951   *Notes and Queries on Anthropology.* London: Routledge and Kegan Paul.

Connerton, Paul
    1989   *How Societies Remember.* Cambridge: Cambridge University Press.

Cornford, Francis Macdonald
    1961   *The Origin of Attic Comedy.* Garden City, N.J.: Doubleday.

Connor, Steven
    1989   *Postmodernist Culture: An Introduction to Theories of the Contemporary.* Oxford: Basil Blackwell.

Cox, Harvey
    1969   *The Feast of Fools: A Theological Essay on Festivity and Fantasy.* Cambridge: Harvard University Press.

Darwin, Charles
    1965   *The Expression of the Emotions in Man and Animals.* Chicago: University of Chicago Press (orig. 1872).

David, Douglas M.
    1967   *The World of Black Humor.* New York: Dutton.

Davies, Christie
    1984   Commentary on Anton C. Zijderveld's Trend Report on "The Sociology of Humour and Laughter." *Current Sociology* 32:j142–57.
    1990   *Ethnic Humor Around the World: A Comparative Analysis.* Bloomington: Indiana University Press.

Davis, Natalie Z.
    1971   The Reasons of Misrule: Youth Groups and Charivaris in Sixteenth Century France. *Past and Present* 50:49–75.

de Sousa, Ronald
    1987   When Is It Wrong to Laugh? In *The Philosophy of Laughter and Humor,* ed. John Morreall. Albany: State University of New York Press.

Diaz, Bernal
    1967   *The Conquest of New Spain.* London: Penguin Books (Sp. orig. 1570).

Doran, John
    1966   *The History of Court Fools.* New York: Haskell House (orig. 1855).

Dwyer, Tom
   1991   Humor, Power, and Change in Organizations. *Human Relations* 44:1–19.

Edman, Irwin
   1947   *Philosopher's Quest.* New York: Viking Press.

Ekman, P.
   1980   *The Face of Man: Expressions of Universal Emotions in a New Guinea Village.* New York: Garland STPM Press.

Erasmus
   1971   *Praise of Folly.* London: Penguin Group (Lat. orig. 1511).

Feinberg, Leonard
   1978   *The Secret of Humor.* Amsterdam: Rodopi.

Ferdon, Edwin N.
   1987   *Early Tonga: As the Explorers Saw It 1616–1810.* Tucson: University of Arizona Press.
   1981   *Early Tahiti: As the Explorers Saw It 1767–1797.* Tucson: University of Arizona Press.

Fewkes, Jesse Walter
   1891   A Few Summer Ceremonials at Zuni Pueblo. *Journal of American Ethnology and Archaeology* 1:1–61.

Fiedler, Leslie
   1971   *The Collected Essays of Leslie Fiedler.* Vol. 2. New York: Stein and Day.

Foucault, Michel
   1973   *Madness and Civilization: A History of Insanity in the Age of Reason.* New York: Random House (Fr. orig. 1961).

Freud, Sigmund
   1960   *Jokes and Their Relation to the Unconscious.* New York: W. W. Norton (Ger. orig. 1905).
   1928   Humor. *International Journal of Psychoanalysis* 9:1–6.

Friedman, Bruce Jay
   1965   *Black Humor.* New York: Bantam Books.

Fry, William F., Jr.
   1963   *Sweet Madness: A Study of Humor.* Palo Alto, Calif.: Pacific Books.

Gell, Alfred
   1975   *Metamorphosis of the Cassowaries: Umeda Society, Language and Ritual.* London: Athlone Press.

Gleick, James
   1987   *Chaos: Making a New Science.* New York: Viking USA.

Gluckman, Max
   1945   *Rituals of Rebellion in South-East Africa.* Manchester: Manchester University Press.

Introduction 49

  1955 *Custom and Conflict in Africa.* Glencoe, Ill.: Free Press.
Goffman, Irving
  1956 Embarrassment and Social Organization. *American Journal of Sociology* 62:264–74.
Goldstein, Jeffrey H. and Paul E. McGhee
  1972 *The Psychology of Humor: Theoretical Perspectives and Empirical Issues.* New York: Academic Press.
Groos, K.
  1898 *The Play of Animals.* New York: Appleton.
Handelman, Don
  1981 The Ritual-Clown: Attributes and Affinities. *Anthropos* 76: 321–70.
Handelman, Don, and Bruce Kapferer
  1972 Forms of Joking Activity: A Comparative Approach. *American Anthropologist* 74:484–517.
Harpham, Geoffrey Galt
  1982 *On the Grotesque: Strategies of Contradiction in Art and Literature.* Princeton: Princeton University Press.
Hassan, Ihab
  1987 *The Postmodern Turn: Essays in Postmodern Theory and Culture.* Columbus: Ohio State University Press.
Hau'ofa, Epeli
  1975 Athropology and Pacific Islanders. *Oceania* 45:283–89.
  1988 Oral Traditions and Writing. Paper presented at the Commonwealth Institute, London.
Hazlitt, William
  1819 *Lectures on the English Comic Writers.* Philadelphia: M. Carrey & Son.
Hieb, Louis A.
  1972 Meaning and Mismeaning: Toward an Understanding of the Ritual Clown. In *New Perspectives on the Pueblos,* ed. Alfonso Ortiz. Albuquerque: University of New Mexico Press.
Hill, Willard W.
  1943 *Navaho Humor.* General Series in Anthropology 9. Menasha, Wis.: George Banta Publishing Co.
Hobbes, Thomas
  1967 *Leviathan, or the Matter, Forme, & Power of a Common-wealth Ecclesiasticall and Civill.* Oxford: Oxford University Press (orig. 1651).
Holdaway, Simon
  1988 Blue Jokes: Humour in Police Work. In *Humour in Society:*

Resistance and Control, ed. Chris Powell and George E. C. Paton, New York: St Martin's Press.

Howe, Irving
    1970   *The Decline of the New.* New York: Harcourt, Brace and World.

Janko, Richard
    1984   *Aristotle on Comedy: Towards a Reconstruction of Poetics II.* Berkeley and Los Angeles: University of California Press.

Jenkins, Ron
    1980   The Holy Humor of Bali's Clowns. *Asia* 3:28–35.

Joubert, Laurent
    1980   *Treatise on Laughter.* Birmingham: University of Alabama Press (Lat. orig. 1560).

Kallen, H. M.
    1911   The Aesthetic Principle in Comedy. *American Journal of Psychology* 22:137–57.

Kalvodova, Dana
    1965   Clowns in the Szechuan Theatre. *Bulletin of the School of Oriental and African Studies* 28:356–62.

Kapferer, Bruce
    1983   *A Celebration of Demons: Exorcism and the Aesthetics of Healing in Sri Lanka.* Bloomington: Indiana University Press.

Kayser, Wolfgang
    1981   *The Grotesque in Art and Literature.* New York: Columbia University Press (Ger. orig. 1957).

Keith-Spiegel, Patricia
    1972   Early Conceptions of Humor: Varieties and Issues. In *The Psychology of Humor: Theoretical Perspectives and Empirical Issues,* ed. Jeffrey H. Goldstein and Paul E. McGhee. New York: Academic Press.

Kern, Edith
    1980   *The Absolute Comic.* New York: Columbia University Press.

Lancy, David F.
    1980   Play in Species Adaptation. In *Annual Review of Anthropology,* ed. Bernard J. Siegel et al. 471–495. Palo Alto, Calif.: Annual Reviews.

Lawick-Goodall, Jane van
    1971   *In the Shadow of Man.* Boston: Houghton Mifflin.

Leach, E. R.
    1966   Ritualization in Man in Relation to Conceptual and Social Development. *Philosophical Transactions of the Royal Society of London,* 251:403–08.

Introduction

Lever, Katherine
    1956   *The Art of Greek Comedy*. London: Methuen.

Levy, Robert I.
    1973   *Tahitians: Mind and Experience in the Soceity Islands*. Chicago: University of Chicago Press.

Linstead, Steve
    1988   "Jokers Wild": Humour in Organisational Culture. In *Humour in Society: Resistance and Control*, ed. Chris Powell and George E. C. Paton. New York: St Martin's Press.

Lowie, Robert
    1920   *Primitive Society*. New York: Horace Liveright.

Lutz, Catherine, and Geoffrey M. White
    1986   The Anthropology of Emotions. *Annual Review of Anthropology* 15:405–36.

Lyotard, Jean-Francois
    1984   *The Postmodern Condition: A Report on Knowledge*. Manchester: Manchester University Press (Fr. orig. 1979).

MacAloon, John J., ed.
    1984   *Rite, Drama, Festival, Spectacle: Rehearsals Toward a Theory of Cultural Performance*. Philadelphia: Institute for the Study of Human Issues.

Makarius, Laura
    1970   Ritual Clowns and Symbolical Behaviour. *Diogenes* 69:45–73.

Malinowski, Bronislaw
    1966   Introduction to *The Savage Hits Back*, ed. J. Kips, pp. vii–ix. New Hyde Park: University Books.

Marcus, George E., and Michael M. J. Fischer
    1986   *Anthropology as Cultural Critique: An Experimental Moment in the Human Sciences*. Chicago: University of Chicago Press.

Martin, Lilian J.
    1905   Psychology of Aesthetics: Experimental Prospecting in the Field of the Comic. *American Journal of Psychology* 16:35–116.

Martin, Mike W.
    1987   Humor and Aesthetic Enjoyment of Incongruities. In *The Philosophy of Laughter and Humor*, ed. John Morreall. Albany: State University of New York Press.

Mayo, Elton
    1933   *The Human Problems of an Industrial Civilization*. New York: Macmillan.

McGhee, Paul E.
    1979   *Humor: Its Origin and Development*. San Francisco: W. H. Freeman.

McGhee, Paul E. and Jeffrey H. Goldstein, eds.
    1983   *Handbook of Humor Research.* 2 vols. Springer-Verlag: New York and Berlin.

McNamara, Brooks, and Richard Schechner
    1982   General Introduction to the Performance Studies Series. In *From Ritual to Theatre: The Human Seriousness of Play*, ed. Victor Turner. New York: Performing Arts Journal Publications.

Mead, George Herbert
    1934   *Mind, Self and Society from the Standpoint of a Social Behaviorist.* Chicago: University of Chicago Press.

Merchant, W. Moelwyn
    1972   *Comedy.* London: Methuen.

Meredith, George
    1906   *An Essay on Comedy and the Uses of the Comic Spirit.* London: Archibald Constable (orig. 1877).

Milner, George Bertram
    1972   Homo Ridens: Towards a Semiotic Theory of Humour and Laughter. *Semiotica* 5:1–30.

Monro, D. H.
    1951   *Argument of Laughter.* Melbourne: Melbourne University Press.

Morreall, John
    1983   *Taking Laughter Seriously.* Albany: State University of New York Press.

Morreall, John, ed.
    1987   *The Philosophy of Laughter and Humor.* Albany: State University of New York Press.

Murphy, Robert F.
    1990   The Dialectics of Deeds and Words: Or Anti-the-Antis (and the Anti-Antis). *Cultural Anthropology* 5:331–37.

Nachman, Steven R.
    1982   Anti Humor: Why the Grand Sorcerer Wags His Penis. *Ethos* 10:117-135.
    1986   Discomfiting Laughter: Schadenfreude Among Melanesians. *Journal of Anthropological Research* 42:53–67.

Nelson, T.G.A.
    1990   *Comedy: An Introduction to Comedy in Literature, Drama, and Cinema.* Oxford: Oxford University Press.

Newman, Charles
    1985   *The Post-Modern Aura: The Act of Fiction in an Age of Inflation.* Evanston: Northwestern University Press.

Introduction

O'Connor, John
    1978   Physical Deformity and Chivalric Laughter in Renaissance England. *New York Literary Forum* 1:59–71.

Oliver, Douglas L.
    1974   *Ancient Tahitian Society.* Vol. 1, *Ethnography.* Honolulu: University Press of Hawaii.

Olson, Elder
    1968   *The Theory of Comedy.* Bloomington: Indiana University Press.

Oring, Elliott, ed.
    1984   *Humor and the Individual.* Los Angeles: California Folklore Society.

Parsons, Elsie Clews and Ralph L. Beals
    1934   The Sacred Clowns of the Pueblo and Mayo-Yaqui Indians. *American Anthropologist* 36:491–514.

Pascal, Blaise
    1941   Letter XI: To the Reverend Fathers, the Jesuits. In *Pensées and The Provincial Letters.* New York: Random House (Fr. orig. 1656).

Pasternak, Burton
    1988   A Conversation with Fei Xiaotong. *Current Anthropology* 29: 637–62.

Peacock, James L.
    1967   Javanese Clown and Transvestite Songs: Some Relations Between "Primitive Classification" and "Communicative Events." In *Essays on the Verbal and Visual Arts,* ed. June Helm pp. 156–77. Proceedings of the 1966 Annual Spring Meeting of the American Ethnological Society.

Piddington, Ralph
    1933   *The Psychology of Laughter: A Study in Human Adaptation.* London: Figurehead.
    1952   *An Introduction to Social Anthropology.* 2 vols. Edinburgh: Oliver and Boyd.

Pirandello, Luigi
    1960   *On Humor.* Chapel Hill: University of North Carolina Press (Ital. orig. 1908).

Plessner, Helmuth
    1970   *Laughing and Crying: A Study of the Limits of Human Behavior.* Evanston: Northwestern University Press (Ger. orig. 1961).

Poland, Warren S.
    1990   The Gift of Laughter: On the Development of a Sense of Humor in Clinical Analysis. *Psychoanalytic Quarterly* 59:197–225.

Potter, Sulamith Heins
    1988   The Cultural Construction of Emotion in Rural Chinese Social Life. *Ethos* 16:181–208.

Plato
    1937   *The Dialogues of Plato*, vol. 1. New York: Random House.

Powell, Chris, and George E. C. Paton, eds.
    1988   *Humour in Society: Resistance and Control.* New York: St. Martin's Press.

Prescott, William H.
    1873   *History of the Conquest of Mexico*, vol. 2. Philadelphia: Lippincott.

Radcliffe-Brown, A. R.
    1940   On Joking Relationships. *Africa* 13:195–210.

Radin, Paul
    1956   *The Trickster: A Study in American Indian Mythology.* New York: Greenwood Press.

Roethlisberger, F. J., and W. J. Dickson
    1939   *Management and the Worker.* Cambridge: Harvard University Press

Rosaldo, Renato
    1980   *Ilongot Headhunting 1883–1974.* Stanford: Stanford University Press.

Rose, Margaret A.
    1991   *The Post-Modern and the Post-Industrial: A Critical Analysis.* Cambridge: Cambridge University Press.

Rosenthal, Frantz
    1956   *Humor in Early Islam.* Philadelphia: University of Pennsylvania Press.

Roth, Paul A.
    1989   Ethnography Without Tears. *Current Anthropology* 30:555–61.

Sands, Steven
    1984   The Use of Humor in Psychotherapy. *Psychoanalytic Review* 71:441–60.

Sangren, P. Steven
    1988   Rhetoric and the Authority of Ethnography: "Postmodernism" and the Social Reproduction of Texts. *Current Anthropology* 29:405–35.

Santayana, George
    1896   *The Sense of Beauty.* New York: Scribner's.

Saper, B.
    1988   Humor in Psychiatric Healing. *Psychiatric Quarterly* 59:306–19.

Introduction

Schechner, Richard
    1985   *Between Theater and Anthropology*. Philadelphia: University of Pennsylvania Press.

Schulman, David Dean
    1985   *The King and the Clown in South Indian Myth Poetry*. Princeton: Princeton University Press.

Schultz, Max F.
    1973   *Black Humor Fiction of the Sixties*. Athens: Ohio University Press.

Shershow, Scott Cutler
    1986   *Laughing Matters: The Paradox of Comedy*. Amherst: University of Massachusetts Press.

Shore, Bradd
    1982   *Sala'ilua: A Samoan Mystery*. New York: Columbia University Press.

Siegel, Lee
    1987   *Laughing Matters: Comic Tradition in India*. Chicago: University of Chicago Press.

Siegel, Rudolph E.
    1973   *Galen on Psychology, Psychopathology, and Function and Diseases of the Nervous System: An Analysis of His Doctrines, Observations and Experiments*. Basel: S. Karger.

Sorell, Walter
    1972   *Facets of Comedy*. New York: Grosset and Dunlap.

Spencer, George Herbert
    1891   *Essays: Scientific, Political, and Speculative*, vol. 2. New York: Appleton.

Stevenson, Matilde Coxe
    1904   The Zuni Indians: Their Mythology, Esoteric Fraternities and Ceremonies. *Annual Report of the Bureau of American Ethnology* 23:1–608. Washington: Government Printing Office.

Swain, Barbara
    1932   *Fools and Folly During the Middle Ages and the Renaissance*. New York: Columbia University Press.

Sweet, Jill D.
    1989   Burlesquing "The Other" in Pueblo Performance. *Annals of Tourism Research* 16:62–75.

Swortzell, Lowell
    1978   *Here Come the Clowns: A Cavalcade of Comedy from Antiquity to the Present*. New York: Viking Press.

Thompson, Stith
    1973   *Tales of the North American Indians*. Bloomington: Indiana University Press.

Towsen, John H.
    1976   *Clowns.* New York: Hawthorn Books.
Toynbee, Arnold
    1954   *A Study of History,* vol. 9. London: Oxford University Press.
Turner, George
    1884   *Samoa: One Hundred Years Ago and Long Before.* London: Macmillan.
Turner, Victor
    1977   Frame, Flow and Reflection: Ritual and Drama as Public Liminality. In *Performance in Postmodern Culture,* ed. Michel Benamou and Charles Caramello. Madison: Coda Press.
    1982   *From Ritual to Theatre. The Human Seriousness of Play.* New York: Performing Arts Journal Press.
Tyler, Stephen A.
    1987   *The Unspeakable: Discourse, Dialogue, and Rhetoric in the Postmodern World.* Madison: University of Wisconsin Press.
    1984   The Poetic Turn in Postmodern Anthropology: The Poetry of Paul Friedrich. *American Anthropologist* 86:328–36.
Vaillant, George C.
    1941   *The Aztecs of Mexico: Origin, Rise and Fall of the Aztec Nation.* New York: Doubleday, Doran.
Welsford, Enid
    1966   *The Fool: His Social and Literary History.* Gloucester, Mass.: Peter Smith.
Werbner, Richard P.
    1989   *Ritual Passage, Sacred Journey: The Process and Organization of Religious Movement.* Washington: Smithsonian Institution Press.
Wierzbicka, Anna
    1986   Human Emotions: Universal or Culture-Specific? *American Anthropologist* 88:584–94.
Wikan, Unni
    1990   *Managing Turbulent Hearts: A Balinese Formula for Living.* Chicago: University of Chicago Press.
Wilde, Alan
    1987   *Horizons of Assent: Modernism, Postmodernism, and the Ironic Imagination.* Philadelphia: University of Pennsylvania Press.
Willeford, William
    1969   *The Fool and His Scepter: A Study in Clowns and Jesters and Their Audience.* Evanston: Northwestern University Press.
Wolfenstein, Martha
    1954   *Children's Humor: A Psychological Analysis.* Glencoe, Ill., Free Press.

Zijerveld, Anton C.
- 1982 *Reality in a Looking-Glass: Rationality Through an Analysis of Traditional Folly.* London: Routledge and Kegan Paul.
- 1983 The Sociology of Humour and Laughter. *Current Sociology* 31:1–100.

Zucker, Wolfgang M.
- 1969 The Clown as the Lord of Disorder. In *Holy Laughter: Essays on Religion in the Comic Perspective,* ed. M. Conrad Hyers. New York: Seabury Press.

"DANCE WHEN I DIE!":
CONTEXT AND ROLE IN
THE CLOWNING OF MURIK WOMEN

Kathleen Barlow

THE MURIK OF Papua New Guinea engage in an elaborate array of joking and respect relationships among specific categories of kin. The whole set of joking and respect relationships includes inter- and intragenerational, cross-and same-sex categories of kin.[1] These relationships constitute an extremely complex commentary on problematic aspects of Murik social life and cultural values. The contexts in which obligatory joking and clowning occur include public, private, collective, and individual settings. In this chapter, I consider only the clowning of inherited female joking partners—classificatory father's sisters and brother's daughters[2] Their clowning plays an important role in socialization and in the reproduction of social organization by juxtaposing subversive assumptions about human nature with the requirements of social structure and personhood. More specifically, their activities constitute a commentary on the role and powers of women.

The first part of the discussion reviews early structural and more recent contextual analyses of joking relations and clowning behavior. This is followed by a brief discussion of the relevance of clowning to gender status. In order to contextualize the clowning behaviors considered here, I present a general introduction to Murik society, emphasizing social organization and gender. The subsequent discussion considers the instructive intent of Murik women's clowning and its subtext on the contradiction between human desires and the formal requirements of social life as a potential source of power for women. Rites of passage contexts that evoke clowning are distinguished from those that do not. Clowning performances in the context of death and mourning are interpreted as crucial elements in the reordering of social relationships following a death (see also Mosko, this volume) and as an affirmation of cultural values.

Analytical Approaches to Joking and Clowning

Early analyses of joking relationships describe them as one component of contrasting sets of social relationships characterized by required expressions of respect and avoidance in some relationships versus privileged familiarity or license in others (Eggan 1937; Lowie 1920; Radcliffe-Brown 1940, 1949). In particular, Radcliffe-Brown emphasizes that extremes of avoidance and joking occurred when the authoritative prerogatives of certain roles produced conflicting demands on the same person or imposed contradictory emotional elements on the actors. The joking relationships I am considering here are indeed part of a more extensive pattern of both respect and joking relationships in which rights and obligations with regard to sexuality and work are potentially contradictory.

Eggan (1937:75-81) suggests that the tension of contradictory obligations may be suppressed in the relationships themselves by avoidance but expressed as joking in relationships with greater emotional and social structural distance between the participants. Displacement of potential conflict onto a relationship that is in structural terms both identified with but safely removed from the context in which conflict is both likely and inappropriate is evident in the Murik joking complex. Conflicts generated by the socializing responsibilities of parents, mother's brothers, and father's sisters are expressed only by *classificatory* mother's brothers and father's sisters.

Subsequent discussions of joking and clowning from a contextual perspective have raised other questions. The most persistent question in the anthropological literature concerns the effects of *as if* performances (e.g., ritual, theater, storytelling) that comment upon the existing social order. Gluckman (1954), Turner (1969), and Geertz (1973) all observe that while such performances express alternative social worlds they often leave the existing social structure undisturbed and even serve to reinforce it. The central question is: In what sense do joking and clowning matter? Do such performances change the social world and, if so, how is it different? Are jokes as a social phenomenon only what Freud (1916) argued they are for the individual, an escape valve for the unconscious? Certainly some of the examples from the Pacific in this volume support the interpretation that the effect of joking and clowning is at least partly to relieve inherent tensions. However, joking and clowning are discrete social forms that occur only in some situations. It seems important, then, to investigate the properties of occasions when they do occur.

Two analyses are helpful in trying to understand the circumstances and effects of clowning in Murik society—one by Geertz (1973:412–53) of imaginative cultural forms, the other by Douglas (1968:361–76) of joking and ritual.[3] In analyzing the Balinese cockfight, Geertz considers the effects on social life. Because the Balinese cockfight allows the audience to perceive directly the emotional dynamic of social hierarchy, he considers it both reflexive and interpretive. Geertz claims that the cockfights are a device through which each Balinese "forms and discovers his temperament and his society's temper at the same time. . . . Or, more exactly, he forms and discovers a particular facet of them" (Geertz 1973:451). Their main effect is to clarify meaning. Although such performances clearly do not alter the status quo, they have important effects. By dramatizing the emotional underbelly of status and hierarchy, the cockfight articulates the meaning of the larger social order, thus creating a different subjective understanding of this order. Without such arenas of expression the Balinese would inhabit a quite different social world, and as a result would be quite different people. In Bateson's (1972:187) terms, these are modes of metacommunication that alter entirely the contextual framing of events and their meanings.

The Murik recognize and exploit the explanatory power of dramatic performance. They use various kinds of performances to accuse and to shame, to depict ideal situations, and to teach through mockery and example.[4] Obligatory joking relationships, and especially the one considered here, are explicitly tutelary and are thought to be essential to becoming a Murik person.

Douglas's (1968:361–76) analysis sheds light on the question of why teaching takes the form of joking and clowning. For her the crucial effect is the juxtaposition of contradictory social structural elements already present in the context in which the joking and clowning occur. Any social situation in which joking occurs, she argues, already contains alternatives. The effectiveness of joking lies in making a submerged alternative form momentarily apparent. Joking has a creative effect because it confronts one relevant social structure that is clearly manifest with another that is less clearly relevant, differentiated, and coherent. It insists on a recognition of at least two simultaneous possibilities. "If there is no joke in the social structure," she concludes, "no other joking can appear" (ibid.:366). For participants and audience, the joke creates a new awareness of social forms, thus posing a question about their ontological status or necessity.

Douglas pays special attention to clowning in ritual contexts. The joke, she suggests, is a rite in and of itself that exploits all available elements.

> Jokes, being themselves a play upon forms, can well serve to express something about social forms. Recall that the joke connects and disorganizes. It attacks sense and hierarchy. . . . If it devalues social structure, perhaps it celebrates something else instead. It could be saying something about the value of individuals as against the value of the social relations in which they are organized. Or it could be saying something about different levels of social structure; the irrelevance of one obvious level and the relevance of a submerged and unappreciated one. (ibid.:370)

As ritual itself is a commentary upon social meanings, joking in ritual contexts is a condensed comment upon the relation of the ritual to its context (cf. Mosko, this volume). Murik women's clowning hinges on a series of paradoxes that comment upon male and female roles, social order, and disorder. The social order (which is predominately but not exclusively male) is hierarchical, ordered, and parental. But the Murik view humans as vulnerable creatures—easily manipulated by their wish to be dependent and cared for and by sexual desire. The persistent tension between emotional neediness and the social order creates opportunities for influence and is a major theme of the secular or mundane joking. Ritual clowning exposes the paradox that membership in secret societies and in descent groups offers opposing but interconnected paths to power.

Clowning and Women's Status

The metacommunicative messages of women's clowning are directly related to ambiguities of women's status in Murik society. The question has been debated whether women fully cognize culture because the public domain is not primarily about them and does not include them (Ardener 1975; Strathern 1976). Murik women are not excluded from public life. First, public culture is structurally and symbolically often about women; the jural domain is not gender specific. Second, the existence and persistence of women's clowning indicate a well-developed awareness of and appreciation for all levels and kinds of cultural meanings.

The low incidence of reports in the ethnographic literature of formalized joking and clowning among women (Apte 1985:43, 69) has led to speculation that the absence of clowning is related to low status. This assumes that those with low social standing (male or female) can less afford the loss of status that asocial behavior may incur. Apte suggests that clowning by men only, or by women only in the company of other women, indicates the inferior status of women. Women refrain from inappropriate behavior in the presence of higher status persons (men). This may be reinforced by norms of modesty and restraint (Fox 1977:807) that inhibit women from performing the immodest behaviors entailed in clowning.

Conversely, Rosaldo (1972:26–27) argues that male prestige and status are maintained by an appearance of dignity that requires separation from the intimate, domestic realm. Women's constant engagement in face-to-face interactions in intimate contexts precludes them from using this technique to gain prestige. This argument implies that when status is precariously preserved by an appearance of dignity and control, it is jeopardized by evoking associations with the intimate domestic realm. However, when status is based on firmer ground within the political and economic structure, men or women can better afford to break the norms of socially acceptable behavior. Given this framework, public clowning by women may be an indication of relatively high status based on factors outside the norms of self-presentation or etiquette and outside the domestic realm.

Cases from the Pacific bear out this association of status and clowning, and in some Pacific societies women's clowning enhances rather than jeopardizes prestige. Ortner (1981) points out that in Polynesian societies rank (age hierarchy) overrides gender subordination. Women consistently achieve high status in descent groups and in the economic realm because they do not give up rights to rank or property in their natal group at marriage.[5] The Murik provide a Melanesian case that confirms this association. As described in the chapters on Polynesian societies (Samoa and Rotuman), Murik women have access to important statuses through both economic and political means. Clowning is an additional means of acquiring status, though it stops short of parity. Although some women are entitled to more respect than some men, Murik women as a group defer to men in many contexts,[6] and they must never joke or clown in the presence of senior male affines.

There are symbolic reasons why in some situations it is appropriate for women to clown. The interdependent yet separate gender and age hierarchies create implicit contradictions. The Murik model of social relationships is based explicitly on an image of a

The Clowning of Murik Women

resourceful and generous mother. Men compete to fulfill these expectations by providing abundant food and by teaching and protecting, activities directly associated with mothers (Barlow 1985; Lipset 1984). Thus, for many public and male-dominated activities, the submerged scenario is one of women's work and productivity, and women's clowning points out this interdependence.

For example, elaborate feasting and dancing accompany all ritual performances. The feast-givers attempt to feed all participants lavishly. When the men dance, a senior woman noted for her ability to clown signifies that women are the ultimate source of the men's performance by dancing around the periphery flouncing her skirts and breasts. She mocks the men's stamping dance step with exaggeratedly female prancing.[7] Her dance movements emphasize the skirt, which men also wear for dancing. The skirt stands for abundance, especially food. Younger onlookers laugh to see a prestigious woman flaunt herself, but senior women nod their approval. The dance is a comment on the otherwise hidden source of the men's splendid performance. She reminds them that those who stand behind their success are women, whose productivity and nurture enable trade and ritual work, and that in relation to women's power to nurture, the men are still children who play. The woman's dancing surrounds the male performance with a maternal presence (Lipset 1984).

The father's sister–brother's daughter relationship teaches women how to exploit opportunities for legitimate authority and unassigned power in this basic scenario of female production and male performance. To understand the dynamics of this relationship requires an understanding of the cultural context in which it occurs.

The Murik of Papua New Guinea

The Murik (approximately 1,500 population) are fisher folk and traders who preside over an extensive mangrove region at the mouth of the Sepik River on the north coast of Papua New Guinea. Living in five villages spread along the coastal sand banks, they harvest fish and shellfish from the mangrove area and trade extensively in the lower river, coast, and offshore islands region. They are known for the beautiful plaited bags made by women, which they trade for garden produce, tobacco, pigs, and other luxuries. In this trade network they exchange rituals and ritual objects as well as many kinds of subsistence goods and manufactured commodities. In a sense, the Murik have made a virtue of their limited natural resources, for they have accumulated a rich repertoire of ritual and material wealth by elaborating trade activities. Trade relationships are based on intermarriage, adoption, "fictive kin," inherited trade partnerships, and historical descent from related ancestors. The underlying philosophy of prestige competition is based on nurturance—influence over others achieved through generous hospitality and gift giving.

Murik social organization can be described as a system of competitive ranking. Perhaps because of their reliance on trade and their identity as a migratory group composed of members from throughout the region, in Murik social organization access to resources is maximized through multiple forms of affiliation. Within Murik villages, ambilineal descent, descent group exogamy, and adoption allow individuals to access resources from the broadest possible base rather than proscriptively. Claims to membership and resources are heavily prioritized and manipulated, but many types of claims are recognized as legitimate. The limiting factors are work, time, resources, proximity, and loyalty. In the world beyond Murik villages, fictive kin ties, adoption, and intermarriage and hereditary trade partnerships are all important means of establishing relationships and claims on resources.

The ambilineal descent groups are based on sets of siblings. The groups are residentially dispersed throughout five villages. In each generation, the eldest member of a sibling set is entitled to inherit certain types of property belonging to the descent group or groups of his or her parents. Choice and sponsorship affect the eldest sibling's ultimate active descent group affiliations.[8] The corporate property of the descent group includes village land, mangrove channels, and ritual property, the most important of which are the descent group insignia, called *suman*[9]

Firstborns must constantly legitimate their claim to leadership by progression through the age sets of the men's or women's secret society and by organizing trade expeditions, feasts, and life-cycle rituals on behalf of members of the descent group (Lipset 1984; Barlow 1991). The paramount obligation of a firstborn is to retire the parent from whom such status is claimed by sponsoring the ceremony for transferring the *suman*. They may be challenged by an ambitious junior sibling who may acquire the *suman* by staging ritual feasts to retire the parent and intervening siblings.

Most often, men hold leadership status and women, as sisters and wives, stand behind them as supporters and contributors. Nevertheless, high status is directly attainable by women, especially firstborns. Women, who make baskets and harvest shellfish, control important resources required for trade. They inherit potentially prestigious descent group affiliations and trade partnerships throughout the extended trade network, and a firstborn woman sponsors prestigious ritual work assisted by her husband and her siblings, who amass the necessary resources.

The openness and flexibility of ambilineal kinship and the combination of ascription and achievement in the prestige system create competition among descent groups for membership and work. Although the ideal world of social relations is one of hierarchy, seniority, respect, and decorum, competition results in a social field that is rife with opportunities for conflict, contradiction, and manipulation. Into the fray and often to the rescue come the jokers and clowns, who occupy liminal statuses — usually classificatory, affinal, and junior. They mediate a social arena characterized by contested membership claims, manipulation of resources, and a conscious intention to push the rules to their limits.

A special category of classificatory or fictive kin performs all ritual work related to status transition. Their kinship status is prefaced with *mwara*, the Murik word for valuable.[10] The obligations and privileges of *mwara* kin are great. They are both ritual actors and joking partners who must be paid with food for their performances. On ritual occasions, they must present money (formerly shell and teeth valuables) to those whom they sponsor. Their behavior clearly distinguishes them from nonclassificatory kin. For example, a woman's actual father's sisters assist her with resources and teach her important skills such as dancing and basket weaving, and they have an important symbolic role in assisting childbirth. The *mwara* father's sister, a classificatory relative, performs the lifecycle rituals and teaches proper social behavior through mockery and burlesque.

Mwara kin relationships are inherited through the opposite sex parent. Multigenerational sets of *mwara* kin are composed of fathers and daughters linked with mothers and sons as opposite sex pairs in each generation. The genealogical origins of sets of *mwara* kin are not known.[11] Each relationship has well-defined obligations for ritual performance, tutelage, and protection associated with it, but the outstanding characteristic of all of them is the preponderance of joking and clowning through which these duties are carried out.

The *Mwara* Father's Sisters and Brother's Daughters Clowning Relationship

Here I am concerned only with clowning by the *mwara* father's sister–brother's daughter pair and hereafter refer to them as father's sister and brother's daughter. However, it is important to keep in mind that these are distant classificatory or even fictive kin statuses. Murik kinship terms are of the Hawaiian type; therefore the classificatory element of *mwara* kinship means that each individual has multiple *mwara* partners,[12] both senior and junior, in her own village and in each of the other Murik villages. The extent to which a relationship is actualized depends upon multiple factors, including proximity, resources, and personality. The duties of *mwara* relationships are well-defined for everyday life and ritual contexts. First, I consider their role in ongoing daily life throughout the life cycle and subsequently discuss status transitions and ritual performances.

The father's sister is first of all an intermediary between the domestic group and the community. In Douglas's (1968) terms, as quasi-kin she may evoke the paradoxes of domestic and public life and the obligatory versus optative qualities of kin and nonkin relationships Malefijt (1968) points out that joking often establishes socially appropriate behavior and eligibility for group membership. The relevant groups for the father's sister are both the wider society and the women's secret society.[13]

The father's sister transforms her junior partner into a social individual by teasing and badgering her into taking an active part in social interaction. What is at first an extremely asymmetrical relationship of senior to junior becomes over time less and less imbalanced as the junior partner becomes more competent. Over the course of the life cycle the junior partner moves from an inferior pupil whose behavior and obligations are defined by the senior partner to a guardian who defines and enforces the status of the senior partner as an ancestor spirit after her death. In at least one dimension, the role displays a dynamic similar to that of parenting and senior siblingship. In all three relationships, junior partners eventually reverse the initial asymmetry by acquiring the skills with which they have been kept in their place. Formally, they succeed their senior partners when they die. The analogy and contrasts with actual kin relationships are a key element in the joking. Parents and older siblings are supposed to be giving and indulgent, but the joking partners mock the dependent role of the child and younger sibling.

The Clowning of Murik Women 67

The father's sister begins to play her role as soon as the baby brother's daughter can leave the house.[14] She challenges her junior partner to reject the helplessness of infancy and to become resourceful and skilled at manipulating others' indebtedness. Most of the joking directed at babies plays upon the similarities of infancy and old age. It is often based on a play upon names in which the father's sister refers to the baby by the name of the baby's paternal grandmother, her own senior joking partner. Thus the father's sister insults her senior partner at the same time that she mocks her junior one.

When younger partners are subjected to mockery, onlookers encourage them to respond to their partner's taunts. A girl's father and the older female joking partners in her group of *mwara* partners offer her witty responses to parrot back when her father's sisters taunt her. The senior partner tries to prolong the interaction and thus build the child's skill. When an adult woman commits a faux pas, her father's sisters recruit her brother's daughters to join them in mocking her, thus teaching them how to turn the tables. Successful joking replies, even if they are merely repeated, are applauded by women bystanders with a prolonged "Heii!" of approval. Some young children (usually eight to twelve years old) are sufficiently adept at the meanings entailed in joking relationships to perform successfully. If their performance is a bit too outrageous or insulting, this is ignored in favor of applauding their potential as future performers.

Among the first requirements of proper self-presentation for female children is that they learn to cover their genitals properly. Young girls go naked, and if they should sit down and fail to fold their hands demurely over their laps, their father's sisters start making remarks about harvesting clams, the conventional metaphor for female genitalia, while grabbing at the little girls' crotches. The humor is enhanced by an intergenerational identity in kinship terminology of grandmother and granddaughter, but it is funny to different people for different reasons. It is funny in an unthinkable sense because an adult woman would never make such a lapse, and funny but true to knowledgeable senior women, who dance naked during the initiation ceremonies of the women's secret society.

Equally as basic as the norm of modesty is the ability to move about gracefully. Lapses are one of the most enthusiastically exploited opportunities for clowning by both older and younger partners. The Murik virtually live in narrow dugout canoes without outriggers and in houses built above the water with unstable ladders and often deteriorating bark floors. For the most part, they are adept at moving through their watery and delicate environment. To them, outright clumsiness, especially falling down, is hilariously funny. The joking partners go wild imitating a faux pas. Whether they witness it or hear about it later, they appear at the scene of the incident and receive precise instructions in order to reenact the mishap. With exaggerated effort and energy bordering on outright aggression they hurl themselves to the ground or capsize a canoe. Most often the audience collapses, nearly weeping with laughter at the sight, while the clowns perform with deadpan faces, fixing their gaze on their hapless victim. The person so attacked hides her face and when possible her person.

Goody (1969:41) suggests that joking relationships may be as much a form of privileged aggression as an expression of familiarity. On many occasions the vigor of the Murik performance conveys unmistakable antagonism toward the subject's ineptitude, but the clowning precludes her from responding with irritation or anger. She is not just the subject of the performance but subjected to it. The father's sisters' and brother's daughters' performance requires them to disgrace themselves in public in order to teach their clumsy subject a lesson. For this they require payment in the form of a meal. They evoke a social world of disorder and destruction in contrast to the preferred social milieu of control and careful handling of objects. Their purpose is to instruct by exaggeration, and one inference is that the conduct of the junior partner reflects on their competence as teachers. Young children, unsure of their competence, interpret these mocking displays as hostile rather than entertaining.

The following example underscores the obligatory nature of this type of clowning. One afternoon a heavy, middle-aged woman was leaving the house where a group of women kept vigil over a dying senior woman. She was going home to relieve those who sat with her own mother, another senior woman who was gravely ill. The atmosphere in the village during these days was very somber. This woman was a *mwara* brother's daughter to the dying woman. (As such, her presence was important in a protective sense that will be described later.) The group in the house included both the dying woman's female kin and her *mwara* brother's daughters. The second step on the house ladder gave way under the departing woman's foot, and she plummeted about four feet to the ground, landing on her hands and knees. The composition of the groups meant that many of her senior and junior *mwara* partners were among the

The Clowning of Murik Women

women inside the house. They emerged from the house and one by one plummeted from the broken ladder. A few onlookers standing outside laughed, but the proximity of the spirit world and the threat of imminent death reduced an otherwise hilarious occasion to one in which some women felt compelled to caution each other not to be too strenuous in their mimicry lest they truly injure themselves. Nevertheless, the mishap could not go unmarked by the joking partners.

Insufficiency and need always provoke clowning. The scene of a nursing infant is the prototype of both satiated bliss and complete dependency, and joking partners often suggest that their partners have never given up their childish desire to keep on nursing. Father's sisters who are lactating respond to a greeting from a brother's daughter (especially a child) by squirting her with breast milk, saying, "Is this why you call to me?" or "Oh, it's you! Come and drink!" Adult partners amuse each other and onlookers by mimicking the familiar pair of a whining toddler and indulgent mother offering her breast.

Other types of need are ridiculed with an aggressive presentation of surplus. One woman was observed by her father's sister going to the bush near the village to collect a few small branches for her morning cooking fire. The father's sister quickly spread the word that this adult woman with a family to cook for had no firewood. A long line of male and female *mwara* kin, including senior, junior and same-generation partners assembled from throughout the village, each with an absurdly large load or hunk of firewood on his or her shoulder.[15] The procession advanced, prancing, stamping, and shouting, to the foot of her house ladder where they dumped it. She then spent several days in the mangroves gathering crab and fish to make a meal and pay them back for their performance.[16]

The realm of behavior that most consistently inspires clowning from the *mwara* kin is sexuality. The ideal Murik woman is maternal and to an extent asexual. She is nurturant and resourceful. Her main concerns are the well-being of her husband, children, and kin. She works hard and does not roam around the village, gossip idly, or draw unwarranted attention from men outside her family. The father's sisters and brother's daughters police each other's activities, inferring illicit motives in everyday activities. They initiate a repartee of innuendo whenever they hear mention of or see one of their partners. They call out, "I know where *you're* going. Just like your grandmother." "See that skirt fly," and especially, "Look out for the man with the crooked leg" (in English, the "man with the 'third' leg"). The Murik assume that the extreme modesty of ideal public demeanor conceals aggressive sexuality. Myriad jokes revolve around false modesty and domestic industriousness as a thin disguise for rampant marital infidelity.

Joking dialogue is often accompanied by mimicry and sometimes horseplay. Any time a woman is bent over from the hip in public rather than squatting, a nearby joking partner is liable to goose her, replacing the image of the hardworking, asexual woman with the lewd figure of one being accosted from behind. Any time a woman seems to be complaining, her joking partner is liable to murmur in consolation and try to shove her breast into the complainer's mouth with an aggressive thrust and grunt, gaining mileage from the double reference to eating and copulation. The implications are that the complainer is whining like a baby, unable to control her appetite for food or sex.

Learning to engage in this kind of horseplay is easy enough for rowdy younger children, but it becomes increasingly more embarrassing and difficult for girls and adolescents. Young girls, proud of their newly developing breasts as signs of impending womanhood, learn not to parade themselves too brazenly through the village. Their father's sisters suddenly chase and grab at them, educating them in the dangers of becoming desirable to men — the obligations of motherhood soon follow. At large-scale events adolescent girls huddle together and try their best to escape the attention of their father's sisters, who harrass and terrify them with their assaultive clowning.

Surprisingly, women do not respond to insinuations of ribald sexuality by asserting their modesty and sexual restraint. They assert their sexual prowess or further exaggerate an inadvertently immodest pose or demeanor, completing the inversion of dominant and background images begun by the joke. In so doing, they shift the joking to another level of dialogue, which evokes the arena of the women's secret society. The joking partners are not just enforcing proper behavior but suggesting an alternative realm for the exercise of female powers, neither blatantly displayed nor relinquished. The father's sisters play with the notion of sexuality as power and resourcefulness, a dominant metaphor of the women's secret society. In the initiation ritual, in which the father's sisters act as guides, the brother's daughters learn that sexuality strategically deployed (especially outside of marriage and organized through the secret society) is the means to resources and great prestige. Thus from the point of view of the father's sister–brother's daughter relationship,

The Clowning of Murik Women 71

the admirable woman is not so much the faithful wife as the woman who knows how to present the image of the faithful wife and mother and to manage her affairs with discretion. Power exercised behind the scenes is better than power forsaken (Barlow 1989).[17] The following exchange between joking partners illustrates one such metadialogue concerning sexuality, resourcefulness, and generosity.

In the verbal combat between two adult joking partners, each response is an attempt to one-up the other's last comment. Here the first woman initiates the exchange by accusing her partner of being stingy with betel nut. Bespelled betel nut is a conventional means of inviting (compelling) a lover to an affair. Two betel nuts and a single betel pepper, representing male genitalia, are often offered by a female joking partner, who says "Eat and be happy." In the following exchange translated from *Tok Pisin*, the lingua franca, "bush" is a double entendre referring to both the forest and female genitalia.

> *First:* You don't give me even one betel nut.
> *Second:* There's betel nut. You go look for it. Lots of it in the bush.
> *First:* Ahh, too hard to pull it out. You pull it out and give it to me.
> *Second:* So! You don't know how to get it out? You must do it yourself!

Though ostensibly discussing how to obtain betel nut, the women are covertly enjoying a rather obscene exchange about each other's sexual prowess and voraciousness. The double entendre of getting betel nut and sex create a metadialogue about each other's capacities to obtain resources—a major form of prestige competition denoted here by an inconsequential exchange about betel nut. The first partner plays the role of supplicant, challenging her partner to be generous. The second woman responds by mocking her partner's lack of initiative and know-how.

The use of sexuality as a metaphor for resourcefulness is drawn from the context of secret women's ritual and helps to explain the appropriate response to the father's sister's attacks of joking and clowning. They can be stopped only by an active response—counterattack, not submission. The goals of the apprenticeship are initiative, risk taking, and self-assertion rather than conformity or obedience.

Though the father's sisters most often interact by mocking, teasing, and clowning, this is only one means of developing their brother's daughters' ability to present themselves well in all contexts. Their duties include real assistance and protection when circumstances call for it. For example, a woman who must suddenly host a trade partner and is caught short of resources for legitimate reasons should ask her father's sisters to help her.[18]

When a brother's daughter is threatened with physical danger, the father's sister comes to her rescue. On one occasion a girl (about eight years old) who had repeatedly defied her mother was being followed through the village by her shrieking mother, who was swatting the girl's legs with a mosquito broom. The little girl's bawling brought her father's sister down from the house to rescue her. Without a word to the mother, she took the little girl by the hand and led her into her own house. The mother turned and went back home. After calming the girl and feeding her a meal of sago pudding and fish, the father's sister escorted her home again.

The prototype of protection is that extended to women whose husbands beat them. (The only acceptable reasons for wife beating are sexual infidelity and failure to cook.) The father's sisters never intervene directly, but a woman so endangered should run away to her father's sister's house and take refuge there. When her husband has calmed down, the woman is escorted home by her father's sister carrying the descent group insignia as a sign that there must be no further violence, or compensation in the form of pigs will have to be given. Such protection is infrequently performed, but is often given as the reason that a husband's violent outburst was suppressed. It is always mentioned as one of the most important duties of a woman's father's sisters.

The clowning of the father's sisters and brother's daughters in mundane contexts highlights the contrasts between human impulses and appetites and socially acceptable behavior. It plays off two contrasting images of woman—the maternal, domestic woman of modest demeanor and the mature sexual woman astute in controlling resources. The father's sister's goal is primarily to instruct naive individuals in the forms of social competence and to demonstrate the proper contexts for expressing different dimensions of womanhood.

Clowning in Ritual Contexts

Ritual contexts highlight other characteristics of the father's sister–brother's daughter relationship. The content of the clowning plays on the same issues as mundane situations with increased emphasis on the issues of debt and exchange. Though the clowning comments on individual behavior, the emphasis is on communications about the

The Clowning of Murik Women 73

state of society. It is important to distinguish the occasions that elicit clowning behavior from those that do not.

Initiation, marriage, and birth are not occasions for clowning. Initiation into the women's secret society takes place in the women's cult house and the mangroves outside the village. (For a discussion of female initiation see Barlow 1989.) The initiation officially marks a transition from a person who plays a supportive role to one who takes initiative. Here mockery and clowning by the father's sisters is completely absent. On this occasion the goal of their long-term tutelage is realized, and they both assist and celebrate their brother's daughter.

The initiates, having been badgered and threatened for years by their father's sisters, fully expect that these women will be the main aggressors in the ordeals of initiation. But the father's sisters act as protectors and genuine, not mocking, instructors throughout. Senior women dressed as male warriors haze the initiates. The father's sisters rescue them at each stage and impart secret knowledge to them. They tell the initiates the names of their lovers in Murik and non-Murik villages—men to whom they go for help in supplying their projects at home. If the junior partners failed to keep this information secret, the father's sisters would be vulnerable to attack from jealous male kin. The father's sisters signify the initiates' membership by entrusting them with this information.

At the conclusion of the initiation, the father's sisters confer beautiful finery on the initiates, which they have made to the specifications of the descent group sponsors. Each group of father's sisters then escorts the newly initiated and decorated woman through each of the Murik villages, carrying the initiate's sponsor's *suman* and receiving on her behalf presents of basket reeds, carved wooden plates, and sago pots—the equipment of a resourceful woman. The father's sisters are paid with an elaborate feast that must include pigs.[19]

Douglas (1968) points out that those who joke often participate in rituals of transition with a certain immunity to the marginality or danger of the ritual redefinition process. Perhaps, she suggests, because the joker apparently is not bounded by the present reality, but has access to alternative frames of reference and possibility, she can provide safe passage when the social reality is at its most oppressive. For example, in the initiation, when the goal of all their teaching is being realized, the father's sisters participate in two social realities. Both of their realms are confirmed. At the same time that the initiate accedes to a position of enormous responsibility and respectability within the descent group (an asexual and ultimately maternal role), she also receives knowledge through the secret society of how to fulfill these obligations by taking control where it is available through sexuality and competitive feasting.

Two other changes in a woman's status occur without the joking and clowning of the father's sisters. Marriage marks the transition from sister and daughter to wife, but in Murik culture there are no irrevocable transfers of property or rights upon marriage. As an institution it is brittle, weakly marked, and involves no ritual. The *mwara* kin have no duties or role to play here. When a woman gives birth she fulfills an important requirement for full adult female status. Because it is a dangerous time and because birth is the ultimate female power, the father's sisters are supportive and help to supply her with food while she remains in the birth house. But here there are few public paradoxes to exploit; only protection and help are offered in a secluded context.

The father's sister–brother's daughter relationship is crucial to rituals surrounding death, mourning, and end of mourning, and the obligations are extensive. At every life-cycle transition marked by the descent group, the father's sisters have given shell valuables to their brother's daughter's parents who retain them on her behalf. These cumulative payments confer a heavy obligation on the brother's daughter. Any time that the father's sister is in mourning for close kin, the brother's daughters must attend to her needs and perform the end-of-mourning ceremony, which brings her back into active participation in society.

When a father's sister dies, the brother's daughters are specifically obligated to see to the preparation of her corpse, mourning, and burial. These impending obligations are a subject of joking among partners in their prime, who threaten to throw each other's corpses away unceremoniously. The *mwara* kin dread the comic dance they are obligated to perform when a partner dies. Because of this, taunts of posthumous indifference are countered with the charge, "Dance when I die. I will leave you this way." If a senior partner requests that a specific dance be performed upon her death, the brother's daughters are obligated to perform it in addition to the clowning dance described below.

On the very serious and unnerving occasion of death, the most outrageous clowning performance of all takes place amid other obligations of support and nurture, a performance that contrasts sharply with genuine sorrow over the loss of the beloved antagonist. When a woman dies, her close kin wail and weep over her body as

The Clowning of Murik Women

the rest of the villagers pass the word and come to the house to show their sorrow. To stay away from the house is tantamount to admitting culpability in the death. Mourning goes on for at least a day and sometimes two or three, as relatives from other villages arrive.

Some time during the first day of mourning the deceased's father's sisters and brother's daughters dress in traditional attire and dance around the corpse. Close kin, who have been weeping over the body, retire to the perimeter of the house and turn away or gaze impassively at the performance. Their own *mwara* kin attend to their needs assiduously. Curious children who have been hushed and sent outside are summoned into the house to watch. The father's sisters and brother's daughters come into the house calling the dead person's names and making a great commotion that shakes the entire house. Kicking the bier and goading the dead woman to get up and dance with them, they try to revive their partner from her passive and asocial state. The inertness of the body in comparison to the vigor with which the living would respond to such taunts is ludicrous and strikes many onlookers as funny. This is the moment of greatest antagonism from the joking partners and the moment when their efforts are most futile. They shout angrily and strike at the bier with hatchets normally used to chop firewood. The prancing and taunting to revive the dead woman are met with shrieks of cathartic laughter from the assembled women and children made nervous by proximity to death.[20]

After a few moments the dancing becomes formal and honorific. The joking partners dance, holding the implements of their deceased partner's productivity, her basket-weaving needles, canoe paddle, and crab-harvesting stick. Senior women make suggestions about how the dance should be performed and decide which of the *mwara* partners should receive the tools as gifts. Following this more subdued performance the partners file down from the house and return to their own houses. They then begin to cook for the kin who arrive from other villages to mourn. They are taking over the obligations of hospitality that neither the deceased person nor her close kin are able to accomplish under the circumstances.

The body is always buried at the end of the first day, and a dummy of pillows covered with layers of cloth and the deceased's clothing is laid in its place near the hearth of the house. This forms the centerpiece for arriving mourners and for father's sisters and brother's daughters from other villages. *Mwara* partners come from other villages to fulfill their obligation to dance around the corpse. By the time they arrive, the tension of the original performance has been relieved by time and the absence of the corpse. They are obligated to dance in their traditional regalia, but their clowning performances are rather different. Their performances are longer, more burlesque and outrageous than the original performance, and they direct their attention to their brother's daughters in the audience. This provides these more distant *mwara* partners with a greater variety of raw material and more audience participation, which inspires them to greater exploits. The close kin who are confined to the house disengage themselves from these activities. They are not yet ready to be drawn back into the ongoing concerns of the community.

Following the mourning period, usually about one year later, the kin of the deceased combine their resources to sponsor the end-of-mourning ceremony. The *mwara* partner of the deceased are compensated then for their clowning performance and their hospitality to nonvillage kin at the time of death. They give their final performance.

The end-of-mourning ceremony begins at dusk. The spirit of the deceased is summoned from the outskirts of the village by the kin and *mwara* kin. The deceased's *mwara* partners dance with her throughout the night. At this ceremony, clowning plays a major role in establishing the end of the transitional period of mourning. Men and women begin and end the celebration together, but during the long night of dancing they occupy separate houses belonging to their respective secret societies. The joking partners put on their dance decorations for the all-night performance. As they enter the house where the community of women will dance all night with the spirit of the deceased, the joking and clowning begin. The themes of the joking are, as always, the vulnerability produced by human appetites for food and sex.

The women's dancing alternates between clowning and seriousness. The clowning burlesques flirtatious females and males driven mad with desire. This is followed by the dignified dancing of high-status senior women. Younger women are encouraged to participate in order to learn both kinds of performance. First the *mwara* father's sisters goad their seated partners to respond to the clowning. Then the actual father's sisters, who always represent the obligations of descent relationships and affinity, invite their brother's daughters to learn the slow and rhythmic formal dance steps.

The clowning attacks take several forms. A *mwara* father's sister may goad her partner to get up and dance with her by dancing toward her like a rapacious male or backward like a tempting

The Clowning of Murik Women

female. The person so attacked is swarmed by more father's sisters, until she gets up to dance with them. The male taunt is met with a flirtatious skipping away as if to say, "You can't catch me," while the attacker lumbers behind. The female taunt is repulsed by grabbing whatever remotely phallic object lies at hand and rushing toward the challenger. The victim so beset by father's sisters that she cannot move is often helped by her own female kin who share the same set of relationships. They come to her aid by approaching the father's sisters and drawing them off with seductive antics of their own. The scenario for the audience is a hilarious pantomime in which males are depicted as sexually voracious and clumsy, while women run circles around them.

The other theme of the clowning, closely equated with sexuality so that the gestures play off one another, is the dependence of nursing in which the power of feeding is asserted and the weakness of hunger is mocked. One or more women hover over a partner with dangling breasts, offering to let her suckle (given that she is sitting passively like a dependent child). The father's sister declares she will act as a mother to the brother's daughter, implying that she is a desolate orphan with no supportive kin group. One response is to grab the father's sister's breasts, commenting on how fallen, small, flaccid, and dry they are and implying that she is unable to provide nurture. Another response emphasizes that one's kin are resourceful and stand ready to humiliate (and indebt) the father's sisters with a grand presentation of many plates of food.

Just before dawn everyone is awakened and encouraged to join the singing and dancing. As dawn breaks and the spirit is sent away with a special lament, the close kin of the deceased are escorted by their *mwara* father's sisters and brother's daughters to the sea to bathe and be cleansed of the death pollution. At this point in the ceremony some of the *mwara* kin and mourners are moved to tears of sadness by the imminent departure of the ghost. The Murik say of this final performance that it is very hard work, even though they are playing and clowning. Therefore, the assembled father's sisters and brother's daughters who have come to send the spirit away on good terms and to remove the pollution from the mourners must be well paid. The sponsors say that they must be well fed during their visit and given gifts of sago bread and pig meat to take home.

The ritual clowning of the father's sisters and brother's daughters displays many of the aspects common to such performances identified by Makarius (1970:44–73). Performers who clown on such occasions behave in an asocial manner for the ultimate benefit of society. Their perfomance expresses a social conflict or problem that must be met by a pacific response. Although they appear to attack, they are appeasable in specific ways. By taking a social dilemma upon themselves in the role of clown, they rescue the community. For this, others are indebted to them, and they must be paid.

The Murik father's sisters assume the tasks of transforming the soul or ghost into an ancestor spirit and of transferring the active *mwara* relationships to the next generation. Their clowning near the time of death confirms the absence of the soul from its body and dramatizes the change in status from living to dead. At this point the structural paradoxes upon which the clowning depends become clear. First of all, the contrast of person as an individual versus a social person defined by a web of social relationships is displayed. The clowning attack on the corpse is a failed attempt to directly interact with the individual. This is followed by a symbolic gesture indicating a change in the person's place in the social structure, the dance with the woman's tools. As an individual she is gone, but as a social persona she is now being transferred to a new role.

These contrasting conceptions of the individual and social person parallel a further contrast in the conceptualizations of society marked by the clowning. In this contrast the clowning is a comment on the relationship of the ritual to the wider social structure. Douglas (1968), following Turner (1969), observes that clowning in funeral contexts brings into high relief the contrast between social structure (formal sets of relationships) and *communitas* (affective bonds of solidarity created through direct interactions).

In the Murik case, formal mourning procedures emphasize the gaping hole rent in the social hierarchy by a death. The mourners keen for the dead person, not by name, but by relationship. They cry out over the loss of mother, wife, and sister. In the midst of this formalized keening over the corpse, the clowning confirms the absolute death of the individual and simultaneously draws attention to the less apparent but quite essential *communitas* among the bereaved. The close kin move aside. They are a passive audience, whose separateness defines the community. This clowning performance is for the larger assembled group that sits surrounding the corpse. The clowns make them laugh as a chorus of voices, and in that tenuous moment their performance highlights the immediate and unstructured bonds among them (Turner 1969:132f). To the Murik, the company of others is important protection against the longing created by death, and in this sense the clowns actually do save the community (Makarius 1970) by redirecting attention to the living and reaffirming the presence of community. The moment of clowning reveals the contradictory relationship of the mourning ritual to the rest of social life. The purpose is ostensibly to mark the loss resulting from the death of a member of society. The overall effect is to underscore the vitality and persistence of the community.

The generational transition among the *mwara* kin that results from a death is first announced by the exchange of implements following the clowning around the body and confirmed in the subsequent duties and performances by the father's sisters and brother's daughters during the mourning. It is ultimately declared by the *mwara* kin from all of the villages in a crescendo of clowning at the end-of-mourning ceremony. Then the *mwara* performers demonstrate the victory of the living over the dead and affirm the continuity of *mwara* relationships into the next generations. Nominally, they join the deceased's spirit to perform together the final status transition of her life, but tangibly they dance and clown with their remaining, especially their junior, partners. The clowning at the end of mourning is a culmination of the adjustment of social reality to a death.

Conclusions

The data that have been presented bear out certain insights of the contextual analyses discussed above. In relation to Geertz's (1973) formulation of the effects of such play, it is now apparent that in Murik society individuals acquire certain abilities for interpreting social life and for perceiving alternatives to the dominant social forms by their participation in joking relationships. The Murik case emphasizes the instructive potential of such performances, turning the father's sister–brother's daughter relationship into a long-term and very active context for cultural learning. The further insight — that play, of which joking and clowning are but one form, takes its meaning from the larger social context — is amply borne out.

Douglas (1968) points out that joking and clowning in particular depend upon contradictory messages inherent in the social context. As such they represent a form within a form with very specific prerequisites in terms of context. The creative exposure of underlying contradiction conveys a metacommunication about the significance of the social forms and attributes invoked by the joke. An investigation of joking and clowning in Murik culture is particularly revealing, not just of structure and antistructure, but of consciously held convictions about the paradoxical nature and requirements of status and human desires. The dynamic of social life depends directly upon it: what people desire in the form of cultural achievements is inevitably opposed to what they might desire as impulsive (and unsocialized) individuals. For women, the contrast is especially compelling because of the demands placed on them in the roles of mother, sister, wife, and affine.

The *mwara* relationships of Murik women concern the opposition between the status and prestige systems and the affective and dependent bonds of domestic, intrafamilial life. By contrasting the public and domestic realms in which they operate (realms of performance both spatially and temporally in very close proximity), the joking and clowning blur the boundaries that maintain gender hierarchy by proposing an opposite reality. The activities that characterize the fathers' sister–brother's daughter relationship express the necessities and problems inherent in growing up female. In order to meet the requirements of family, kin, and community, a woman must express herself as both a sexual and a nurturant being—a wife and a mother—thus becoming the object of others' desire and hunger. Uncontrolled sexual appetite is satirized as slavish. Hunger and dependency are both epitomized and mocked in the image of the sucking child. Satisfying these appetites in men and children is the stuff of women's lives, but the clowning affirms that it need not consume them.

The ritual performances of the father's sister–brother's daughter are addressed to the community as well as to individuals. They accomplish the transition of individuals from one status to another throughout their lives and are thus integral to reproducing the social order. The clowning of the *mwara* father's sisters appears when individual desires run contrary to the requirements of status, and their antics express these implicit conflicts. Their message is that it is possible to surmount the difficulties of formal status by acquiring certain skills and insights. In so doing one becomes able to control rather than be controlled by the terms of conflicting domains—the world of sexual appetite and of longing for maternal nurture versus the normative world of social obligations and work.

Every woman plays the role of brother's daughter and father's sister throughout her life, a role that contrasts sharply with the confines and hard work of, for example, being a good mother, sister, daughter, or wife. This *mwara* relationship affords women the opportunity to comment upon the restrictions and work demanded in these roles and on the irrepressible play of urges and appetites that inspire and threaten the moral order. At initiation, the novices approach new understanding of the affective domain and new status in the social structural domain.

Upon death, the deceased is assumed to be unwilling to relinquish either her attachment to the living or her role in the community and to be reluctant to assume a new status. Her junior *mwara* kin are also expected to resist assuming the more difficult obligations of seniority. As they do in mundane situations where individuals balk at progress toward greater competence and status, the *mwara* kin clown to enlighten and to compel the necessary transition. The totality of the clowning performances associated with a death brings the community, including the bereaved and the deceased, into line with its structural principles.

By the completion of the end-of-mourning ceremony, the community has been fully reconstituted around the changes in status necessitated by the death. At this point attention returns to the social processes and contradictions among the living that continue to require the joking and clowning of the *mwara* kin. Their antics create a particular awareness of antagonistic processes, which are the wellsprings of social interaction. That the joking and clowning are an effective means for individuals to triumph over the dilemmas that these contradictions produce is evident in the earnestness and enthusiasm with which many embrace the joking relationships and in the insistence that the partners dance their mockery even in the face of death. The dancing by the junior brothers' daughters at the death of their senior father's sisters evokes both the fragility and the resilience of Murik society. It is a simultaneous expression in one fleeting moment of the elaborate forms that constrain and the turbulent emotions that propel Murik social life.

NOTES

I am especially grateful to the Murik women who tolerated and educated this stranger, for whom the effort to understand their laughter was both engaging and strenuous. The subtlety and polysemy of their clowning is barely suggested by this analysis, and for what I have misunderstood and just plain missed, I ask them to extend yet again their tolerance and humor.

The fieldwork on which this paper is based was supported by the Wenner-Gren Foundation for Anthropological Research and the Institute for Inter-Cultural Studies (February 1981–August 1982) and the Sepik

Documentation Project of the Australian Museum (June–September, 1986 and 1988). The work was carried out primarily in the Murik villages of Darapap, Karau, Mendam, and Big Murik and the Murik settlements of Wewak town (Kreer Beach and Nambatu Basis), East Sepik Province, Papua New Guinea.

I would like to thank Bill Mitchell for substantial assistance in clarifying the analysis presented here. David Lipset, as always, improved the analysis by suggesting refinements and counterinterpretations based on his understanding of Murik male culture.

1. Respect and avoidance relations are mandatory among women and their husbands' senior male kin. There are four kinds of joking relationships. One is among women and their husbands' younger brothers. This is the only affinal joking relationship. There are two intergenerational, same-sex joking relationships among classificatory mother's brothers and sister's sons and classificatory father's sisters and brother's daughters. These relationships also define a same-generation joking relationship among classificatory cross-sex siblings. This chapter discusses only the father's sister–brother's daughter relationship. The parallel male relationship of mother's brother–sister's sons is similar in terms of responsibilities and ritual roles, but the content of the clowning is strongly differentiated by gender.

2. It should be noted that clowning—active pantomime and burlesque—as Mosko (this volume) notes, is often separated analytically from joking, but it is not clearly separated in the relationships I am discussing and cannot be used to distinguish contexts, actors, or situations. Both joking and clowning occur with respect to dyads and groups, and much of the humor derives from the fact that these activities simultaneously affirm and negate or invert relationships.

3. Mitchell (introduction, this volume) uses the terms *secular* and *sacral* where I use the terms *mundane* and *ritual* to describe the contexts in which clowning occurs. In general, his *secular* and my *mundane* are equivalent. I prefer the term *ritual* in the Murik case to *sacred*. Ritual is used here in a broader sense to include activities in which prescribed form carries meaning about the event but is not necessarily a communication about what is sacred.

4. A dramatic example of this occurred when a woman paraded to the men's house in full initiation regalia the morning after her younger brother had undergone initiation. According to the rules of seniority, her descent group sponsors should have initiated her, the eldest sister, first. When she appeared on the village path so attired, the senior descent group leader sitting in the men's house burst into loud wailing.

5. See also Gailey (1980) for Tonga.

6. The Murik data on women's status vis-à-vis men raise interesting questions about the criteria for evaluating status and the distinctions between authority and power. From the point of view of Murik men and

women, men are more appropriate public actors in official capacities and have better access to arenas of decision making, namely the men's house. Pollution associated with menstruation and birth further restricts women's participation in public life.

7. Gell (1985:195) describes a similar expression of gender contrasts in Umeda dance. See also Mead (1963:256) for a danced demonstration of an underlying contradiction in gender roles among the Tchambuli (Chambri), a Sepik society with marked similarities to the Murik.

8. For example, a firstborn daughter may have a mother who is also a firstborn but a father who is a younger sibling. Her sponsorship and opportunities for leadership are stronger through maternal links, and these are more likely to be acted upon both by her and by the descent group. However, certain circumstances may require or encourage her to activate the paternal links, and she may legitimately do so, but her claims are weak if she has not contributed resources and work to this group.

9. *Suman* are arrangements of boars' tusks, fruit, flowers, and leaves that are assembled and displayed for all official activities of the descent group. Each group controls a number of such insignia, which have power to command peace or to instigate war.

10. *Mwara* kin are addressed either by the kin term without its prefix, *mwara*, or by some colorful substitute. In Melanesian pidgin the most common term of address for women is *kateres*, from English *cutlass*, meaning sparring partner or "one who spears me." Plates of food exchanged in this relationship are "spears" and presenting them is said to "kill" or "knock out" the recipient.

11. Sometimes generational overlap means that partners are nearly the same age. I do not know of any instances in which the age relationship and seniority were reversed. Marriage ties occasionally convert joking partners to affines who should show respect and avoidance. If this happens, the two partners must agree which relationship to acknowledge. A *mwara* relationship that has a history of ritual payments and performance behind it usually takes precedence over an affinal one.

12. I use the term *partners* because joking and clowning exchanges are often dyadic interactions, but each woman has approximately five to ten *mwara* father's sisters and five to ten *mwara* brother's daughters in each of the Murik villages. On public occasions, when many women gather to share a meal, the horseplay of the *mwara* kin takes place among groups of women who belong to the same set of *mwara* relationships, and it has more the character of team sport. In each generation a group of same-sex siblings share the same *mwara* affiliations. In the course of an individual's lifetime, specific *mwara* relationships assume great importance, while others are almost never brought into play.

13. Membership in the women's secret society is determined by sponsorship. A woman's father decides to sponsor his daughters for initiation singly or together, depending upon his ability to acquire pigs and

other trade goods to contribute to the ritual. A woman who has been initiated into the secret society is decorated with the descent group insignia that her parents choose and thus acquires the right to initiate trade and ritual activities in her own name. The secret society is mainly composed of firstborn daughters and sometimes second- or thirdborn.

14. Until a child is old enough to laugh and to recognize a person at a distance (about six months old), the Murik say, he or she is not ready to leave the home of its mother and maternal grandparents. Such a child is entirely dependent on its mother and has no social persona.

15. This is a case where the opportunity for mockery was seized by all possible participants and even some affinal joking partners who were not technically *mwara* kin. Bateson (1958:14) notes a similar "spreading" or contagion in *naven*, first-accomplishment celebrations, among the Iatmul.

16. The tenor of such a meal is one of great satisfaction on the part of everyone, for at this point all obligations have been fulfilled. The performance that necessitated the feast is recounted in great detail for everyone's enjoyment, and further teasing and joking ensue.

17. Initiated women are expected to maintain extramarital relationships in the extended trade network, men whom they can call upon for support in supplying their ritual work. This privilege is guarded by the power of the *suman*, which the women may carry on behalf of each other to prohibit violence from a jealous husband or disapproving father or brother.

18. Legitimate reasons include bad weather that prevented fishing, absence from the village of other kin who might assist, or depletion of the family food supply due to recent ritual work. Trade partners arrive completely unannounced and may very well appear at times that are less than ideal for making a good showing of hospitality and abundant resources.

19. The sponsoring descent group is the one that obtains and presents the pigs for the *mwara* father's sisters. It may be one of the mother's or father's descent groups, and occasionally more than one group presents pigs and displays insignia on behalf of the same individual. These presentations are the result of a long-term effort (typically a year or more) to amass resources through trade.

20. Scheff (1979;118f) describes the cathartic function of laughter evoked in ritual contexts as an important balance of tension and emotional distance. The clowning performance allows those experiencing loss and fear to participate in and observe their own distress, relieving it with laughter. Those who are too threatened or emotionally involved and those who are uninvolved will not respond with laughter, but those in an intermediate range of emotional distance will. In this case the poles of too close proximity and too much distance were represented by the close kin, who seemed numb in the face of the performance, and by the ethnographers, who were puzzled and fascinated but did not sufficiently comprehend the situation to laugh spontaneously.

REFERENCES

Apte, Mahadev L.
- 1985 *Humor and Laughter: An Anthropological Approach.* Ithaca: Cornell University Press.

Ardener, Edwin
- 1975 Belief and the problem of women. In *Perceiving Women,* ed. S. Ardener, pp. 1–28. New York: Wiley.

Barlow, Kathleen
- 1985 Learning Cultural Meanings Through Social Relationships: An Ethnography of Childhood in Murik Society, Papua New Guinea. Ph.D. thesis, University of California, San Diego.
- 1989 Achieving Womanhood and the Achievements of Women in Murik Society: Puberty Rites, Cult Initiation and the Cultural Construction of Gender. Author's files.

Bateson, Gregory
- 1958 *Naven: A Survey of the Problems Suggested by a Composite Picture of the Culture of a New Guinea Tribe Drawn from Three Points of View,* 2nd ed. Stanford: Stanford University Press.
- 1972 *Steps to an Ecology of Mind.* New York: Ballantine Books.

Burnand, Gordon
- 1977 Teasing and Joking in Isolated Societies. In *It's a Funny Thing, Humour,* ed. Antony J. Chapman and Hugh C. Foot, pp. 437–38. New York: Pergamon Press.

Douglas, Mary
- 1968 The Social Control of Cognition: Some Factors in Joke Perception. *Man* 3:361–76.

Eggan, Fred
- 1937 Respect and Joking Relationships Among the Cheyenne and Arapaho. In *Social Anthropology of the North American Tribes,* ed. Fred Eggan, pp. 75–81. Chicago: University of Chicago Press.

Fox, G.
- 1977 "Nice Girl": Social Control of Woman through Value Construct. *Signs* 2:805–17.

Freud, Sigmund
- 1916 *Wit and Its Relation to the Unconscious.* Trans. A. A. Brill. London: Fisher & Unwin.

Gailey, Christine Ward
- 1980 Putting Down Sisters and Wives: Tongan Women and Colonization. In *Women and Colonization: Anthropological Perspec-*

tives, ed. Mona Etienne and Eleanor Leacock, pp. 294-322. New York: Praeger.

Geertz, Clifford
    1973   Deep Play: Notes on the Balinese Cock Fight. In *The Interpretation of Cultures*, ed. Clifford Geertz, pp. 412-53. New York: Basic Books.

Gell, Alfred
    1985   Style and Meaning in Umeda Dance. In *Society and the Dance: The Social Anthropology of Process and Performance*, ed. Paul Spencer, pp. 183–205. New York: Cambridge University Press.

Goody, Jack R.
    1969   *Comparative Studies in Kinship*. Stanford: Stanford University Press.

Gluckman, Max
    1962   *Essays on the Ritual of Social Relations*. Manchester: Manchester University Press.

Lipset, David M.
    1984   *Authority and the Maternal Presence: An Interpretive Ethnography of Murik Lakes Society* (East Sepik Province, Papua New Guinea). Ph.D. thesis, University of California, San Diego.

Lowie, Robert
    1970   *Primitive Society*. New York: H. Liveright.

Makarius, Laura
    1970   Ritual Clowns and Symbolic Behaviour. *Diogenes* 69:44–73.

Malefijt, A. M. deW.
    1968   Dutch Joking Patterns. *Transactions of the New York Academy of Sciences*, ser. 2, 30:1181–86.

Mead, Margaret
    1963   *Sex and Temperament in Three Primitive Societies*. New York: Morrow Quill.

Ortner, Sherry B.
    1981   Gender and Sexuality in Hierarchical Societies: The Case of Polynesia and Some Comparative Implications. In *Sexual Meanings: The Cultural Construction of Gender and Sexuality*, ed. Sherry B. Ortner and Harriet Whitehead, pp. 359–409. Cambridge: Cambridge University Press.

Radcliffe-Brown, A. R.
    1940   On Joking Relationships. *Africa* 13:195–210.
    1949   A Further Note on Joking Relationships. *Africa* 19:133–40.

Rosaldo, Michelle
    1972   Woman, Culture and Society: A Theoretical Overview. In *Woman, Culture and Society*, ed. Michelle Zimbalist Rosaldo

and Louise Lamphere, pp. 17-42. Stanford: Stanford Univ. Press.

Scheff, T. J.
    1979 *Catharsis in Healing, Ritual and Drama*. Berkeley and Los Angeles: University of California Press.

Strathern, Marilyn
    1976 An Anthropological Perspective. In *Exploring Sex Differences*, ed. Barbara Lloyd and John Archer, pp. 49–69. London: Academic Press.

Turner, Victor
    1969 *The Ritual Process, Structure and Anti-Structure*. Ithaca: Cornell University Press.

EXAGGERATION AND REVERSAL:
CLOWNING AMONG THE LUSI-KALIAI

David R. Counts and Dorothy A. Counts

THE LUSI-KALIAI people live along the coastal fringe of the northwest part of West New Britain Province of Papua New Guinea and are physically isolated from the main centers of Papua New Guinea.[1] Their five villages are buffered by about one hundred kilometers of sea from the nearest roads or airstrips. One result of their isolation is that they, along with many other rural peoples of the world, usually must provide their own entertainment. (At least this was the case until recently. A village correspondent has recently informed us that a local entrepreneur bought a generator, VCR, and monitor for a new business, where, for a small fee from his audience, he shows rented videos.)

We anthropologists often write as if the people among whom we live and study go about their whole lives—working in gardens, building houses, holding ceremonies, exchanging wealth, rearing children—with deep seriousness. After all, if our accounts of their lives are to be taken as serious business (and our careers depend upon it), then those lives must themselves be serious matters. But of course, it isn't so, or at least it isn't so that they spend their *whole* lives in seriousness. They also spend a good deal of time and energy amusing themselves. There are a number of ways that the Lusi-Kaliai provide their amusement. One way is the telling of Aesoplike folktales, called *ninipunga* in the Lusi language (Counts 1982).

Ninipunga are literally stories that are told for fun—a form of pure entertainment. They often feature animal characters whose actions burlesque the behavior of objectionable or stupid humans in such a way as to make high comedy of low behavior. A visit to a village by a person who has a reputation as a skilled storyteller is a notable event, and a large crowd will gather in the evening to call for their favorite stories or the visitor's specialties. Since storytelling

Clowning Among the Lusi-Kaliai

form among the Lusi-Kaliai requires that the narrator quote the actual dialogue of the characters, each performance becomes a local theatrical event that is entertaining and exciting.

Events staged for the primary purpose of entertainment are not the only ones that provide it. Serious events also entertain and amuse. The ceremonies to claim a firstborn child are important and serious matters for the parents, as their standing in the community for years to come rests on the successful performance of the ceremony (Scaletta 1985). Similarly, sponsoring a visit to the village by a set of spirit beings is a major undertaking for the organizers. Yet, for other villagers and for visitors to the community, such events may be a welcome form of entertainment. Outsiders attending the festivities bring with them news and gossip; there are public performances that break the routine of day-to-day life; major ceremonial events often involve dancing and singing from dusk until dawn, with the attendant satisfied exhaustion of the participants afterward. On the periphery of these activities, tied only loosely to the central purpose of the ceremony, clowns often perform and offer social commentary. Clowns are entertainers, often hilarious ones, but there is frequently a solemn undercurrent to their performance, for like medieval jesters, they also address serious business.

There are two kinds of Lusi-Kaliai clowns: those who participate in ceremonial events and those who perform outside a ritual context. The distinction that we make between them is a heuristic one for our own analytical purposes and not one that our friends would recognize as culturally significant. The remainder of this chapter concerns these two sorts of clowns, who operate in different contexts and vary in the style and content of their social commentary.

The Lusi-Kaliai

There are approximately a thousand Lusi-speaking people living in hamlets and villages along the northwest coast of New Britain in the Kaliai political subdivision. Lusi is an Austronesian language, part of a patchwork of related Melanesian languages that constitute the Bariai family of languages stretching from northwest New Britain across the Dampier Straits to northeastern coastal New Guinea. While they make use of the sea at their doorstep for the provision of ready protein, the Lusi-Kaliai are not primarily seafarers or fisher people. Rather, they are gardeners, producing taro, sweet potatoes, and other vegetables and fruits in shifting plots periodically cleared of light secondary forest, burned, and then planted using digging sticks. In the past half-century the Lusi-Kaliai have also begun planting coconut plantations and have added the production of copra as a cash crop to their gardening activities.

The growth of the town of Kimbe, capital of the Province of West New Britain, less than two hundred kilometres away from the Kaliai area, is part of the inexorable process of Papua New Guinea's recent development. Kimbe has brought markets for Kaliai copra, sources of goods for their trade stores, and access to Western-style entertainment (like videos) within easy striking distance for the first time. Still, without roads to link the Lusi-Kaliai to Kimbe, their isolation—and with it much of the colonial and precolonial pace and preoccupation of life—remains strong.

The Lusi-Kaliai have an ideology of patrilineality and virilocality. Their basic coresidential unit is the hamlet, which typically is occupied by the agnatically related men of a *kambu*—the named patrikin group—and their wives and children, who live as nuclear families in houses built either around a central plaza or in lines facing each other across a common area. Much of hamlet life focuses on the men's house belonging to the *kambu*. It is in the men's house that resident bachelors and visiting males sleep and where ceremonial paraphernalia is stored. The *kambu* is the primary cooperative unit. It organizes ceremonies, fences gardens, pools wealth when its sons marry, and shares bride-wealth when its daughters do. Most of the ceremonial activity of the *kambu* centers upon life events, especially marriage, firstborn ceremonies, and mortuary ritual. It is also the kin group that supplies the clowns for ritual events.

Ritual Clowning

There is no Lusi term that can be translated as *a clown*. Clowning is an action; the term for it is a verb, *sega* (to clown; to act the fool).[2] Ritual clowning, the doing of *sega*, is tied to the central and serious ritual events that are the focus of community interest. The actions of the clown provide a commentary on the ritual work that is of overriding importance to the community. The examples we have of the public clowning that occurs in conjunction with ceremonial activities all share at least two elements. First, ritual clowns usually perform as transvestites. Women costume themselves as men and

Clowning Among the Lusi-Kaliai

perform exaggerated parodies of selected aspects of male behavior. We also have been told of men dancing *sega* dressed as women, but we have not witnessed it.[3] Second, clowns parody certain kinds of behavior. Specifically, female clowns mock the stereotypical male behavior of warriors, village leaders (especially the leader who is chief sponsor of the ceremony at which they are performing), guitar-strumming youths, and drunks. They also burlesque the actions of outsiders: overweight, pompous white men; self-important politicians who wear shoes, socks, and dark glasses and jingle keys in their pockets; and urban dwellers who walk the town streets carrying ghetto blasters. They probably also mimic actions of resident anthropologists, but we are mercifully unaware of examples of this type of clowning.

Ritual clowns regularly perform at weddings and at rites for firstborn children. An example from each will illustrate the way in which Lusi-Kaliai clowns provide both entertainment and social commentary.

The formal ritual culmination of a Lusi-Kaliai marriage—the wedding—occurs when the groom's family have accumulated the appropriate bridal gifts, no easy task. The bridal gifts include arrays of Sio pots, Siasi carved wooden bowls (cf. Harding 1967), and huge matched quantities of pandanus sleeping mats and fathom lengths of *vula* (shell currency).

When all is in readiness, the bride's patrikin escort her, in costume, weighted down with shell currency, her skin shining with coconut oil, from her home to the home of the groom. Near the destination the groom waits with his supporters and the piles of gifts. The two *kambu* meet, the bride is handed over to the care of her husband, and the gifts are publicly counted and given over to the bride's family. Throughout this process, from the beginning of the procession until the end of the distribution of bride-wealth, some of the women—usually old women—of the bride's *kambu* perform *sega*. Dressed as warriors ready for battle with their loins wrapped in bark cloth, breasts restrained by bands of cloth, skin whitened with powdered lime, battle emblems (albino cowries or boar's tusks) clenched between their teeth, and brandishing fighting clubs or spears cut from slender branches, they leap and rush about, threatening onlookers with their weapons. The clowns concentrate their attack on members of the groom's party, especially the men.[4] The chosen victim of an attack is expected to flee until the clown is distracted and finds someone new to threaten. Those not party to the chase flow with the action, sometimes aiding the clown by threatening to trip her victim and always finding hilarity in the sight of an old woman putting a strong young warrior to flight.

The second illustration of ritual clowning is drawn from performances at firstborn children's rituals of validation. Scaletta (1985) provides a detailed discussion of these rituals, which also form a central part of the ceremonial and political life of the Kabana people living to the west of the Lusi-Kaliai. Kabana and Lusi-Kaliai adults compete for prestige and standing in their communities in part through the lavishness of the ceremonies held to honor their firstborn children.

Among Lusi-Kaliai, parents who aspire to important social standing ritually recognize nearly every first achievement of their firstborn child: the child's first step, for example, or its first time to dance in public. The major rites, which validate the claim of the father's *kambu* to the child and formalize the relationship of the child with its mother's kin, are highly elaborated formal public ceremonies that usually occur some time between the child's sixth and eleventh years. These rites include the presentation of a young woman on the occasion of her first menses, the ceremony of penile supraincision for a young boy, or its analogue for a young girl when her ears are pierced.[5] The last two rites, called *vaulo*, are events of great moment for the parents. The ceremony is usually held for a number of children at the same time, and if possible, it should take place when there are *aulu* (spirits) resident in the men's house of the hamlet. For the fathers and their kin, the *vaulo* is an enormous undertaking, for the potential rewards of great prestige are balanced by the risk of excruciating humiliation if they lack sufficient resources to feed all guests and present generous gifts of shell currency and pandanus mats to the children's mother's patrikin (Counts and Counts 1970).

For the sponsors it is a time of worry and tension. For others it is a time of festivity. The action usually begins at dusk, as singers and dancers, sometimes including masked spirit beings, begin their performance in the village plaza, and it lasts through the night. Soon after dawn, the serious business of shell currency presentation begins, as the name of each recipient is called and his or her gift is publicly counted by a master of ceremonies. When this is over, the honored children are brought out.

All the children are decorated: their bodies and faces are painted, they are dressed in dance costume, and they are bedecked with shell currency and dog's tooth, *nassa* shell, or cassowary quill ornaments. The children are the center of the attention, and each one is brought through the middle of the village, either surrounded by a crowd of supporting adults and perhaps also by the stately masked *aulu* figures or carried standing on a shield above the heads of the crowd.

Leading the crowd, dancing backward just in front of the children to be presented, are the clowns, usually women and usually from the initiates' mother's patrikin.[6] The clowns' dress is variable. Unlike the wedding clowns who wear warrior attire, all of the clowning for children that we have witnessed has parodied the dress of young modern men. *Dress* is used loosely here; the clowns wear shorts and T-shirts, and long socks and shoes if they can find them. They also often sport sunglasses and carry radio-cassette recorders, and rather than charge the crowd as they might do at a wedding, they are more likely to stagger around drunkenly, falling down and shoving at the spectators.

The more somber side of clowning behavior may also be expressed at the ceremonial presentation of a child, for the same women who burlesque the *man bilong gita* (literally, guitar man in Tok Pisin, but figuratively a lazy layabout) that the newly supraincised boy may become also mourn his passage through the cycle. After the surgery a clown may throw herself, still in her costume, on the newly bloodied mat and weep for the child's suffering and shed blood. When this happens the keening clown remains prone on the mat until one of the child's agnatic kin compensates her for her grief.

Ritual clowns do not perform gratis. As is true of everyone else who participates in honoring a celebrant, they must be paid. Clowns are compensated, consultants tell us, "to buy their shame," to repay them for having shed their dignity to play the fool in public.

Informal Clowning

Informal clowning differs from ritual clowning in a number of significant respects. First, it may have a restricted audience rather than a general and public one. Second, it may exist on the sidelines, associated with but not an integral part of a ritual, or it may occur in a context that is unrelated to any formal event. In the latter case it is wholly impromptu, sometimes triggered by the behavior it ridicules and sometimes by the behavior of those for whom the clown is performing. Third, it may not involve gender role reversal, and even on those occasions when the parody apes the behavior of a person of opposite sex, the gender reversal may be only incidental and not an integral part of the clowning performance. Fourth, the clown dons a costume only if dress is an unmistakable element of the target's identifying features. Otherwise the buffoonery may mock the target's walk, speech habits, or some other behavior characteristic. Finally, the humor of the performance comes from the exaggeration of the target's identifying features.

Informal clowning occurs in association with the ritual presentation of firstborn children, but is separate and distinct from the formal *sega* already described. It is especially likely to happen if the ceremony involves the participation of a powerful spirit figure whose presence drives women from the village. In 1981, when our twelve-year-old son was one of the children ceremonially introduced to a local men's house, Dorothy fled with the other women, retiring to an enclosure at the far end of the village where the women distributed among themselves some of the food that had been prepared for the men. After the feast, the women began to *sega*. Some imitated the men, pretending to shout instructions and announcements in English and charging the giggling women, while one woman imitated the leader of the kin group who had sponsored the ceremony, strutting back and forth and ordering all the women to run away.[7] When a young man came to tell the women they could return, they chased him from the enclosure, throwing things at him and hitting him with sticks.

According to our consultants, when women retire further from the village, they usually strip naked to bathe, and then dance, sing, and *sega*, parodying the supposedly secret activities of the men. Had that been the case in this instance, we were told, the women would have cut spears and used them to threaten the young man who came to call them back to the village. Again there is a dark side to the event, for our consultants claimed that in earlier times any man caught spying on the women at such a time would have been surrounded and killed at the order of the senior women. Word would have then been sent back to the village that the female spirit named *Vovonga* had caught and killed him, just as a woman who was caught spying on men's secret activities would have been killed by a male spirit.

Other informal clowning among Lusi-Kaliai is, like ritual clowning, −1 public. But while ritual clowning takes place in a context where a crowd already exists for another purpose, this informal clowning is impromptu and is itself the focus of action. If it is successful, it creates a public for whom it is the central attraction. In the remaining section of this chapter we discuss two impromptu clown

Clowning Among the Lusi-Kaliai

actors: one, called Antu Kikira, was a commentary on villagers' views of whites; the other parodied the arrogant stupidity of a Papua New Guinean official.

Antu Kikira is best described first. The clown's head was an old white volleyball, split to go over the wearer's head. Below the volleyball there appeared to be a grossly fat person wearing an old suit, dress shirt, and worn leather shoes. For several months in 1975, Antu Kikira would appear from time to time, usually from the vicinity of a men's house, and slowly and ponderously parade up and down the village thoroughfare, the open space across which the houses faced each other. Commonly, he would emerge at a time of day when young children were about, playing in the sand or under the verandas of the houses. The children would run screaming in all directions searching for the nearest parent or appropriate substitute to throw themselves on for protection from the monster. The children's screams of fear brought the adults out to shriek, point, and hold their bellies with the pain of laughter. Occasionally a parent would take a child toward Antu Kikira, thrusting it at him and telling the Antu, "Here, you can eat this one—he's a bighead!" The proffered child would scream even more loudly, while the watching adults would laugh harder.

What was happening here? First, Antu Kikira was a white man: his bald, white, featureless head, his inappropriate clothing, and his threatening pomposity clearly identified him. These same features made him a perfect parody of the most objectionable features of the stereotypical colonial European. To see such persons being aped was genuinely funny. Second, Antu Kikira was an *antu* (ghost, spirit being): he usually emerged from behind the men's house, as did the equally ponderous *aulu*, and from the same area whence came the voice of the *antu*, the bull-roarer. As a white *antu*, Kikira was a barbed and ambivalent joke about the belief of the ancestors (and of unsophisticated contemporary people of the New Britain interior) that Europeans were in fact ghosts. The children's reactions—their fear and screams—were themselves a parody of the ancestors' own fear of the whites who came to the Kaliai area about a century ago, so that too was part of the humor of the performance.[8]

Several people performed Antu Kikira during the months of his residence in Kandoka. The performers were mostly young and middle-aged men, though occasionally a young woman would don the attire and make the rounds. On one occasion Antu Kikira was performed by a young woman at the request of some parents in the village whose children persisted in playing in the puddles left after a hard rain. The parents, concerned that pig feces had contaminated the water and were endangering their children's health, wished to frighten them. The children soon left their play.

The Antu Kikira clown had a short life. After a couple of months, some of the younger children who were old enough not to be afraid, but young enough to spoil the effect for toddlers, began to use the volleyball (and sometimes an old torn sheet as clothing) to frighten the younger children on a daily basis. As the character became familiar, he lost his power to amuse as well as to frighten. Eventually the torn, discarded, volleyball shell became part of the trash swept up and thrown out to sea.

Our second example of impromptu clowning occurred during our residence in Kandoka village in 1981. At that time the Department of West New Britain (the arm in West New Britain Province of the national government) dispatched several teams who were charged with visiting all the villages in the province, explaining to the local people proposed constitutional amendments, and attempting to gauge public support for the changes. The teams were led by a national civil servant—in the case at hand, an information officer—who was accompanied by the locally elected member of the provincial legislative assembly and the member of the local government council from each council district. The information officer assigned to patrol in the Kaliai area was a man whom we will call Maringe. For the Lusi-Kaliai, Maringe was a target for clowning. Indeed, some suggested that he *was* a clown! One member of the provincial legislature told David the following story:

> You know, we in West New Britain are really lucky—really lucky. The national government wanted our province to have at least one of everything. They knew we were nearly complete, so they sent a man to find out what we were lacking. After careful study he found that we were short only one thing: West New Britain had *no* clown! Once they knew, the people in Moresby had pity on us. They sent us Maringe. Now we have a clown. Now we are complete![9]

From the perspective of the Lusi-Kaliai, Maringe started with a disadvantage. He was a foreigner; he spoke atrocious Tok Pisin; his incompetence was legendary, for he had but to touch a piece of equipment for it to cease working; and finally, he was gullible. As if these severe deficiencies were not enough, he was known throughout the village within hours of his arrival as a person both arrogant and offensive.

He did not walk through the village, he swaggered and strutted. He showed no deference to big men and big women. Rather he

Clowning Among the Lusi-Kaliai

presumed familiarity, entering houses without invitation, staying where he was not welcome. Villagers felt that he talked down to them in the public information sessions, that he lectured them as if they were children for whom his visit was a gift of the gods. He did not ask where he might stay but commandeered the just-completed Young Men's Social Club building for his own use. Finally, the villagers quickly realized that he was spending more time trying to set up assignations with young village girls than he was in doing his job.

His lust for the unmarried girls of the village was the opening the people needed. As Maringe chose to base his team in Kandoka and go out to the other Kaliai villages rather than patrolling and staying in each one, he was at the mercy of the Kandokans for the better part of a week. During that time they played on his gullibility; conspiring to lead him down the proverbial garden path, taking him for what they could. Young girls would be sent to inform him that a desirable young woman would meet him in the bush far from the village late at night. Then a crowd would hide and watch as he went secretly, with no light, to meet his imaginary paramour. When he returned hours later, he would be given a message from the girl that she had waited and waited, but he had gone to the wrong place. When the amusement of watching Maringe being led by his penis began to pall, one of the village men suggested to Maringe that perhaps he would like to marry his daughter. All that was needed was a down payment on the bride-price.

Maringe paid over 50 kina (about US$75) and his stereo radio-cassette player. From then on, members of the girl's kin group began to call him by in-law terms, ask him for gifts, and require that he honor all the taboos restricting a person's behavior with respect to his in-laws. They also successfully demanded that he make available for their use his house in Kimbe, when they went there. All of this was done with complete gravity as far as Maringe was concerned, though every move had been carefully planned and the entire village was privy to the scam. For days the gossip focused on the latest coup that the villagers had counted against this oaf. Needless to say, the marriage was never consummated.

The clowning picked up on Maringe's identifying characteristic. One was a pet phrase: "No problems!" When informed that his movie projector used in the information session was not locally repairable after he broke it, his response was "no probs!" Indeed, any difficulty was met with a "no probs" response. Yet, from the point of view of the Kandokans, this was a man with *many* problems.

For the rest of our stay, when someone in the village was informed of a difficulty or asked for something that he or she could not possibly provide, the response was an exaggerated "no probs!" and laughter from everyone within hearing. The second characteristic that was clowned was Maringe's walk—indeed, his swaggering strut was sometimes aped in his presence, the clown remaining out of Maringe's line of sight. More frequently, someone would simply parade down the middle of the village, waving condescendingly, and shouting "No probs!" to the delight of onlookers.

Now, without question, the treatment given to Maringe was harsh. He was both ridiculed and gulled, and the conspiracy to do it was virtually villagewide, wider than that if we take note of the quote from the Talasea-area provincial parliament member with which we opened this discussion of Maringe. It sometimes seemed to us that people were testing how far they could push Maringe before he would realize that he was being made a fool of and decamp. His departure was what the villagers wanted, but being powerless to effect that goal directly, they used the ridicule available to them. They also used direct action to express their anger, by urging their local parliament member to file a formal complaint against Maringe when the patrol returned to the capital. In fact, a formal complaint was lodged, and Maringe was suspended from further patrols while it was investigated.

During Maringe's stay in the village, the people did what they could, and what they could do was to make a fool of the offender and amuse themselves. The point on which to leave this discussion is just that: amusement. Through the actions of those who clowned at Maringe's expense and the hilarious gossip provided by those who managed to gull him, the village was entertained for weeks. Just a "no probs!" or the recounting of one of the Maringe stories in which the villagers won and he lost were enough to provoke laughter. He was very offended when he lost the girl, too, and threatened to sue for the return of his goods, but to no avail.

Conclusions

We suggest that the two sorts of clowning we have described are dissimilar in form, employ disparate strategies, and deliver different messages: the contexts in which ritual clowns perform and the comments on social affairs that they convey are not the same as those of informal clowns who perform on an impromptu basis. Our analysis of the content of clowns' messages is necessarily inferential, for we have never systematically pursued the meaning of clowning with our consultants. The following interpretations of Lusi-Kaliai clowning seem to us, from what we understand of Lusi-Kaliai culture, to be reasonable; they are possibilities that we want to explore with our friends and either verify, revise, or reject the next time we have the opportunity to reside in West New Britain.

Ritual clowns perform in view of the persons whose behavior is the topic of comment: they are, in fact, performing for two distinct audiences and, perhaps, providing for each a separate message. One message for the general populace is that the models of the adult male who embodies the qualities of the male ethos (a model to which the newly supraincised boys aspire)—including the men's posturing as warriors or as modern men with their socks and shoes, ghetto blasters, sunglasses, key chains, and guitars—are ridiculous. No particular male is singled out as a representative of the category (although clowns and audience alike may have a prototype in mind to add content to the performance). Rather, the target is an archetypal one, and therefore, any particular individual who took offense would be nominating himself as an example of the category, not a role to which anyone would likely aspire.

Punctuating this statement that the strutting adult male is really pretty silly is the sadness women feel as they see their sons move from the female sphere (literally out of their mother's house and into the men's house) into the male sphere of influence, or their daughters move from their natal home to that of their husbands where they might be unprotected. We think, although we do not have a single quotation from an informant to substantiate this, that Lusi-Kaliai women are ambivalent about the ceremonies. They are sorry to see their little boys grow up and their daughters become exposed to the potential dangers of marriage. As Dorothy Counts argues elsewhere (1987, 1990), marriage for Lusi-Kaliai women is dangerous, for most will be the victims of male violence at one time or another, and some may be driven to suicide. Unable or unwilling to prevent a daughter's marriage, with its attendant dangers, women can at least comment on it by clowning. The ambivalence of the women is illustrated by the earlier description of a clown weeping on the mat where the blood of her grandchild was shed to facilitate his becoming a man.

Another message, this time focused on particular individuals, is to the groom and his kin who are threatened by the clowns from the bride's family. First, the relationships between the two groups of affinally related kin are characterized by competition as well as cooperation. Her relatives have the right to call on him and his kin for contributions of pork and shell money when they sponsor important ceremonial distributions. They also may claim the children of the marriage if the husband and his kin fail to pay all of the bride-wealth or neglect to perform the *vaulo*, thereby demonstrating their inability to meet their obligations to the children. Although a marriage allies the two groups, there is underlying tension between them. This tension is acknowledged by the avoidance rules that severely limit interaction between a person and his or her affines. It is also expressed by the sham battle in which clowns from the bride's family attack the groom's kinsmen with mock fighting clubs and spears. This attack is done in fun, but it also includes an element of aggressive and violent behavior that carries a message from the bride's family to that of the groom.

On one level, the clowns demonstrate the commitment of the bride's relatives to defend and support her if she is abused by her husband or his kin. Domestic violence, especially wife beating, is an expected part of married life in West New Britain. The amount of punishment a husband can inflict on his wife is limited by the presence of her relatives and their willingness to intervene in her defense if he beats her excessively. The attack of the clowns reminds (perhaps warns) the groom and his family that there will probably be conflict between the two kin groups if he abuses her.

An important distinction between our examples of formal and informal clowning is that informal clowning takes place out of the sight of the persons being aped. Any messages, including those about what is unacceptable social behavior, are therefore for the benefit of someone other than the victim of the ridicule. In this case the clowning targets an individual who may be a prototype of the stereotype being lampooned in formal clowning: *this particular person* personifies those qualities that clowns in another context have demonstrated as absurd, ridiculous, laughable, and not to be imitated by those who do not want to be seen as fools.

In all the instances we have seen of informal clowning, there is a power differential between the goat and the clown, and this inequality is part of the structure of the performance. The informal setting permits relatively powerless persons, as clowns, to use ridicule to comment on the unsavory or foolish qualities of more powerful persons whom they would not dare ridicule to their faces or in public. Thus women go off by themselves to parody their menfolk, but they do not *publicly* ape their husbands, fathers, village elders, or older brothers with impunity. Villagers imitate the gross and unendearing qualities of whites or government officials, but not where the victims can exact angry retribution against them.

Once again, however, we can see the reciprocal side to this humor, because the other message being communicated is that the powerful are not invulnerable and the weak may have their own sources of strength. Maringe, the powerful fool, was in fact vulnerable to village anger and resentment and, when the game was over, he was poorer, still unmarried, and reported to the government for incompetence. Women, who were required to submit to their menfolk, claimed the right to attack and kill any man who invaded their private domain (as men could kill women who saw the sacred masks or entered the men's house), and they still exercise their prerogative to attack any male—even a messenger—who trespasses on their territory. In spite of the perceived inequality, those without power are not bereft of resources: there is a time and a place when, as clowns, they can assert authority and can successfully challenge the establishment.

It would be a mistake to end this chapter on such a somber note. It is important to remember that the serious side of clowning behavior among the Lusi-Kaliai is inseparable from behavior that brings light and laughter and pleasure into the lives of people and provides them with entertainment. Clowns comment, but they comment with mirth.

NOTES

The research on which this essay is based was conducted in West New Britain, Papua New Guinea, in 1966–1967, 1971, 1975–1976, 1981, and 1985 with the support of the National Science Foundation, the Social Sciences and Humanities Research Council of Canada, the Wenner Gren Foundation, McMaster University, and the University of Waterloo.

1. We have agreed with scholars in Papua New Guinea to try to standardize our usage of terms for the people who have been our hosts since 1966. The people with whom we have lived are called the Lusi-Kaliai. We have chosen this awkward hyphenated term because the language spoken by our friends is called Lusi, while the region where they live (essentially a political division deriving from colonial times) is called Kaliai. In this chapter when we refer to the inhabitants of the region generally, we call them Kaliai; otherwise our references are to the Lusi-Kaliai and to their language, *Lusi*.

2. Verbs in Lusi-Kaliai never stand alone as uninflected forms, hence

there is not really such a form as *sega* (to clown, play the fool) as an infinitive form. *Someone* must clown, as in *ti-sega*, (they clown), or, a kind of noun can be formed from the verb, as in *sega-nga*, (clowning). In this chapter we ignore these linguistic niceties and treat *sega* as though it could stand without an affix.

3. We have also been told of one man in Kandoka village who is known for clowning naked (to the embarrassment of his wife and the amusement of everyone else). Our consultants suggest that naked clowning by both men and women was once more common. In addition, a lot of clowning that goes on today involves sexual burlesque, for example women sporting huge penises and lunging lasciviously at the men, or men equipped with the appearance of enormous breasts and women's skirts performing impromptu bump and grind acts to the great enjoyment of all but their respective spouses.

4. The ritual opposition of patrikin groups in mock battle is not restricted to the wedding events described here. We suggest that the clowns' attacks pass the message to the bride's new affines that she is protected by her patrikin's interest in her well-being. That interest extends to her children, as well. The most graphic example of such mock strife between affinally linked Lusi-Kaliai *kambu* that we have witnessed took place in 1967, following the death of a young boy. When his mother's patrikin group arrived to participate in mourning the boy's death, the men marched in a phalanx through the village center bearing spears and painted for battle. The dead boy's patrikin lined side by side with shields facing the oncoming spears to bar their "enemy's" path. When the two groups met the spears were thrust into the waiting shields. Then everyone dropped their weapons and embraced, weeping for their joint loss. The bereaved mother's patrikin had been given opportunity to express their rage that those responsible for their child had been negligent and had permitted his death.

5. The purpose of penile supraincision is the same as that of circumcision—to expose the glans penis. Rather than removing it Lusi-Kaliai make an incision along the top of the foreskin, allowing it to drop back from the glans. Initiates are usually from about six to eleven years when the incision is made.

6. Lusi-Kaliai are reluctant rule makers about what there *must be* to make events proper in the abstract. In specific cases, of course, they will tell an inquirer precisely what went wrong, and with glee if the error is someone else's. We never have heard a statement that "there ought to be clowns," but we also have never seen clowns at minor rites and never have seen a major one take place without them. We surmise that if there were no clowns at a *vaulo* the spectators would be highly critical afterward about the ability of the child's relatives to do things right.

7. It is important to note here that women maintain the fiction that what the men do is secret from them. The women, who are driven away to

protect them from these powerful spirit beings that only men can control, gleefully celebrate their possession of knowledge thought to be the property of the unsuspecting men.

8. We hasten to add that our own two-year-old also found Antu Kikira terrifying, even though we promised him that we wouldn't let it eat him.

9. This anecdote was told to David while he was sitting on the beach with some members of the provincial legislative assembly awaiting transport to Kimbe, the capitol of West New Britain. The conversation was in Tok Pisin, and the term used to describe the need filled by Maringe was *klaun*.

REFERENCES

Counts, David R., and Dorothy Ayers Counts
    1970   The Vula of Kaliai: A Primitive Currency with Commercial Use. *Oceania* 41:90–105.

Counts, Dorothy Ayers
    1982   *Tales of Laupa*. Boroko: Institute of Papua New Guinea Studies.
    1987   Female Suicide and Wife Abuse: A Cross-Cultural Perspective. *Suicide and Life-Threatening Behavior* 17:194–204.
    1990   Beaten Wife, Suicidal Woman: Domestic Violence in Kaliai, West New Britain. In Special Issue: Domestic Violence in Oceania, *Pacific Studies* 13(3):151–70.

Harding, Thomas G.
    1967   *Voyagers of the Vitiaz Strait: A Study of a New Guinea Trading System*. American Ethnological Society Monograph 44. Seattle: University of Washington Press.

Scaletta, Naomi M.
    1985   Primogeniture and Primogenitor: Firstborn Child and Mortuary Ceremonies Among the Kabana (Bariai) of West New Britain, Papua New Guinea. Ph.D. dissertation, McMaster University, Ontario.

CLOWNING WITH FOOD: MORTUARY HUMOR AND SOCIAL REPRODUCTION AMONG THE NORTH MEKEO

Mark S. Mosko

IN HIS SYNOPSIS of the cross-cultural study of humor, Apte observes that, historically, "joking relationships" and ritual "clowning" have received the most attention from anthropologists (1985: 152). Indeed, ever since Lowie's (1909, 1920), Radcliffe-Brown's (1952), Steward's (1931), and Evans-Pritchard's (1929) early treatments, joking relationships and clowning have held the status of virtually formal types in the comparative study of kinship. Thus Apte is led to suggest how, typically, the two categories are doubly differentiated: on the one hand, joking relationships consist of dyadic exchanges between individual persons, whereas ritual clowning involves group performances; on the other, joking tends to affirm or epitomize relations, while clowning characteristically reverses, inverts, or negates them (1985:30–66, 152–61).

This essay attempts to subvert these formal differentiations through an examination of ritual burlesque as practiced among the North Mekeo peoples of Papua New Guinea. The ritual clowns or jokers in this instance are affinal relations. And, unsurprisingly for Melanesians, their humorous performances, staged in the context of mortuary ceremonies and exchanges, consist of obligatory public demonstrations of exaggerated eating and bravado, termed *ipani* (literally, eating). As I shall describe, *ipani* eating and burlesque involve groups rather than individual persons and, hence, would constitute ritual clowning in Apte's classification. But according to the actors' own categorizations, mortuary eating is included among additional humorous ritual forms in which affines interact as individual persons, that is, in joking relationships. In this respect, the criterion of personal dyad versus group seems irrelevant. Moreover, I shall attempt to show how exaggerated mortuary *ipani* both affirms and reverses differentially the ordinary terms and values of

North Mekeo kinship and affinity, thereby also confounding Apte's second criterion for the joking/clowning distinction.

But as important as the choice between formal and indigenous classifications is, North Mekeo *ipani* eating illustrates even more forcefully how humor can perform social functions that are anything but trivial. *Ipani* eating plays more than the merely symbolic role, say, of passively projecting indigenous terms of relationship, whether through their expression or their inversion; rather, the humor of mortuary eating and the laughter it elicits actively facilitate the ritual transformation of certain types of nonmarriageable kin into their opposites — specifically, into nonkin and hence potential affines. In this sense, *ipani* could be seen as an "anti-rite," to borrow Douglas's phrase (1968:369–70). The crucial point is not merely whether *ipani* eating satisfies the formal criteria of joking or clowning (or both), but that, viewed in the context of indigenous categorizations and social organization, its intrinsically humorous properties contribute to reproducing society itself.

The North Mekeo

In order to deal with these conceptual or theoretical issues, I must first sketch out the more salient features of North Mekeo culture and society generally — among them, aspects of the geographic and ecological setting; tribal, moiety, and clan organization; marriage exchange and regulation; hereditary chieftainship and sorcery; the system of reciprocal mortuary feasting between clans; and the broader symbolic setting of affinal relations and humor.

Geographic Setting

The North (Bush) Mekeo[1] are an Austronesian-speaking people living along the middle reaches of the Biaru River at the western edge of the Central Province of Papua New Guinea. Their habitat varies from grasslands and swamps on the coastal plain to primary rain forest along the foothills of the Owen Stanley Range. The population is distributed in some seven nucleated villages established along the main course and tributaries of the river. Depending upon immediate ecological circumstances, villagers subsist on a variety of vegetable foods — sweet potato, plantain, banana, taro, coconut, breadfruit, rice, pumpkin, pitpit, and sugarcane — grown in swidden gardens. Domesticated pigs and fowl are consumed only on ceremonial occasions, but given the sizable expanses of uninhabited territory the North Mekeo are blessed with an abundance of wild game and fish: pig, cassowary, wallaby, crocodile, many species of birds, mullet, barramundi, and prawns. Villagers are thus usually able to subsist in modest comfort, and when food resources do fall short, as they occasionally do, they can still rely on sago to carry them through.

Tribal, Moiety, and Clan Organization

Just prior to "pacification" and colonial domination late in the nineteenth century, the North Mekeo were organized into two politically autonomous tribes, the Amoamo and the Kuipa. Relations between the two tribes consisted of a state of perpetual war. Since members of different tribes were prohibited from marrying, they regarded one another as nonkin or nonrelatives. By contrast, fellow tribespeople were prohibited from warring among themselves and were supposed to acquire their wives and husbands from among their own numbers. Thus peace, kinship, and affinity distinguished relations within each tribe from those between tribes. Because of this—and it is of particular relevance to the subject of contemporary mortuary ritual and *ipani* eating burlesque described below—members of the same tribe, and only they, should feast one another on the occasion of death. For although the circumstances of intra- and intertribal relations have changed considerably since Western contact, the precolonial attitudes toward peace and war have persisted largely unchanged.

Marriage Exchange

While villagers are traditionally required to marry endogamously as to tribe, they are prohibited by rules of exogamy from marrying persons of the same patrilineal descent groups.[2] To explain: each tribe is ideally bisected, first, into exogamous patrilineal moieties, and then each moiety is bisected into two patrilineal clans, giving a total of four per tribe. Members of the same clan or moiety share the "same male (i.e. agnatic) blood;" members of clans of opposite moieties correspondingly possess "different male blood." Thus, it is persons of different male blood belonging to different clans in the opposite moiety whom villagers consider their potential spouses.

But every villager is additionally prohibited from marrying

members of his or her own mother's clan of the opposite moiety. While these persons do not possess the same male blood, they are considered to share the "same female (i.e. cognatic) blood," and on this basis they reciprocally refer to one another as "women's children," *papie ngaunga*. Villagers must choose their spouses, then, in a clan of the opposite moiety from which their own mothers did not come.

These kin, clan, and affinal distinctions figure critically in the practice of exaggerated *ipani* eating burlesque specifically and in the logic of mortuary exchange generally, as I shall describe below.

Hereditary Authority

Like their closely related neighbors, the Central Mekeo and the Roro, the North Mekeo possess an elaborate division of ritual and political authority within each clan composed of four patrilineally transmitted offices—peace chief, peace sorcerer, war chief, and war sorcerer—and four correspondingly specialized lineages.[3] Ideally, each officeholder is the genealogically most senior member of his lineage within the clan. War chiefs and war sorcerers were responsible in earlier times for organizing their clansmen in war and the negative intertribal reciprocity of violence, death, and male blood (cf. Sahlins 1972:191; Mitchell 1988). The expertise and authority of the tribe's peace chiefs and peace sorcerers, now as before, concern the complementary reciprocities of female blood by means of intratribal marriage and mortuary feasting.

The intricate and detailed interconnections among these latter exchanges especially will be unraveled in the following sections of this chapter. For now, in laying out their wider context, I merely emphasize that as *ipani* is performed by persons and groups linked by ties of marriage, on the one hand, who have assembled specifically on the occasion of mortuary feasting, on the other, it falls doubly under the nominal authority of clan peace chiefs and sorcerers.

Mortuary Feast Exchange

Roughly consistent with Hertz's (1960) classic formula, the North Mekeo stage two kinds of mortuary feasts: a preliminary burial feast soon after a clan member dies, and a final, larger-scale, charcoal-carrying feast where all clanspeople who have died since the last such great feast are celebrated and their survivors' mourning observances are ended.⁴ In most respects, the ritual procedures for the two kinds of feast are identical. *Ipani* eating and burlesque, for example, can be performed amid the preparations for either type of feast, and its acknowledged role in each instance is the same.

The central exchange in both feasts is termed *pange* (literally, lost), and consists of certain categories and quantities of raw vegetable and meat foods. *Pange* foods are given by the deceased's clan peace chief to peace chiefs of clans in the opposite moiety. The host peace chief is supported ritually by his own peace sorcerer. Materially, he is supported by all members of the mourning clan and their cognatic kin, the women's children. The category *women's children* here includes the children of the host clan's outmarrying women as well as members of the deceased's own mother's clan. The peace chief who receives the *pange* food distributes it among his clanspeople and those women's children of their clan who do not belong to the deceased's clan. *Pange* prestations are reciprocal and ideally equivalent. When a feast-receiving peace chief subsequently has deaths in his clan, he, his sorcerer, and the other survivors will return the identical quantity and quality of goods that they had previously been given.

One of the stated purposes of mortuary feasts is to end the deceased's clan's mourning ordeals so they can return to ordinary village life. But this involves a reassortment of the blood identities of the survivors and thereby a reorganization of their relations and affiliations to the other clans of the endogamous tribe. These restructurings occur specifically in the exchange of the *pange* feast foods representing certain female or female-derived bloods of the deceased and his or her relatives—specifically, those female bloods originally derived from the deceased's lineal grandmothers.⁵ As I describe more fully below, the exchange of *pange* feast foods unmixes and returns to the clans of their origin the bloods of the deceased's grandmothers, which had been mixed together in the deceased's conception via the parents' sexual union. The blood identities of the deceased and the deceased's survivors as traced through him or her are thereby deconceived or reconceived (*engama*, which also means conceive, begin, end, and happiness; see below). In essence, mortuary deconception and reconception allow the long-term reproduction of ties of strictly male blood within agnatic moieties and clans as well as the abrogation of female blood between members of clans linked in the short run through affinity and cognatic kinship.

It is worth emphasizing that *ipani* burlesque and the laughter thereby elicited in making the bereaved survivors "happy" again contribute directly to the deconception and reconception of the male and female blood relations and identities, through which the total tribe and its constituent units are composed.

Ipani Eating

The term for mortuary eating, *ipani*, means in its broadest sense simply "to eat." Alternatively, villagers refer to mortuary *ipani* performances as *konga keaniani*, "they eat coconut," *akole keaniani*, "they eat sweet potato," *foa keaniani*, "they eat banana," *angai keaniani*, "they eat mullet," and so on (any staple food category may be so mentioned). Most curiously, as I discuss below, the term *ipani* also has the meaning of "poison."

Ipani eating involves the public consumption of food in quantities considerably beyond the usual point of satiation. The people who do the eating are "laborers" (*ipa ngaua*, literally, "sibling-in-law, parent- or child-in-law"), consisting of the husbands and wives of the feast "owners" (*ina ngome*).[6] The owners, again, are the members of the deceased's clan and their women's children affiliates, and until the mortuary feast is concluded they remain in a condition of mourning. So when the laborers stage an *ipani* spectacle, they do so to entertain the owners in a quite specific way.

Typically, *ipani* is performed amid the laborers' other work and activity in preparation for the peace chief's official presentation of the lost *pange* foods. Immediately after the announcement of a death within the clan, the peace chief summons the owners of the death (i.e., his clanspeople and their women's children) to return to their home village. Their spouses, the feast laborers, accompany them. As the owners arrive and gather around the corpse collectively expressing their grief, the laborers assume all of the "work" (*pinaunga*) that the owners would ordinarily do in life but of which they now, in a condition of pain, unhappiness, and mourning, are undesirous and incapable. For with the death of a person, all his or her clanspeople and women's children "die" (*kemae*) too. Removed from life, it is claimed, they can do no work. For them, work and the other things of life that are ordinarily "sweet" (*mitsia*; see below) are reversed and become "unsweet" (*etsiu*); the owners do not want or like them. They shun, for example, the singing, drumming, decorating, and other activities associated with courting. Each of the owners similarly abstains from one category of food which he or she frequently shared or associated with the deceased in life. But the things and activities in life that the owners had earlier found to be unsweet — practices such as crying, grieving, abstaining, and so on — become sweet in the sense that now in death they are desired.

Since the laborers are persons of different blood from the deceased and the owners, they remain in life. It is thus left to them to perform the tasks for which the owners are inhibited but that must be accomplished nonetheless in readying the village for the mortuary feasts and the eventual return of the owners to life. On a daily basis, female laborers work in the owners' gardens, retrieve the produce, carry firewood and water, cook, and so on. Male laborers, for their part, build and repair the platforms necessary to house the expected guests, and they are regularly sent hunting and fishing in the bush. The male laborers are also required to stay awake at night in shifts in order to keep lighted the smoking fire by which the accumulating meat is preserved for the feast.

These various feast labors come under the official authority of the clan peace chief. But often he appoints a clansman to act as "bossman," whose responsibility it is to convey the chief's directives to the laborers. However, the laborers are also obliged to obey any owner who, frequently enough over the course of a feast, may call out an order.[7] This is because the laborers' work at feasts is one form of the obligatory "compensation" or "payment" *(kaua)* that every married person is expected to contribute to his or her spouse's relations — in particular, to spouse's clanspeople and women's children.[8] Indeed, the duty to participate in *ipani* burlesque is one element of affinal payment or compensation.

Laborers' work and exertions at mortuary feasts, however, have strong symbolic associations with food, with ordinary eating, with procreation, and with life generally. Villagers acknowledge that bodies must eat to work; yet bodies, to eat, must work to produce and prepare the food required for life. The converse of this relation between work and eating is also maintained: bachelors and practicing sorcerers who do no work, for example, are expected to "eat nothing" (Guis 1936:176; Mosko 1985:87). And, perhaps closer to the specific logic of exaggerated eating in humorous *ipani* performances, new brides who are engorged with food are prohibited from working, but their superfluous consumption is diverted toward the conception and life of other bodies (i.e., the bodies of their offspring) (cf. Strathern 1989).

All the while that feast laborers work on behalf of the grieving owners they are fed generous quantities of food several times each

North Mekeo Humor and Social Reproduction 111

day—staple foods as well as foods considered to be delicacies—in accordance with these assumptions. A major share of the food resources the owners expend in subsidizing their death feasts is in fact consumed by the laborers, and a correspondingly large portion of the laborers' efforts is directed toward generating and processing the food that they, the laborers, are presented to eat.

Now it is from feeding the laborers for their daily work that the impetus for ritual *ipani* eating and burlesque arises. By prearrangement, characteristically, one of the laborers requests, or just casually mutters a wish for, some coconut, some chicken, some bush pig, some freshwater mullet—any food they have perhaps not yet been given or would enjoy more of. The implication of the request, though, is that laborers as well as owners have been greedy—laborers for their lack of satisfaction with the food they have eaten, owners for failing to feed the laborers sufficiently. And greediness, especially when charged between affines, is possibly the most severe moral deficiency in the North Mekeo register of values. Predictably, the owners respond in mock anger and indignation. They dispatch the laborers to collect large amounts of the one food they had found wanting. And to ensure that the laborers have no cause for additional hungers, they are ordered to retrieve great quantities of other foods, along with the firewood and water necessary to prepare them.

After one, two, or even three days have been devoted to procuring the designated foods, the assembled laborers are directed to sit in two circles—one for men, one for women—on the ground of the village thoroughfare or "abdomen" (see below) directly in front of the owners gathered at the clan clubhouse. Then, as the laborers are presented with numerous large basins of the prepared foods and commanded to eat them, the overtly comic aspect of *ipani* is manifested. The laborers start to eat, greedily and with great bravado. They eat, and eat, and eat some more. Gradually, the laborers' abdomens begin to swell, and many make a show of intentionally extending their bellies outward and grabbing and massaging them so they will hold even more food. Soon, however, the laborers' gesticulations, facial expressions, and body contortions start to reveal momentary signs of growing satiation and physical discomfort. Still, the laborers call out for more, more, and more food.

It is this exaggerated eating and greed on the part of the laborers that constitutes the essential point of humor for the owners watching. Although they remain in death and sadness and are expected to cry and grieve rather than laugh, the vision of their overeating spouses and affines involuntarily elicits from them considerable laughter, mirth, and, in their terms, "happiness" *(engama)*. And just as the laborers punctuate their greedy demands for more and more food with groans and gestures reflecting their sated conditions, the owners occasionally interrupt their own belly laughs and near-hysterical derision to shout further commands in sham outrage.

In the two *ipani* exhibitions I witnessed in 1974 involving burial feasts for Nganga clan of Akabe village, the feeding, eating, laughter, and haranguing went on for approximately one and one-half hours. On the first occasion, a female laborer had asked one of the male owners if she could have a bit of coconut. With that, the four male laborers present were sent hunting, and the seventeen female laborers were directed to bring large quantities of coconut, firewood, and bananas from the gardens. After the women returned with their goods in the afternoon, two of the men reported they had shot two bush pigs, one very large. While the pigs were being fetched, the women built two large cooking fires on the ground of the village abdomen—something not done for ordinary consumption. One fire was for boiling, the other for roasting. Once the male laborers had finished butchering the pigs, the women cooked all the food and transferred it to large bowls and platters. The women divided some of each kind of food into two piles on the ground. The male and female laborers then sat in separate circles around the food piles and, at the command of the bossman and other owners, commenced to eat.

As they ate, one after another of the laborers got up and walked to the bush, presumably to go to the toilet, returning a few minutes later. Each time, this provoked protests from one or more of the owners. At one point, two female laborers had been absent for ten minutes or so, and the bossman sent for them to be brought back. As it was explained to me, laborers are suspected of leaving for the bush only to vomit secretly the food they had by then eaten or to avoid eating their share with the others. Thus, if laborers are caught vomiting or malingering in the bush, the bossman can order them to pay a special fine to the clan peace chief, although none was levied on this occasion.

The engorging, clowning, laughter, feigned anger, and so on continued until both groups of laborers conceded they could eat no more. First the women lined up in front of the clubhouse, holding before them four bowls of uneaten food. The peace chief's own wife addressed the owners, saying, "Thank you greatly, we have eaten coconut and had enough." The chief indicated that each of the women was fined one tin of mackerel and one tin of bully beef.

When the male laborers next lined up, they similarly admitted they could not eat all the coconut, whereupon they were individually fined one bottle of beer and ordered to contribute money toward the purchase of one bottle of gin.[9] The female laborers then retreated to the domestic houses of the village, and the male laborers joined the male owners at the clan clubhouse.

The second instance of *ipani* I observed proceeded much as had the first. One of the male laborers was overheard to say he hoped they might get some of the mullet that were then migrating in the river. So over the next two days, while the female laborers were commissioned to the gardens for vegetables and firewood, the men, laborers and owners alike, went spearfishing. Since fishing and hunting are not classified as "work," owners—unless they are appointed to a special mourning status *(oaifa)* —are not prohibited from joining laborers in these activities during feast preparations (see Mosko 1985:chaps. 3, 7). On the evening of the second day, the laborers staged the eating ceremony, this time with plenty of mullet included among the piles of other foods. And since both female and male laborers were again unable to finish the foods presented to them, they were ordered to pay fines to the owners' peace chief.

Three additional features of *ipani* burlesque should be emphasized. First, toward the end of the performances I observed that the intensity of the laborers' exclamations and visible efforts to eat more and more food diminished as they gradually approached their absolute eating capacities. Having experienced more than an hour of eating, the laborers arrived at a point where they were taking only the smallest of bites, holding and slowly chewing each in their mouths for as long as five minutes, say, before taking another. By this time their greedy calls for more food were coming less frequently and forcefully, and their faces betrayed what can only be described as maximum discomfort. By the end of it all the laborers had eaten themselves into a state of virtual immobility. I shall comment on this detail below.

Second, it was explained to me that if one of the laborers vomited in the course of the eating, it would count as though the whole group of them (as differentiated by gender) had failed to eat all of the food proffered.

Third, there is the possible (and I suspect hypothetical) conclusion to *ipani* that I did not witness wherein the female or the male laborers are able to eat everything. In such a case, apparently, the group would not be fined. However, according to my informants, this rarely if ever happens.

Interpretation and Analysis

Part of what makes the mortuary eating humorous for the owners is the laborers' apparent earnestness. Although their discomforts visibly mount as the eating progresses, the laborers continue to call out stridently for more and more food. Clearly, the juxtaposition of uninhibited greed with grossly exaggerated satiation is responsible for much of the laughter; the humor here, as we might say, arises from "too much of a good thing" (cf. Young 1977:81–82). There is, however, a parallel and additionally provocative incongruity in the activity of the owners, for frequently it seems the very sternness and feigned anger of their commands and harangues also elicit immediate laughter.

But there is more to the meaning of this mortuary humor, just as there is considerably more to the laborers' overall role at feasts and, indeed, to the social function of the feasts themselves. The analysis and interpretation of *ipani* will therefore require tracing out further detailed connections among related social and cultural contexts—some of which I have already mentioned—looking particularly to the distinctive contributions of *ipani* to the processes of mortuary deconception and reconception and, thereby, to the reproduction of social relations.

Affinal Relations: Playing and Paying

When villagers say that *ipani* involves a kind of payment or compensation, they mean that it is obligatory and one of a broad range of debts every married person, male or female, owes his or her affines.[10] When asked why a man or woman should be beholden in all these ways to a spouse's kin, villagers quite simply and consistently respond, "He married their sister (or daughter)" or "she married their brother (or son)."

In the same respect that *ipani* is regarded as a kind of paying or compensation, villagers conceptualize it as just one variety of humorous "playing" *(bakau)*.[11] Typically, different types of playing are associated with distinct categories of social relationship. Since *ipani* involves playing among affinal relations, it is specifically included in the class of playing known as *ipaipa*, which I shall gloss as affinal "joking" (literally, "sibling-in-law–sibling-in-law" or, alternatively, the diminutive of "sibling-in-law").

Some conventionalized types of affinal *ipaipa* involve dyadic or person-to-person interactions; others implicate groups. Among affines interpersonally, for example, a woman's brother might visit her house and remove any object of her husband's that he might see and fancy. Similarly, a woman is entitled under the rules of affinal joking to take anything she desires from her brother's wife. In any event, husbands and wives are expected to take these losses in good cheer. And even when, on occasion, parties to these actions do not publicly exhibit their amusement at these exploits, other villagers do.[12]

Still another variety of dyadic affinal joking or playing involves opposite- as well as same-sex siblings-in-law.[13] Ordinarily, people are expected to exhibit respect toward their spouses' siblings—in particular, never to say or do anything publicly that might shame or insult them. If a man or woman should do so, directly or indirectly, then the offended party will run immediately toward the offender's house with the intent of taking a seat beneath it. The element of humor enters when the interaction turns into a race between the two in-laws. If the person who caused the offense can get there first, there will be no fine or compensation; if not, then the offended brother- or sister-in-law must be given a pig or another valuable (e.g., armshell, pearlshell, string of cowrie shells or dog's teeth, or bird of paradise skin). Regardless of who wins, the exchange typically elicits pronounced laughter and mirth from actors and spectators alike.

With reference to Apte's formal distinction between joking relationships and ritual clowning, the definitive feature of *ipani* eating burlesque specifically and *ipaipa* joking or playing generally is not whether the interactions are collective or individual in scale; rather, it is the affinal character of the relations themselves. Between agnates or between cognatic kinsmen and kinswomen of other categories (e.g., women's children), mortuary eating and affinal joking and playing are strictly inappropriate.

Food Symbolism and Ipani *Eating*

Of all types of affinal humor, *ipani* uniquely and explicitly concerns food. For the North Mekeo as for other Melanesians, the production, exchange, and consumption of food in any interactive context symbolically expresses important aspects of the social relationships involved. In the following sections, I describe how bombastic North Mekeo eating thus signifies transformations in the relations of feast owners and laborers in terms of gender, affinity, and agnatic and cognatic kinship. At the same time, though, I attempt to show how the humor evoked in mortuary eating itself contributes actively to producing and reproducing those relationships.

With regard to food generally, the feast laborers as eaters contrast with the owners who have denied themselves foods specifically associated with the deceased person. Life and death are thereby symbolically contained in the mortuary *ipani* eating of the laborers and the funerary abstinence of the owners.

Villagers also distinguish the two kinds of food, "plant" or "vegetable food" *(fokama)* and "meat food" *(tsitsi)*. Ideally, laborers consume both in any given eating performance. Generally speaking, plant food is associated with femininity and the abdominal region of the body, and meat with masculinity and the throat. Plant and meat foods, furthermore, contain distinct elements, both of which are considered necessary in the formation of human blood and other body tissues. Villagers claim that both vegetable and meat foods are required for the sustenance of human bodily life. When properly prepared, combined, and consumed, plant food and meat are "potent" or "hot" for making blood and sustaining the health or life of the body. The lack of either one of them is correspondingly "cold" or "not enough" for bodily sustenance and can lead to hunger, starvation, or death.

In this respect, plant food and meat are to the body of the living human being as procreative bloods — womb blood and semen — are to the initial formation of the human fetus. In human conception, mother and father are understood to contribute roughly equal proportions of the two fluids (Mosko 1983). On the basis of this analogy, plant and meat foods — including those eaten to excess in feasting *ipani* performances — are expressive of "blood" relationships or "kinship" (*atsi atsitsi*; literally, "senior/junior siblings") traced bilaterally through both females and males.

Sweet Versus Unsweet

Directly pertinent also to the symbolism of exaggerated *ipani* eating and relations between owners and laborers is the cultural distinction between sweet and unsweet mentioned earlier with reference to the contrast of life and death. In the context of food and eating, sweet ordinarily refers to cooked or transformed food (e.g., boiled sweet potato, roasted pig, ripened coconut) as distinct from unsweet, that is, raw or untransformed food. When it is shared or exchanged among persons, sweet food signifies the existence of a kin or blood tie. The refusal to share sweet food, or the giving or exchange of raw unsweet food, connotes the absence of such blood or kin relationship. Similarly, among blood relatives sweet food should never have to be requested; rather, it should be shared before anyone might be called to ask for it.

In the various aspects of their play upon the opposition sweet versus unsweet food, owners and laborers thereby predicate the uniquely ambiguous or contradictory character of their own relations; this is, as to whether, cognatically calculated, they are of the same blood or of different blood. Villagers claim, on the one hand, that they should marry persons of "different [cognatic] blood," or nonrelatives; but, on the other, since the tribe is an ideally endogamous unit, all potentially legitimate marriages unite persons who share some degree of the "same [cognatic] blood" and count terminologically as kin. Owners and laborers, tied to one another through marriage and affinity, thus conflate the same blood/different blood distinction.[14]

For this reason, I suggest, laborers comprise an especially appropriate category of relations for representing to owners the ambiguity and conflation of the values *sweet* and *unsweet*. Villagers attribute the values sweet and unsweet to their social relations in particular contexts of activity just as they do in all other dimensions of their experience, such as eating. Ideally, people regard their (same blood) relatives as sweet: they like to be together, to talk, to visit, to share and eat food together, and so on. To do these same things with nonrelatives, with persons of different blood, is in principle unsweet. Yet, where persons of the same blood are unsweet for sexual relations and marriage, persons of different blood are in this context sweet. So in these matters as elsewhere, sweet and unsweet are contrastively defined relative to given contexts. But since laborers, from the perspective of owners (and vice versa), are regarded as persons of both the same and different blood, they are simultaneously and hence ambiguously or contradictorily sweet and unsweet.

At mortuary feasts, consequently, the owners' failure to provide sufficient sweet cooked food and the laborers' need to have to ask for it each invoke the recurrent issues as to whether the two are the same or different blood or, with respect to any particular activity, whether their interaction is to be regarded as sweet or unsweet. In greedily withholding sweet food or greedily requesting it, both parties, partly defined as kin, in effect deny that kinship.

Now, on most social occasions, the accusation of greediness or implied denial of blood relationship (the two amounting essentially to the same thing) is just about the most severe and provocative public recrimination one villager can make of another, particularly when they are reputed to be close genealogical or clan relatives. Denying blood relationship with a full sibling, a clansperson, or a woman's child, for example, is considered much more serious than disavowing a more distant cognate. In the universe of tribal sociality, the relations between owners and laborers are unique. On the one hand, they consist of the same (cognatic) blood, thus binding the parties by obligations of kinship, even if weakly; on the other, they are categorically nonrelatives possessing different blood, leaving them minimally bound by kin responsibilities if at all.

With regard to *ipani*, it is interesting to compare the owners' hypergenerosity with the hyperconsumption of the laborers. As noted above, activities considered to be sweet and unsweet to owners during their mourning ordeals are regarded as unsweet and sweet, respectively, to laborers in the ordinary condition of life. For owners, singing, courting, laughing, and expressions of happiness generally are unsweet, while crying, wailing, sexual abstinence, and sadness are sweet; and for laborers, the same practices are inversely valued. At the extremes of *ipani* eating and burlesque, however, these distinctions and inversions are eclipsed. Ordinarily in the condition of life, say, when a person's abdomen or throat is lacking food and feels unsweet (i.e., hungry), he or she "desires" *(emitsia)* food; food is "sweet" *(mitsia)* to him or her. Then, upon eating, the subject reaches a condition of bodily sweetness or satiation. But eating to the point of oversatiation transforms the sweet abdomen or throat to a paradoxically, undesirable or unsweet condition of being too sweet. The feast owners' overfeeding of the laborers and the laborers' overeating of the owners' food thus jointly conflate the sweet/unsweet and the same blood/different blood distinctions.[15]

Life Versus Death

A parallel conflation occurs in *ipani* with respect to the life-death opposition. The sweet foods the laborers eat and the position they as spouses and mates hold vis-à-vis the owners signify both life and blood or kin relationship. But by eating themselves well beyond the state of sweetness and satiation in the presence of the owners even to the point of vomiting and immobilization, the laborers achieve a condition paradoxically resembling death. Indeed, the ritual transformations of the two seem to be in reverse: where dead owners laugh themselves to life (albeit a life substantially different from that which they earlier departed; see below), living laborers eat themselves to death (cf. Young 1977).

Death, Ipani *Poisons, and Dirt*

Death and eating are implicit in the name for the eating ritual, *ipani,* in yet another way. Among the meanings of *ipani* is "poison." *Ipani* poisons are distinct from food of all types. They are not sweet or unsweet, they are "dirty" *(iofu).* In fact, all dirty substances qualify as poisons, and if human beings eat them they will produce illness and death instead of health and life.

Dirty things primarily consist of the body leavings and bloody residues of humans and the analogous bodily remains of certain animal species associated with humanlike spirit beings of the bush. The most dangerous of all dirty substances are the bloody remains of dead humans. Dirty things are thus doubly associated with death, being both its cause and its result.[16]

Dirty substances bring about illness and death by reversing the ordinary bodily processes of health and life, including the blood- and body-manufacturing effects of food. As described earlier, when sweet food is properly prepared and eaten it sustains the body's blood and other tissues. The body's blood and tissues are ordinarily sweet to it; hence they remain inside while the bloodless unsweet inert elements of food are regularly excreted. When dirty *ipani* poisons are eaten, however, the body's own blood and tissues become unsweet to it, and substances ordinarily excreted are made sweet. The result of eating poison is to excrete blood and to retain bloodless wastes, precisely the condition of illness *(eisaoa;* literally, "see inside") that, if carried far enough, results in death.

Mortuary Transformations

A crucial aspect of indigenous understandings about *ipani* poisons, then, is that they can invert the processes of life and death in their ability to affect transformations between sweet and unsweet, especially as regards matters of blood. *Ipani* eating and burlesque at mortuary feasts have the capacity to affect analogous transformations between life and death, sweet and unsweet, sadness and happiness, and so on—not just upon the laborers doing the eating but among the owners who witness it.

Life and Death, Sweet and Unsweet

When someone dies, members of his or her clan and their women's children avoid all public expressions of life. They suspend work, courting, singing, decorating, drumming, and dancing, and as owners they each abstain from a particular food that they individually associate with the deceased. In life—that is, before a given death occurs—doing all of these things is sweet, avoiding them is unsweet, and the people are happy. With death and the assumption of their mourning regimen, everything is reversed. What in life was sweet is now unsweet, what was unsweet becomes sweet, and they are sad and unhappy.

These inversions are produced by death itself, for like all "dirty" things including poisons, death has the capacity (i.e., hot or potency) to change sweet to unsweet and vice versa, and happiness to unhappiness.

One of the ultimate aims of mortuary feasts is to reverse these transformations yet again so that the owners can return to an ordinary life of happiness. Following the feast, the peace chief of the clan that has received the formal prestation of raw "lost" foods ritually replaces the owners' mourning garments and paraphernalia with colorful clothes, decorations, tools, and foods that in sadness and death they regarded as unsweet. Immediately the released owners join the mass of resplendent guests from other clans of the tribe in singing, drumming, dancing, and courting. No longer sad and unhappy, the owners exhibit and experience the sweetness of life, as it is defined in the culture, in its purest form.

Deconception and Reconception: Blood Relations and Nonrelatives

The significance of *ipani* eating humor specifically and mortuary feasting generally, however, extends beyond actors' personal interests, attitudes, and capacities. For, in the process of returning the owners to ordinary life, the boundaries comprising the tribal society and its subgroupings are also redrawn and thereby reproduced. In this respect, the ritual efficacy of North Mekeo humor is most evident.

The owners' sweet and unsweet predilections at the end of their mourning ordeal are identical to the ones they had in life prior to their "dying" *but for two critical differences*: they lack, of course, the deceased, and with that the raison d'être for including certain survivors among their cognatic kin relations. With the loss of their

North Mekeo Humor and Social Reproduction 121

common blood relative (i.e., the deceased), some of the owners' fellow tribesmen and tribeswomen who were previously bound to them by sharing the same blood traced indirectly through the deceased become, once the feast is concluded, unrelated or of different blood as regards that relationship. Who is sweet or unsweet to whom and with respect to whichever activities—those appropriate to kin relations and those appropriate to nonkin—is therefore different after a mortuary feast as compared with before death arose in the community.

These particular mortuary transformations involving categories of kin and nonkin are intricately connected with the indigenous theory of human procreation, the structure of marriage rules, and the overall system of clan reproduction. In North Mekeo culture, fathers and mothers are understood to mix their procreative clan bloods (i.e., semen and womb blood) in the act of sexual intercourse. By thus "conceiving" *(engama)* children, parents' sexual bloods give form and substance to their children's bodies. The result of this mixing socially is that new relationships by cognatic blood connection are also "conceived" or "begun" *(engama)*. Once born, a child lives its life with a body composed of the mixed bloods of distinct moieties and clans as derived through its parents. Consequently, the child also shares or possesses some portion of the same (cognatic) blood as all its bilateral kin or relatives.

When the child ultimately dies, however, its clan peace chief and surviving relations (i.e., clanspeople and women's children) make mortuary feasts for him or her, and in those feasts the cognatic bloods of conception are *un*mixed. Procreation, in essence, is undone. The formal feast exchange—the lost raw *pange* foods exchanged by peace chiefs—returns some of the cognatically derived bloods of the deceased's conception to the clans and moieties of their origin. The deceased is thereby *engama de*conceived. And since in life the feast owners were identified as possessing some of the same (cognatic) blood as the deceased, some portion(s) of the blood that they, the owners, unmix or undo in the event of the deceased's death is blood of their own. All who have "died," in other words—the owners as well as the deceased—are *engama* deconceived as regards certain aspects or elements of their blood or kin identities; simultaneously, they are *engama* begun or rebegun and, as regards the living at any rate, made *engama* happy.

For the sake of clarification, the relations from whom the deceased and the owners are deconceived at mortuary feasts are the members of the deceased's two grandmothers' clans (i.e., the deceased's father's mother's clan and mother's mother's clan).[17] And prototypically it is these people who, through their own peace chiefs, receive the lost raw feast foods *(pange)* and cook and eat them. These feast receivers are persons who shared with the deceased in the interim of his or her lifetime a portion of same (cognatic) blood originally derived from the deceased's two grandmothers. The grandmothers, of course, conveyed their female-derived bloods to the bodies of their children, among them the deceased's parents, who likewise contributed portions of those bloods to the bodies of their children in conception, including that of the deceased. The deceased's two grandmothers' bloods are, up until that moment, widely shared among the deceased's fellow clanspeople and women's children (i.e., the feast owners) on the one hand, and the surviving members of the deceased's grandmothers' clans on the other.

When the former give away the feast foods and the latter reclaim and reassimilate them, the two female-derived, grandmaternal bloods of the deceased's conception are effectively returned to the clans from which they originated. For both feast givers and feast receivers, then, mortuary deconception is also a reconception or redefinition of their respective personal and group or clan identities in terms of the opposition of same and different bloods.

It is worth noting that the site of mortuary feast deconception or reconception is the precise spot where just earlier in the feast preparations the laborers had staged their *ipani* eating burlesque, similarly transforming the owners to a state of happiness. This place, the "abdomen" or "womb" *(inaenga)* of the village, is where the dead were buried in precolonial times, and it is linguistically connected with the womb of the female body, where the mixing of procreative bloods and conception occur, as well as with the kin category "mother" *(ina)*.

According to the rules of marriage, a person's nonrelatives are his or her potential spouses; that is, villagers must choose their spouses from among their fellow tribesmen and tribeswomen with whom they share no agnatic or cognatic blood. However, as already mentioned with respect to the tribe's endogamous constitution, all members of both moieties, including supposedly legitimate spouses, are already cognatic kin sharing some degree of female-derived bloods by implication of the procreative mixing of bloods through numerous prior generations. As I have discussed at length elsewhere (Mosko 1983, 1985, 1989), this contradiction—marrying nonrelatives ideally of different blood who nonetheless share the same blood—is resolved in mortuary feasting, deconception, and reconception. Certain categories of the owners' cognatic kin who were previously unsweet as potential spouses are transformed by means of the feast exchanges into nonrelatives unrelated by blood. Henceforth, they are sweet to the owners for the sake of potential marriage. Little wonder that owners, as soon as they are deconceived, throw themselves into the singing, dancing, courting, and so on with such abandon!

The humor evoked in ritual *ipani* facilitates these several mortuary transformations. Owners and laborers, as I have described, are related in terms of ambiguity and conflation. They are spouses and affines, supposedly unconnected by ties of the same blood; thus they are sweet to one another for sexual relations. But except for prior acts of feasting deconception, they too would share, as cognates and fellow tribesmen and tribeswomen, the same blood and regard one another as sexually unsweet. So when laborers and owners act as both kin and nonkin; when same blood is different blood; when sexually sweet is sexually unsweet; when sweet food is eaten to the point it becomes unsweet; when generosity becomes greediness and greediness becomes denial; when paying and being paid take the form of playing, the humor and incongruities of the eating spectacle transform the owners' sadness and pain of death into the happiness of life.

The laughter elicited by *ipani* thus begins the deconceiving and reconceiving of relations between the owners and other groups of the tribe. And taking deconception and reconception to their conclusions in the formal feast exchanges, the categories and relations composing North Mekeo society, in whole and in part, are reproduced.

Conclusions

By way of summary, I can now enumerate the major claims warranted by this examination of North Mekeo eating burlesque in its wider cultural and social setting.

With respect, first, to the individual dyad versus group criterion in Apte's attempted differentiation of joking relationships and clowning, *ipani* seems initially to involve interactions between groups. However, I have suggested that this practice is more meaningfully understood alongside other forms of obligatory affinal humor or playing that consist, instead, of persons in dyadic interactions. Here, the individual dyad-group dichotomy is not a salient one.[18]

Second, consistent with Apte's other criterion for joking relationships, some elements of *ipani* symbolically *affirm* or *epitomize* the terms of the relations between owners and laborers, kin and affines, same blood and different blood, and so on; but other features of *ipani*, in accordance with Apte's specification for ritual clowning, *invert, reverse,* or *negate* them.

On either analytical axis, then, *ipani* eating burlesque partially conforms with as well as deviates from both comparative categories, *joking relationships* and *clowning*. Yet, regardless of whether or to what degree indigenous constructions approximate formal Western distinctions, the important anthropological questions and issues in this case seem to me to lie elsewhere—most obviously, regarding the role *ipani* eating and humor play in the wider system of symbols and relations. Moreover, the meaning and function of *ipani* performance do not stop at the level of the merely symbolic or humorous. For, as I have tried to show, the practice of *ipani* and the laughter it elicits contribute to the systematic shaping and reshaping of the relationships composing society itself.

On this evidence, performative humor (i.e., clowning, joking, or whatever) would not seem to possess a single cross-culturally transcendent value. But neither would it appear simply to project the given social relations of a particular society passively. In the case of North Mekeo mortuary burlesque, at any rate, performative humor can be an active transformer of social relations, even to the point of facilitating the reproduction of the total sociocultural system.

NOTES

Apologies to Michael W. Young for the chapter title, "Clowning with Food." The field research on which this chapter is based was generously supported by the National Institute of General Medical Sciences (Grant 01164), the Research School of Pacific Studies at the Australian National University, and the Board of Trustees of Hartwick College. Numerous colleagues and friends have kindly offered comments and suggestions that in one way or another have proven most helpful in the present effort, among them Michael W. Young, Eugene Ogan, Stephen F. Gudeman, William E. Mitchell, Margaret Jolly, James J. Fox, Connie M. Anderson, David W. Anthony, Michael Monsell-Davis, Epeli Hau'ofa, Michele Stephen, and my anonymous referees. I am particularly grateful to the members and staff of the Department of Anthropology in the Research

School of Pacific Studies at the Australian National University for providing me the opportunity to write this chapter while I was a Research Fellow on the Comparative Austronesian Project over 1989–1991. My wife, Cassandra, and son, Orion, are to be thanked also for bearing so cheerfully my occasional ill humors. My chief debt, however, is to the North Mekeo people who have shared their wisdom and way of life with my family and me. Responsibility for any errors or deficiencies is nonetheless strictly my own.

1. Initial ethnographic fieldwork was carried out among the North Mekeo over twenty six months in 1974–1976 and, subsequently, in May–July 1990. Published accounts of the North Mekeo relevant to the subject of this paper include Mosko (1983, 1985, 1989, 1991a, 1991b); as yet unpublished discussions include Mosko (n.d.1, n.d.2, in press). For comparable data on the closely related Roro and Central or Plains Mekeo, see Seligmann (1910); Hau'ofa (1971, 1981); Davis (1981); and Stephen (1974, 1987).

2. By "traditional" I mean contemporary villagers' own estimations of *kangakanga*—the hereditary customs and practices supposedly bequeathed to them by their ancestors from precolonial times. For a fuller discussion of how certain North Mekeo *kangakanga*, including elements of mortuary ritual, have been transformed over the course of colonial history, see Mosko (n.d.1).

3. The additional division of each clan into senior and junior subclans, and hence the distinction of senior and junior peace chiefs, senior and junior peace sorcerers, and so on, is minimally relevant to the interpretation of mortuary *ipani* and is not described here. Interested readers can consult Mosko (1985:chap. 6, 1991b, n.d.2, in press).

4. Burial and charcoal-carrying feasts are described in greater detail in Mosko (1985:chaps. 7–8, 1989, in press).

5. The complete details of these mortuary blood transformations are exceedingly complex and go considerably beyond the subject of *ipani* eating and clowning per se. In the sections that follow, I have concentrated only on those social and cultural features that are crucial to the analysis of the *ipani* performances. For readers seeking fuller documentation, see Mosko (1983, 1985:chaps. 6–8, 1989, in press). Hau'ofa (1981:133–37) offers a substantially different view of *ipani* eating and mortuary exchange among the related Central Mekeo peoples.

6. The reciprocal term for husband or wife (*akaua*, or spouse) in either reference or address is linguistically related to the indigenous notions of "playing," *bakau* and "paying," *kaua*; see below.

7. Female owners do not take quite the same aggressive role in ordering laborers about, and typically it is they who are selected to play the roles of special ritual mourners *(oaifa)*, whose overt actions in nearly all respects are considerably subdued; see Mosko (1985:chap. 7) and Seligmann (1910).

8. Other examples of *kaua* marital payment include several categories of symmetrical and asymmetrical exchanges of goods (i.e., bride-wealth) between relatives of the bride and groom at the time of betrothal or elopement and afterward and more casual and irregular contributions of labor (i.e., brideservice); see Mosko (1985:chap. 6).

9. Previous to contact and the introduction of money and Western manufactured goods, these payments at *ipani* eating performances were composed of articles of substantial indigenous value (e.g., strings of dog's teeth, armshells, strings of cowrie shells, bird of paradise skins, stone axeheads — the same articles commonly employed in marriage compensation payments or bride-wealth; see Mosko (1985:chap. 6).

10. Clearly, villagers are not referring here just to the payment of fines to the officiating peace chief.

11. In native etymology, the terms *bakau,* "to play," and *kaua,* "to pay," carry related meanings.

12. Most villagers seemed to agree that this kind of *ipaipa* joking was not appropriate between a man or woman and his or her opposite-sex true sibling's spouse, that is, a man and his sister's husband or a woman and her brother's wife, between whom all relations are ideally symmetrical. This kind of *ipaipa* joking, in other words, is appropriate only between classificatory same-sex siblings-in-law.

13. Ideally, true siblings-in-law, or one's husband's or wife's true brother or sister (i.e., same father, same mother) would not engage in this kind of joking, but classificatory siblings-in-law would; see previous note. Also, it would appear that this kind of affinal playing occurred most often between opposite-sex siblings-in-law. This was the case in all instances I observed, but none of my informants categorically stated this to be the case.

14. The identical ambiguity or contradiction is contained also in the common assertion that husbands and wives, although ideally of different blood at the time of marrying, possess the same blood once they have produced offspring. Elsewhere I have discussed the fuller implications of this societal contradiction of same and different blood and its resolution; see especially Mosko (1983, 1985:chaps. 6, 7).

15. Compare with Wagner's (1978, 1986a, 1986b) notion of symbolic "obviation."

16. The concept of *iofu* "dirt," and the related notions of *tsiabu,* "potency" or "hot" and *ekekia,* "impotency" or "cold," are key symbols to the North Mekeo, their various and complex meanings pertaining to virtually every context of the culture; see Mosko (1985, 1991a).

17. For a more complete treatment of these relations, see Mosko (1983, 1985, 1989, in press).

18. Following Strathern's (1988) critique of Western anthropologists' characterizations of Melanesian sociality, I have recently developed this argument with respect to other elements of North Mekeo mortuary feasts and personal agency; see Mosko (in press).

REFERENCES

Apte, Mahadev L.
    1985   *Humor and Laughter: An Anthropological Approach.* Ithaca: Cornell University Press.

Davis, Michael M.
    1981   Nabuapaka: Social Change in a Roro Community. Ph.D. dissertation, Macquarie University, North Ryde, Australia.

Douglas, Mary
    1968   The Social Control of Cognition: Some Factors in Joke Perception. *Man* (n.s.) 3:361–76.

Evans-Pritchard, E. E.
    1929   Some Collective Expressions of Obscenity in Africa. *Journal of the Royal Anthropological Institute* 59:311–31.

Guis, Fr. J.
    1936   *La vie des Papous.* Paris: Dillen.

Hau'ofa, Epeli.
    1971   Mekeo Chieftainship. *Journal of the Polynesian Society* 80:152–69
    1981   *Mekeo: Inequality and Ambiguity in a Village Society.* Canberra: Australian National University Press.

Hertz, Robert
    1960   [1909] *Death and the Right Hand.* New York: Free Press.

Lowie, Robert
    1909   The Hero-Trickster Discussion. *Journal of American Folklore* 22:431–33.
    1961   [1920] *Primitive Society.* New York: Harper.

Mitchell, William E.
    1988   The Defeat of Hierarchy: Gambling as Exchange in a Sepik Society. *American Ethnologist* 5:638–657.

Mosko, Mark S.
    1983   Conception, De-conception, and Social Structure in Bush Mekeo Culture. In *Concepts of Conception: Procreation Ideologies in Papua New Guinea,* ed. D. Jorgensen. *Mankind* (special issue) 14:24–32.
    1985   *Quadripartite Structures: Categories, Relations and Homologies in Bush Mekeo Culture.* Cambridge: Cambridge University Press.
    1989   The Developmental Cycle Among Public Groups. *Man* (n.s.) 24:470–84.
    1991a   The Canonic Formula of Myth and Non-myth. *American Ethnologist* 18:126–51.

1991b   Great Men and Total Systems: Hereditary Authority and Social Reproduction among the North Mekeo. In *Great Men and Big Men: Personifications of Power in Melanesia*, ed. M. Godelier and M. Strathern, pp. 97–114. Cambridge and Paris: Cambridge University Press and Maison des Sciences de l'Homme.

n.d.1   The Sorcerers' Appearance: The Transformation of Hereditary Political Office and Alliance in Early North Mekeo Contact Experience. Paper presented at Comparative Austronesian Project conference, "Hierarchy, Ancestry and Alliance in Austronesian Societies," January 1990, Australian National University, Canberra.

n.d.2   Junior Chiefs and Senior Sorcerers: The Contradictions and Inversions of Meko "Hierarchy." In *Transformations of Hierarchy: Structure, History and Horizon in the Austronesian World*, ed. M. Mosko and M. Jolly. Ms. under review.

in press   Motherless Sons: 'Divine Kings' and 'Partible Persons' in Melanesia and Polynesia. *Man* (n.s.).

Radcliffe-Brown, A. R.
   1952   [1940] On Joking Relationships. In *Structure and Function in Primitive Society*, by A. R. Radcliffe-Brown, pp. 90–104. New York: Free Press.

Sahlins, Marshall
   1972   *Stone Age Economics*. New York: Aldine.

Seligmann, C. G.
   1910   *The Melanesians of British New Guinea*. Cambridge: Cambridge University Press.

Stephen, Michele
   1974   Continuity and Change in Mekeo Society, 1890–1971. Ph.D. dissertation, Australian National University, Canberra.
   1987   Masters of Souls: The Mekeo Sorcerer. In *Sorcery and Witchcraft in Melanesia*, ed., M. Stephen, pp. 41–80. New Brunswick, N.J.: Rutgers University Press.

Steward, Julian
   1931   The Ceremonial Buffoon of the American Indian. *Papers of the Michigan Academy of Science, Arts, and Letters* 14:187–207.

Strathern, Marilyn
   1989   *The Gender of the Gift: Problems with Women and Problems with Society in Melanesia*. Berkeley and Los Angeles: University of California Press.
   1989   Between a Melanesianist and a Deconstructive Feminist. *Australian Feminist Studies* 10:49–69.

Wagner, Roy
    1978   *Lethal Speech: Daribi Myth as Symbolic Obviation.* Ithaca: Cornell University Press.
    1986a *Symbols That Stand for Themselves.* Chicago: Chicago University Press.
    1986b *Asiwinarong: Ethos, Image, and Social Power Among the Usen Barok of New Ireland.* Princeton, N.J.: Princeton University Press.

Young, Michael W.
    1977   Bursting with Laughter: Obscenity, Values and Sexual Control in a Massim Society. *Canberra Anthropology* 1:75–87.

REFLECTIONS OF AN ANTHROPOLOGIST WHO MISTOOK HER HUSBAND FOR A YAM: FEMALE COMEDY ON TUBETUBE

Martha Macintyre

"WHAT IS SHORT, black, and sticks out of the wall?"

"A ceremonial serving fork!"

There were roars of laughter from the people around, and the riddler beamed expectantly at me. I struggled to compose my face so that it did not betray my bafflement in such a way as to mark me as stupid. Not getting the joke is undignified, mortifying. On Tubetube it is also unladylike and gauche.

I was at first puzzled when a group of people returned from visiting a neighboring island and reported a new marriage there. The first question about the bride was, is she amusing? Gradually I realized that the term *talawasi*, which I first understood to mean simply funny or humorous, had more profound implications, especially when applied to women. Anyone can joke, of course, and most people can tell riddles for hours on those days when the rain pours down and everyone is forced to sit indoors. Even I could tell riddles eventually—although I never got the one about the ceremonial serving fork. I was a stranger, so nothing could be expected of me. The comic abilities required of an in-marrying woman from another island are more demanding. Needless to say, when comparing themselves with their immediate neighbors, Tubetube women are described as characteristically beautiful, hardworking, clever, resourceful, loving, and extraordinarily funny.

In exploring the specific relationship between clowning and femininity, I am concerned with the portrayal of clowning events as experiences. For this reason I have chosen to write in a reflexive and descriptive mode. First, in order to communicate something of the humor of Tubetube clowns but also to provide a sense of the interaction in joking and the progression from banter and impromptu forms of clowning to formal comic performance. In this essay I examine two comic events that illustrate the importance of being frivolous on Tubetube. Both are examples of ritual clowning and are essential elements in the ceremonial sequences for mourning and farewell.

Talawasi, as a noun, is probably best translated as "a jest" when it is used to refer to a comic performance. In other contexts, it means "a joke." It can also be used adjectivally to indicate that a person or thing is funny, humorous, droll, or whatever. The suffix *wasi* indicates that this involves social interaction; the term in isolation means "sharing." Jests are social events, normally performed by mature women, although young women who are gifted comics may participate on occasions.

The events discussed in this chapter occurred during my fieldwork on the island of Tubetube in Milne Bay Province, Papua New Guinea, between 1979 and 1981. Tubetube is a tiny island in a group of eight populated islands, which people refer to as the Bwanabwana. The term means "small islands" and has been adopted by the provincial government to refer to the region encompassing the islands from East Cape to the Louisiades, but the people who live in this area reserve the term for the small volcanic and coral islands that lack rich soil and large areas of land for gardens. Bwanabwana people in the precolonial era were traders, producers of specialist products such as pottery, carved wooden utensils, and woven fiber products. Their gardens are relatively small and unproductive, so they continue to depend on the people of the large neighboring islands for feasting yams. The population of the Bwanabwana is about 2000 people, of whom 140 live on Tubetube. These people speak a distinct language, Kaina Wali or Kaina Tubetube.

Formal Jesting

I begin by presenting *talawasi* as a classic *rite de marge*, (liminal rite) focusing first on the form of the ritual and then on the role of senior women in the whole sequence. Although I observed at least five *talawasi* performances, I can only describe the content of one in any detail. The others I observed early in my fieldwork, when my grasp of the language was poor, and I could not follow the stories being told or enacted. The first jest I saw was part of the funeral ceremony of an old man who had been a major *kune (kula)* trader and lineage leader. As I have described the ceremony in detail elsewhere (Macintyre 1989) I shall here focus on the sequence and the jest itself.

The death followed a long illness, so most people were prepared for the three-day mourning period before the burial. Every adult on the island walked or paddled through the pitch-black of a moonless, cloudy, tropical night to sing and weep over the body. The corpse, washed and decorated, was illuminated by the prestigious glow of a large pressure lantern. The central mourner was the deceased's eldest daughter. She sat in the shadows weeping and chanting mourning songs and observed the mourning taboos on eating, washing, and moving about the village. Whereas formerly she would have dressed in special skirts, hacked off her hair, and covered her body in ash and oil, she now marked her sorrowful state by wearing old clothing and covering her head and face with a dark cloth. Her substitution of these coverings is in keeping with the policy of the missionaries, who tried to ban the more severe constraints on mourners. The effect of course is functionally similar; the woman is at once the central *living* figure, but her vitality is muted and her individuality hidden, in contradistinction to the corpse which is washed, dressed in finery, and brightly lit. Both are immobile. The chief mourner's children and a handful of older people, who had been adopted by the deceased in the distant past, kept vigil by the corpse for three days and nights. This group of people is always distinguished from affines and other relatives.

On the day of the burial those who had been mourning for the whole three days (others went home after a day, and interisland relatives arrived at various times over the three-day period) were prostrated by grief. They were exhausted, dirty, and dehydrated. Their eyes were glassy and their manner distracted. These people became the focus of the *talawasi* rite, which was late in the afternoon after the burial.

After the interment a fire was lit inside a small shelter built over the grave. As the fire burned and began to die, various relatives prepared a large feast. As soon as the fire died the jest began. An elderly woman, in this case the deceased's elder sister's daughter (who was in fact about the same age as the man who had died) ostentatiously stepped into the middle of the village clearing. She summoned people in an authoritative but jovial manner, and as they congregated she began to tell stories. Even though I could not understand them completely, I recognized that conspiratorial manner adopted by stand-up comics in our own culture as she drew in her audience with the promise of divulging something hitherto unknown and unsuspected. She shrugged and adopted expressions of disingenuous shock as she described in detail the scandalous

Female Comedy on Tubetube

behavior of some person whose identity "she could not possibly reveal, but . . . " and the sniggers and giggles began as she dropped broad hints so that the butts of her jokes were instantly recognizable to her audience. She cast aspersions widely, directing her satire at anyone pompous, self-important, or boastful. She told several stories against Europeans—simply, and using mime to convey the humor. These were half directed at me and recounted some folly that betrayed the ignorance and ineptitude of European men who tried to teach innovative techniques or, alternatively, tried to learn something like climbing a coconut tree in Papuan fashion.

Mime and mimicry, exaggeration and ridicule were combined to refashion and reinforce a stable, orderly world. The humor was conservative and incorporative—"they" (neighbors, visitors, Europeans) are ridiculous, immoderate, and given to silly excesses. "We," of course, are wise, competent, moderate, and sensible. The woman was a gentle humorist, reserving her biting satire for common enemies so that her audience enjoyed the conviviality of shared condemnation. I realised as I watched that her anti-European humor was implicitly premised on my fictive inclusive status— "*They* were all ignorant aliens, *you* of course are one of us and so may laugh at their mistakes and arrogance." The old lady drew us together into a snug communion, and as the knowing smiles spread, her chat and banter shifted and became the antics of the clown. Slapstick and parody gradually gave way to farce until eventually we were all laughing. Those who so recently were wailing their sorrow were soon roaring with laughter, some wiping away tears and pleading for her to cease as they clutched their stomachs in an effort to control their mirth.

As the mourners were consumed by laughter, others stepped in and gently removed them from the circle. Those who were dirty, hungry, and exhausted were taken away and washed, rubbed with oil on their hair and body, and dressed in clean clothes. Some had flowers put in their hair. Those marginalized by grief were speedily and unobtrusively reincorporated. The *rite de marge* concluded with a distributive feast. Those members of the deceased's lineage who so recently had been immobilized by grief were transformed into gracious hosts. All who came to share their sadness were rewarded with gifts of food.

However, the communion established in the jest is not a commensality. The reestablished social order is one in which the receivers (of comfort, sympathy, assistance) quickly repaid these debts with pots of food and pieces of pork. Those who came as helpers to the villagers weakened by sorrow left as guests, burdened down with lavish gifts of hospitality. The dead in his grave, his family transformed themselves into that social category of persons most respected in the Massim: creators of indebtedness, gracious and hospitable hosts—distributors of food.

It would be easy to see the old woman merely as an entertainer—like the wise fool of Shakespearean drama. For although she is the focus of the jest, there is little that bespeaks her authoritative role in the ritual sequence. However, she is perceived and respected as the director of proceedings, and her skills as a comic are essential for the restoration of order and authority. The means she employs to effect this change—telling jokes, playacting, and assuming grotesque or exaggerated postures—are classically those that propel people from unpleasant to pleasant emotional states, so that laughter is both the precipitant and marker of changed sociality. As a senior woman, her customary demeanor is dignified, her speech measured, and her public voice low pitched. Douglas, in discussing Freud's and Bergson's theories, comments that "the essence of the joke is that something formal is attacked by something informal, something organised and controlled by something vital, energetic" (Douglas 1975:95).

The female comic in *talawasi* rituals might thus be seen not only as the subversive agent but as the embodiment of a role contradiction that is in itself a stimulant of laughter. The dignified matron reveals herself as capable of raucous bawdiness. The lineage leader, whose moral authority is claimed by virtue of her righteousness, suddenly mocks this by exposing the follies of the powerful to the ridicule of the weak. But her audience in this rite is waiting for the bereaved people to laugh, so that her humor has to work; even here she has to prove her effectiveness by provoking laughter. In making people laugh she has enabled them to set out on the path that leads eventually to the great restorative feast that will mark the lineage's triumph over the disruptive effects of death (Macintyre 1989). In her role as jester, the senior woman affirms her status as a leader, an agent of lineage authority. I shall return to this theme later, but turn now to the jest that enabled me to understand the social significance of female comedy on Tubetube.

Teasing and Informal Joking as Performance

By the end of my fieldwork I was aware of the various styles of humor that women performed. I had been their butt many times.

Mary, one of my adopted daughters, epitomized the ideals of Tubetube femininity. She was tall and straight backed with the rounded features so admired in the Massim. More importantly, however, she was gregarious, extroverted in her manner, and very funny. She, like all the other women of my lineage, found my celibate state a source of endless drollery. Mindful always of our relative ages and my status as her fictive mother, her humor remained within the bounds demanded by *yakasisi* (formal respect).

Let me illustrate the difference between her teasing and the more risqué mockery in which women of my own generation could indulge. These examples reveal also that the comic performances of *talawasi* are really very similar in character and form to the badinage and raillery that occurs in everyday life. Whenever hard physical work has to be performed by groups of women, then the gifted comediennes emerge. I assume of course that men engage in similar sorts of banter and joking, but I could not participate in the same way, and of course they would not make risqué jokes about me in my presence. Communal work is either exclusively female or mixed, so that men lack similar opportunities for public performance. When men work in groups digging a new garden they sing, shout, and engage in boisterous competitive activities. But as they are surrounded by women and children who are engaged in secondary garden preparation, such as mounding or pulling out large roots, their joking is constrained by their exertions as well as their audience.

An Impromptu Jest

We were all hard at work digging and planting yams in a new garden. The gradient was incredibly steep and the sun was hot. I dropped my digging stick, wiped some sweat from my brow, and braced my aching back with my hands as I slowly straightened up. Mary, who was standing several yards away, ostentatiously noted my hand on my forehead and drew attention to it by mimicking it, pretending that I was in fact shading my eyes to peer into the dense bush about thirty feet away. With a knowing nod at me, she screwed up her eyes and exclaimed in glee as she sighted an imaginary lover lurking in the bushes. By now all the women were enjoying the light relief of this charade. Mary pretended to converse with the hidden admirer, mouthing and gesticulating so that it was clear that she was trying to help him gain some woman's attention. "This one?" She extended her arm in a grand stage gesture—pointing to a very old woman some distance from me. "Oh, not that one?" She was disingenuous; her face assumed an expression of mock surprise that the Lothario in the shadows should not want the belle of the group. She indicated other ludicrous choices—an infant, another elderly woman—and each time feigned astonishment as he apparently shook his head. She calmed him as he grew impatient with her inability to see which woman he wanted. Finally, she pointed to me and her face lit up as the imaginary lover signaled approval. "Yes, well, as soon as all these other people get back to work we'll arrange an assignation." She gave me a knowing look and gravely resumed her work as if a model for all the other women who were wasting time watching her.

The Anthropologist as Object

Once, after a lengthy recording session, John Wesley and Panetan, the two senior men who were my major informants, asked me what I was going to do with all the myths I had transcribed and translated. I tried to explain something of the interpretative process. They agreed that, like Bible stories, these myths were rich in allegory and that some could be read like parables. We began discussing metaphors and esoteric forms of speech. "But what about the little ones, those short stories that are just told for fun?" Emboldened by my success in explaining some symbolic approaches, I thought I would now offer "potted Freud"; after all, Roheim had offered classically Freudian interpretations of Massim myths. I selected one story in which the protagonist is a small hairy yam with a voracious sexual appetite. It seemed pretty clear to me that here we had a phallic symbol. Panetan and John found this terribly farfetched. One of my older female relatives who had been listening scoffed and laughed. How silly I could be at times!

I should have realized that her mischievous smile disguised a plot. She had me at last! My rigid celibacy had (as she'd predicted) warped my mind. Deprived of sex for months on end, my disturbed mind could no longer distinguish between yams and penises. If I squatted while weeding in a garden she would make some comment about my hoping for my lover to emerge. If I were in a group peeling yams, I was most expressly *not* to be given the small elongated hairy yams—goodness knows what I might do with them! While such sexual jokes could only be private and were never said in front of men or young people, the style was always that of a comic before a large audience. I suspect that in my absence that senior lady will have no compunction about including me in a public *talawasi*, and I may indeed be remembered on Tubetube as the woman who mistook her husband for a yam.

At that time, however, the joking was a means of managing my alien status, of incorporating me with laughter at those points where my behavior or ignorance revealed my relationship as fictive. No woman in her thirties would voluntarily remain chaste while her husband and family were miles away. Well, then, I must have secret lovers, even if they turned out to be yams!

Jest as Gentle Censure and Entertainment

On the eve of my departure there was a feast followed by a vigil through the night. At about two in the morning, when voices were hoarse from singing and spirits were low, three women, my elder sisters, announced that it was time for their jest. They had been whispering in a huddle and shrieking with laughter as they agreed on the form of the performance. This was to make me happy and to liven my feast, which was becoming a very sad affair as I kept bursting into tears at the prospect of my imminent departure.

The jest was performed as a mime, without any speech. At times it seemed like a charade, as standardized hand signals indicated time passing, a change of location, and other information. In style the mime was similar to Mary's garden performance, with large gestures and grotesque facial expressions conveying the complexities of a flirtation, a secret assignation, or a consultation with the audience. The story was of a love triangle, an adulterous husband caught in flagrante delicto by an aggrieved and suspicious wife. The three actresses established their respective characters quickly. Small mannerisms made each one instantly identifiable, for this was a true story involving three people who were in fact all sitting around the fire as part of the audience!

As soon as I realized the import of the story I froze, fearful of an argument if the recently reconciled couple responded negatively to their ridicule. Nobody else seemed perturbed. As I peeped warily at the real wife I saw her laughing. Moreover, the other woman seemed more taken by the humor than by any idea that this was a form of public humiliation. Only the errant husband evinced any discomfort. He shrugged and gave me a sheepish smile as I caught his eye.

The jest was a burlesque in which the wife crept up on the adulterous pair, crawled along the platform, and waited until they were in the throes of passion before seizing the man by the feet and dragging him out of the doorway, naked and in considerable pain. The humor depended in part on prior knowledge of the real protagonists: a sturdy, amiable, but slow-witted husband, a quiet and normally shy wife whose diminutive stature provided much of the humor in the final scene, and a silly young woman. In the performance the husband was played by a small, finely built woman and the wife by her more sturdy sister. The husband's lover was played by a woman who was tall and considered ungainly and unattractive by many people. The casting was in itself a joke.

At the time I observed that *talawasi* is entertainment, light relief in a long night full of sad farewells, reminiscences, and Wesleyan hymn singing. In retrospect it can be reconstructed as a cultural form, an example of a genre.

The subjects of my sisters' satire were known as "little people"— they were poor by local standards, they had many children, and they had no political clout. In discussions with senior men and women, that particular couple was often singled out to exemplify the economic disadvantages that followed from having few senior relatives, limited intelligence, and a lack of sexual restraint. They did not need to be publicly humiliated for they had no reputation to lose. Their sins were little sins.

Cruel Jesting and Public Ridicule

The jest differs in tone from the shaming ceremony, *kiyo*, which is performed to express public disapproval and to exact both revenge and compensation. In 1981 I observed the preparations for a *kiyo* performed on the neighboring island of Naluwaluwali. The preliminary discussions revealed that most of the younger generation of adults had never been part of a *kiyo*. They, like me, were fascinated by an account of a shaming ceremony that had occurred twenty or more years previously. Old people recalled the riotous and ribald assaults on person and property when an aggrieved group chose to humiliate an adulterer and his extremely young lover. Indeed, the younger people were so astonished by these stories of public abuse that they quickly vetoed any similar performances in the current context. They were particularly shocked by the vulgarity of the chants or taunts and by the reports that villagers would insult their victims by exposing their buttocks. A couple of young men denied that this could occur, assuring me that their elders were fabricating events in order to stress their vehemence and forcefulness as young people.

The *kiyo* on Naluwaluwali was performed by the kin of a deceased woman whose widower had remarried before completing the mortuary exchanges for her death. His offense was twofold—he insulted his wife and her kin by failing to observe mourning taboos, and the debts associated with a lengthy marriage were not settled (Macintyre 1989).

In the event, the participants in the 1981 *kiyo* refused to behave in ways they thought were demeaningly vulgar or un-Christian, irrespective of their elders' insistence on the correct form of a *kiyo*. The ritual was divided into two phases. The first was the more humorous or uproarious, a march on the village and the noisy assault on the offenders' house. The second part was not humorous at all and is best glossed as a "verbal duel." The affronted first proclaimed their charges against the villagers and demanded compensation. The leaders of the occupied village defended their kinsfolk and offered valuables or pigs commensurate with their view of the offense as a minor breach. As the debate raged, pigs or valuables (and, for the first time in 1981, money) were proffered. If the offended at any stage believed that the villagers were not readily going to give sufficient compensation, they reverted to the shaming, humorous mode—or threatened to do so. This threat of further public humiliation ensured that demands were met.

Even the modified insults I observed were startling in the ways they departed from norms of polite behavior. People shouted abuse, made explicit reference to sexual activity, and impugned villagers' morality on all matters—all forms of behavior that in everyday life would have incurred wrath or even demands for compensation. But the accounts I collected of *kiyo* ceremonies performed over twenty years ago suggested that, while form remained similar in the past, the content of the humorous section was devoid of any subtlety or sympathy for the objects of censure.

The *kiyo* is a crude and cruel charivari, and those toward whom it is directed lose status and wealth. At a *kiyo* the taunts and ridicule are obscene and derogatory and are performed by men and women. By contrast, the jest at my feast was full of good humor, and because its focus could not possibly be misconstrued as a piece of social criticism or deflation, it was presented for simple enjoyment. Moreover, the performers were all women of relatively high status in the community whose matronly dignity set behavioral boundaries, even when they were simulating sexual intercourse in the dim light of the fire! So far as I could tell, their comic talents enhanced their status as senior women.

Women as Comics

In jests, whether they are of the type performed by the single woman during the mourning ritual or the small group burlesque put on at a feast, women are most often the clowns. As I dredged my memory, my letters from the field, and notebooks for examples of jokes, jests, and other clownish things, I was struck by the repeated confirmation of my impression that women were given credit for their comic abilities, whereas male comedians were rarely public figures. Men tell jokes, perform charades, riddle, and ridicule too—but they are not expected to do so, nor are they expected to do it well.

During the period of my fieldwork there was one man who was in some respects a natural fool. He lived alone in a hamlet where he was left to his own devices and fed by his brother's family. He built fantastical houses that wasted scarce resources, and he made strange sculptures from tree trunks. He often dressed in exaggerated versions of the traditional warrior's clothing and carried spears or flags made from pandanus. His bizarre dress and inability to converse rationally made him an object of fear and fun. However, as he had been a man of substance, a man of renown in *kune (kula)* exchanges before his illness, more often his strange constructions and inappropriate responses evoked pity and a sense of the tragic. Often when younger people laughed at him, their elders would frown reproachfully and tell them that he had once been a man of substance, intelligent and gracious in his ways.

Similarly, a small boy who was a deaf-mute was often encouraged to dance while others drummed or clapped. This usually drew laughter, but the women of his hamlet quickly intervened if they thought the mirth was unkind or if he became embarrassed as older children laughed at him. He seemed to me an intelligent child and he could mimic others very cleverly, but his mother and grandmother discouraged him from playing the fool and chided those who made him a figure of fun.

The protection of the weak, and the insistence that these people were not really funny, indicate a view of humor that emerges more clearly when people assess jokes or clowning, for then it is clear that intention is critical. The reenactment of an intrinsically funny event (with its inevitable exaggerations) is bound to be unequivocal in its humor, whereas the humorous reversals that stimulate laughter are often more ambiguous when they are real-life incidents. This is particularly the case when the subject of the joke incurs an injury. The slip on the banana skin is funnier when the audience is reassured that no physical damage has resulted and the injury is merely to dignity.

Clever reconstructions of events are greatly appreciated by Tubetube audiences, and the revisions or deletions are commented upon by people when they recount successful *talawasi* performances. When I returned to Tubetube after a long absence, several people reported a *talawasi* that reenacted one of my early experiences on the island.

I had been walking for about a half hour with a basket of yams on my head, and my neck ached terribly. As I reached the beach I set the basket down on an old log and sat down to rest. The two young women I was with were sympathetic, but amused by my problems with balance and weight, and waited patiently. When I replaced my load, to my horror I found it had been on an ants' nest. Hundreds of large ants swarmed down my face and began biting me. I dumped the basket on the beach and dived into the sea, desperately brushing the insects off. At the time, the women repressed all giggles and fussed over me, concerned about the bites that covered my neck and shoulders.

Ten years later, this event had been comically transformed. It now exemplified the ineptitude of the novice, and much of the humor was derived from the transformation of the languorous white woman who is prostrated by the most minor exertion—carrying a basket of yams—to a frenzied creature whose undignified leaping and flailing reveals the sham of her exhaustion. The intrinsic slapstick humor was exploited fully by the performer as she bounded about in the water, arms waving frantically.

Intrigued by the construction of my initial tiredness as sham, I asked whether they really thought I had been faking. The reply was ingenuous: no, they actually appreciated my initial problems, but why spoil a good story with the truth? Embroidery upon the facts and minor alterations in order to make contradictions more stark are the marks of the creative skills of a comic performer. Jests that follow these conventions of a recognizable genre are those used in rites, for the form itself signals that they are to be laughed at.

The creation of performance events often flows from initial spontaneous reenactments as people chat over the day's events.

Both men and women can be raconteurs, but even at the mundane level of domestic storytelling female performance is more expressive. Men sit and tell stories, whereas women more often combine gesture, mime, and movement with verbal accounts. Stories told by men are easily redacted, whereas female storytelling and clowning performances defy repetition by imitators.

These differences reflect a broader gender division among those who are lineage leaders. Oratory and the power to influence people are masculine qualities in the sense that they are essential for male leaders, and women who are renowned as orators or *kune* traders are called *tautaune* (manly). But the capacity to jest and thereby direct the mode of sociality in a specific situation is feminine only insofar as it is construed as a necessary skill in social domains that are ordered by women—mortuary ceremonies, feasts, and the rituals of incorporation of visitors into the life of the hamlet. Humor is not a feature of those activities that are central to men's lives—*kune* exchange, forms of litigation, and formerly, fighting. Both men and women can be funny, but situationally women have greater scope and gain prestige through the activity. Elsewhere I argue that ideals of gender difference on Tubetube draw on the historic roles of men as warriors (Macintyre 1987). The qualities of the frenzied warrior that still constitute masculine power preclude a sense of the ridiculous and exclude jokes.

Joking is definitely a feminine social grace, and on Tubetube it is directly linked to other skills of hospitality. Being funny is part of being a good hostess. It is less important than being able to feed guests, but it is an essential element in entertainments of all sorts. Humor that is sarcastic or in any way disdainful or contemptuous of its subject—as when an elder upbraids and reprimands an errant youth in public—is the preserve of senior men or women who are acknowledged lineage leaders. But hospitable humor is restorative and assertive of sociality. In such a small community, where the incidence of adultery is very high, jokes about sex, marital infidelity, and lust are clearly one way of dealing with the anxieties they provoke as sources of disruption and discord.

In clowning rituals, women assume the comic role that we recognize as masculine in the Western tradition, with the comedian as wry observer, distant and bemused. There are no dizzy comediennes or dumb blondes. Indeed, while there is a style of humor where the intelligent and impatient wife is exasperated by a stupid husband, there is very little sexual or sexist stereotyping as the basis for funny story conventions. Situations that border on chaos, slapstick calamities, and the humor of mutual misunderstandings provide the basis for many jests. But verbal jousting, outwitting the vain or boastful, or teasing the lovelorn also rate highly as entertainment.

Conclusion

I have tried to describe and elucidate female jesting on Tubetube. In doing so I am aware that this feminine act may not be unique to Bwanabwana culture; indeed, the contributions in this volume on female clowning in Murik Lakes and Rotuma suggest that women are perceived as comic in a wide range of societies. But in my search for comparisons, I realized that clowning is relatively rarely described, and when *female* clowning does occur it seems more often to be role reversal or ritual inversion, in which women subvert or mock authority in Saturnalia or charivari. In this case the female clowns and comic performances are integral to a wide range of ceremonial activities, and rather than being unusual or atypical, the clowning and jesting is an institutional extension of an aspect of highly valued female behavior. Comedy serves as a means a of social integration in times of stress or disruption within the community. Thus the *talawasi* ritual during the funeral is the *rite de marge* that facilitates movement from the asocial state of grief to reincorporation. The dynamic is similar at feasts, for there laughter is the promoter of conviviality and commensality between diverse and unrelated people. Elsewhere (Macintyre 1987) I describe female agency in its more negative mode, when the threat of witchcraft is used as coercion or sanction by senior women. There I argue that as sisters (and witches) women were able to wield considerable power within their matrilineages. The centrality of the women who are the elder sisters in formal jests indicates that this too is an aspect of female agency in the public arena. Teasing, parody, and burlesque are gentle forms of castigation, reprimand, or disapproval. Laughter and hilarity are more sociable means of unifying people than fear of witchcraft. In tiny communities such as Tubetube, where mistrust would lead to social isolation, the clown role can then be interpreted as the essential inverse of the antisocial witch.

REFERENCES

Douglas, Mary
    1975   *Implicit Meanings*. London: Routledge and Kegan Paul.

Macintyre, Martha
    1987   Flying Witches and Leaping Warriors: Supernatural Origins of Power and Matrilineal Authority in Tubetube Society. In *Dealing with Inequality: Analysing Gender Relations in Melanesia and Beyond*, ed. Marilyn Strathern, pp. 207-28. Cambridge: Cambridge University Press.
    1989   The Triumph of the *Susu*. In *Death Rituals and Life in the Societies of the Kula Ring*, ed. F. H. Damon and R. Wagner, pp. 133–52. DeKalb: Northern Illinois University Press.

HORRIFIC HUMOR AND FESTAL FARCE: CARNIVAL CLOWNING IN WAPE SOCIETY

William E. Mitchell

CARNIVAL, A FESTIVAL characterized by cultural inversions, long has been a favorite topic of scholars and travelers whose rich descriptions of the carnivalesque abound for societies in Europe, the Caribbean, and the Americas.[1] Historically, carnival is associated with the calendrical festivals of stratified European societies, both pagan and Christian, and the latter's colonial possessions influenced by Catholicism. Scholarly usage dictates that the term *carnival* be restricted to this cultural and geographic sphere. Such usage masks the notion that "primitive" stateless societies are not sufficiently evolved to mount large-scale festivals with inversion, including clowns, as a prominent feature. Consequently, the carnivalesque is not reported by ethnographers or historians as present in Melanesia's animistic egalitarian societies. It is not supposed to be there.

Yet there are forest-dwelling Melanesian societies whose festivals do contain dramatic antipodean elements that rival, and in some instances surpass, those of the famous carnivals of ancient Rome and modern Rio de Janeiro. My intention is to extend the idea of carnival—what Turner calls "society in its subjunctive mood" (1967: 76)—far beyond its present parameters to one such Melanesian society: the Wape of Papua New Guinea.

Those scholars who view carnival as a cultural tradition rooted in the Roman Saturnalia and allied to a proseletyzing Catholicism may object to this tactic. However, it is not my purpose to redefine the concept of carnival but simply to liberate it from the ethnocentric confines of European historiography. In passing, we also may learn something more general about human comedy and the extent of humorous inversions.

145

Carnival in New Guinea

Whereas many New Guinea societies focus their indigenous festivals on the harvest, initiation, or death, the Wape, who, live in the Torricelli Mountains of the West Sepik Province, focus their greatest festivals on curing. The Niyel curing festival is the longest and most culturally complex of these, in terms of its interpenetration of Wape everyday life.[2] It is performed every few years at irregular intervals in all Wape villages. As a centerpiece of the Wape exchange system, the Niyel festival generates reciprocal transactions among patrilineages via kinship ties. After several preparatory months involving a series of rituals and exchanges with relatives in other villages, the festival climaxes in a weekend carnival on the sponsoring village's dirt plaza attended by hundreds of costumed people from the surrounding area. The featured spectacle is prancing men in towering body masks symbolizing various Wape demons.[3]

This chapter is concerned with a small but essential part of the Niyel festival's carnival climax, what Bakhtin (1968) and others identify as carnival's subversive or saturnalian—even grotesque—aspect. It is this denormatizing of traditional norms, however transient, by mocking, satirizing, or inverting everyday experience that sets up carnival's exciting and liberating centrifugal force. And, just as carnival disrupts and challenges the orderly procession of everyday life, the antics of carnival clowns disrupt and challenge the fixity of everyday values. But the anarchistic force of carnival is, ironically, also culturally regenerative and conservative. Carnivals are not revolutions; they are only disruptive, not destructive of the status quo. While subversive, their liberating thrills are temporally bounded.

This, then, is the conventional view of carnival. But carnival cannot be dismissed simply as a safety valve against radical change.[4] Ignored by most writers is carnival's substantive and enduring power as a legitimate repository for the heretical. While not immediately transforming, carnival's importance for cultural change is the perpetuation of heretical notions in the imagination of its participants. The sensory experiences of carnival, vivid and emotive, document difference as contested images that linger in the memory.

This is the submerged praxis of carnival, to nourish the representations of difference in the human imagination, where, like avatars, they may eventually emerge to challenge the known and the

Carnival Clowning in Wape Society

now. For example, during an age of privileged birth and absolute monarchs, European carnivals offered a glimpse of democracy in action by momentarily raising the powerless and lowering the powerful, hundreds of years before the French Revolution. In a similar way, Niyel carnival men cavorting in women's skirts and women dancing with men's weapons prefigure a radicalization of Wape gender roles and a view of where power may or might reside. Thus, carnival is not just an episodic event bounded firmly by time, but an event characterized by subversive images that, incubating in the human imagination, continue to impact social practice.

The subversive nature of the Niyel carnival is conveyed through comedic ritual performances parodying everyday life and characteristically violating dogma of kinship and gender. These performances, ranging from the scatological to the silly, are touched with the kind of madness that usually evokes smiles and laughter—or, on occasion, unease and anger—from amused or surprised observers. Wape ritual, like the Umeda (Gell 1975) to the west and the Gnau (Lewis 1980) to the east, is primarily nonverbal and nonesoteric in the sense that explanations of ritual are limited to and known by most men. Consequently, there is no elaborate, indigenous exegesis of Wape ritual, including ritual clowning.

The Wape of Papua New Guinea

The Wape live in sedentary villages in the Torricelli Mountains between Papua New Guinea's northwest coast and the sprawling swamps of the Sepik River. They number around ten thousand and speak Olo, a language of the Torricelli phylum. Wape men have participated in the world market system since the 1930s as contract laborers for Western enterprises, especially copra and gold, in other parts of the country and are fluent in the lingua franca, Tok Pisin, as are most children and some of the women. Western influence is most pronounced at Lumi station, headquarters for the national government and for the regional Catholic (Franciscan) and Protestant (Christian Brethren) missions, each of which have several satellite mission stations scattered throughout the area. Although there are many nominal Christians in Wapeland,[5] traditional religious beliefs and customs remain culturally dominant.

The Wape are organized into patriclans and exogamous patrilineages. Marriage is by bride-wealth, postmarital residence is virilocal, and polygyny is permitted but rare. The Wape are egalitarian in the sense that, other than recognizing hierarchical status differences based on sex and age that advantage men and adults, one may direct others only on the basis of kinship ties.

Although the Wape practice slash-and-burn horticulture, sago is their principle food. Hunting is important in male ritual but in most areas is insignificant as a source of protein. Poor nutrition among the Wape is a problem reflected in one of the world's lowest birth weights, a delay in the onset of puberty, and short adult stature (Wark and Malcolm 1969). Many villagers also suffer from chronic upper respiratory infections, and malaria is holoendemic and uncontrolled. Wape ceremonial life, not suprisingly, is centered on curing.[6]

Comedic Genres of the Niyel Carnival

The term *clowning*, as used here, refers to public performances characterized variously by burlesque, buffoonery, nonsense, and irony.[7] The clowning performances discussed in this chapter are either sacral or theatrical. While both are intensely social, one plays with cosmic forces and the other does not. By *sacral clowning* I mean that the clown performs within a ritual frame in juxtaposition to a deitylike figure in the way that Pueblo clown performances are related to the kachinas (Laski 1958:12-15, 38–59).[8] In contrast, theatrical clowning is nonreligious and ranges in form from tightly orchestrated skits—for example, those performed by "whiteface" and "auguste" clowns in European and Arnerican circuses (Bishop 1976; Bouissac 1972, 1982)—to more extemporaneous and inventive performances, for example, those of the new "postmodern" or "private" clowns influenced by the art of mime (Engibarov 1988; Little 1986:55).

The carnival phase of the Niyel festival occurs on its last two days and nights—Friday and Saturday—and is anticipated by villagers as a colorful change from the predictability of their usual lives.[9] In contrast, the exorcism of the afflicted is a quiet, almost private, affair performed at sunrise Sunday morning after most of the revelers have started homeward or gone to sleep.[10] But during the carnival nights, boisterous throngs of visitors from neighboring villages join their hosts in the village plaza to form a sea of undulating, circling forms decorated with feathers, ferns, flowers, shells, and leaves and who dance and sing by torchlight until dawn. Punctuating the waves of movement like fanciful buoys are the

Carnival Clowning in Wape Society

soaring demon masks. The Niyel carnival affords one of the few opportunities for young men and women from diverse villages to come together in a festive mood to appraise the beauty and verve of likely mates. It is not, however, a time for overt sexual license. The presence of powerful demon spirits easily enraged by human coital fluids precludes any form of bacchanal. But this is a time of high spirits and excitement—and human danger, too—as the commingling of hundreds of celebrants with active sorcery beliefs from different villages, some of whom are traditional enemies, is an unusual activity for these people.

Sacral Clowning

In each village when the Niyel festival is performed, a few men from the sponsoring village usually volunteer to be initiated into the Niyel curing society to replace Niyel adepts who have died or are enfeebled. Initiation entitles them to carry the Niyel masks and exorcise victims of the Niyel, a fish spirit inhabiting rivers and empowered to cause illness to those who enter the river or eat its products. The Wape have several curing societies, each related to a different demon with its peculiar mask, and most men belong to one of them. Of the various curing festivals, the Niyel is the largest, and it alone has clowning performances.[11]

Among the several kinds of demon masks worn by men at the Niyel festival, the only sacred ones are those commissioned by individuals afflicted by Niyel. These sacred masks are carried by adepts of the Niyel curing society as well as by initiates carrying one for the first time.[12] The Niyel masks, especially those of the initiates, are the main centers of attention, and various male and female relatives honor their prancing wearers by dancing with them.

Wape sacral clowning is specifically related to the Niyel mask carriers. Although most of the individuals dancing with a Niyel initiate are his classificatory sisters, there are two other categories of kin who may dance with him and evoke amusement by breaking gender or kinship taboos. One category is a Niyel initiate's wife's parents, who honor their son-in-law by publicly shaming themselves. Painting their faces black, they dance naked behind him in a public exhibition of their genitalia, in a representation of "life as it should not be" (Hieb 1972b:6). Wape men traditionally wore no pubic covering or decoration. To be shamefully exposed, a father-in-law pulls back his peniss foreskin to reveal the glans as he cocks his head to one side and, grinning inanely, extends his tongue from the corner of his gaping mouth.[13] Wape women traditionally wore, as a few still do, a narrow string skirt fore and aft, which the mother-in-law removes to dance with her son-in-law.[14]

Because sexual exhibitionism is tabooed in Wape society, dancing naked before hundreds of people in the presence of one's son-in-law, with whom the relationship is typified by avoidance and decorum, has a certain horrific quality that, while it might momentarily take the observer's breath away, is also described as deeply funny.[15] The nakedness by the initiate's wife's parents becomes a ritual costume that shocks and amuses.[16] Although the couple's ritualized actions are essentially directed toward their son-in-law, it is only within the social context of the carnival throng that these assume meaning. For example, the couple are described as being shamed by their naked demeanor, but it is not, for example, the shame of a person who is caught in flagrante delicto. Their behavior is not so much audacious as ironic. While dancing with their son-in-law to honor him, they also mock their kinship tie to him. In a quotidian frame their actions would be scandalous—even crazy—but in the ritualized frame of carnival their actions, while visually startling, on one plane glorify their relationship while on another negate it in what sociolinguists call a *co-occurrence violation*. Paradox is funny. This kind of "code inconsistency" (Irvine 1979:777) undercuts one message with a qualifying one that in some way negates it.[17] In a similar way, "comedy," as Babcock explains,

> may be a spiritual shock therapy which breaks up the patterns of thought and rationality that hold us in bondage and in which the given and established order of things is deformed, reformed, and reformulated; a playful speculation on what was, is, or might be; a remark on the indignity of any closed system. (1984:103)

The closed system ritually deconstructed by the antics of the naked affines appears to be nothing less than the Wape kinship system itself. In the villagers' shocked laughter we apprehend "a logical moment of truth" (Swabey 1961:v), for in this society where kinship shapes almost all significant relationships, the absence of kinship is chaos; affines gone crazy. By performing obscenely vis-à-vis their son-in-law in a carnival context, the naked couple dramatically dissolves the everyday distinctions between kinship and chaos, right and wrong, ritual and play, serious and silly. Actions unthinkable within any other social frame are here sanctioned and correct. In this sense, the dancers are transformers of boundaries who, in a public contradiction of self, become signifiers of the boundaries that are dissolved. Indeed, they are "'of the boundary' itself" (Handelman 1981:342), quite unlike their son-in-law, whose liminality as a Niyel novice becoming an adept situates him somewhere *on* the boundary but not *of* it.[18]

The second category of kin involved in sacred clowning involves men whose mothers belong to the same clan as the initiate's mother, in other words, these men and the initiate theoretically share the same classificatory mother's brothers. These men, if they wish, may dance with the initiate by assuming female dress and decorations. By the flickering flames of torches it is difficult for the outsider to distinguish them from the initiate's classificatory sisters who also chant and dance with him.[19] In daylight they are more easily identified, especially when dressed in an eccentric fashion to heighten the burlesque. For example, when my neighbor Suwe was a Niyel initiate at the Taute festival, a man from Senem village whose mother belonged to Suwe's mother's clan arrayed himself in a skirt of wild leaves and a headdress of oppossum fur and tossing cassowary feathers. Leaping around the dance ground in a rambunctious and ridiculous manner unlike any woman, he was the cause of much amusement.

Like the naked affinal dancers, cross-dressed male dancers may be interpreted as further deconstructing the kinship system within the frame of carnival as well as attacking the authority of gender. Male transvestites mockingly subvert Wape notions of both gender and kinship by dancing with the initiate as if they were his classificatory sisters. At the end of carnival the initiate pays the women and the transvestite dancers in coins or a mixture of coins and shell money, the latter the traditional form of payment.[20]

There is another form of modified transvestism that involves women, but it is neither as shocking nor as humorous to observers as the examples of sacred clowning given above. It is permissible during Niyel carnival—and at no other time—for a woman to carry a man's bow when she dances. The few women whom I saw dancing with a bow were mature married women who, chanting about the hunt, occasionally called out to dead ancestors and the *mani* demon, two classes of the supernatural who may be appealed to for game. Some of the younger villagers, especially males, find this very amusing, but they keep their levity hidden from the dancer. In this example, kinship is not a factor because the woman dances alone, but her seizing the bow—the quintessential Wape male symbol—calls into question who and what is male and female, further dissolving the everyday sureties of gender.

Theatrical Clowning

As the carnival revelers circle around the plaza, onlookers and resting dancers watch the proceedings, some from the verandahs of the encircling houses, others as they wander along the periphery of the action where humorous skits are enacted. These brief, satirical skits—theater in miniature—antedate contact with the West and are standard features of the Niyel carnival. The skits, mostly lampoons of everyday life, are performed in masquerade by young, mainly single, men; they alone have "license to joke" (Handelman and Kapferer 1972:488) in this way. Unlike sacral clowning that is related to the sacred Niyel masks, the skits are strictly secular and, like a circus sideshow, tangential to the main attraction in the center ring. The youths who perform these ad hoc skits are self-selected, for there is no "clown society" as among the Pueblo Indians (Dozier 1961:115–16). Performers present their short skit before amused knots of observers and then move on, repeatedly circling the arena and performing the same skit again and again. The skit may be one that they originated or one that they saw performed at a previous Niyel festival.

The first time that I witnessed these droll performances was in the village of Otei shortly after I arrived in Wapeland. In one of the skits, two young men wearing women's skirts and blouses with phony breasts had neckerchiefs folded bandit-style around their foreheads to partially mask their faces. With their heads bent downward further disguising their features (although most men are easily identifiable and this is part of the fun) and their arms locked together, they shuffled to an fro while singing in falsetto to mourn their "husbands," who were contract laborers on coastal plantations.

In another skit, two men dressed as husband and wife, their faces similarly masked as the couple above, carried a naked rubber doll. The "husband" handed their "baby" to his "wife," whereupon she pretended to feed it rocks that, I was told by one observer, represented rotten sago. The degree of laughter generated, of course, depends upon the costume and who is wearing it, the skill of the performers, and the receptiveness of the particular audience.

Plot summaries of fourteen skits enacted at the four Niyel carnivals on which I have detailed data appear in table 1.[21] Undoubtedly other skits also were performed at some of these Niyel carnivals but were not observed. The fourteen skits represent twelve different plots (three skits have a common plot of wives mourning absent husbands) enacted by eighteen male performers, ten of whom portray women, seven portray men, and one, a cassowary. Three dolls were used as props to represent babies. In four of the skits, two performers appeared together as women and in one skit as a husband and wife, but the majority of skits were solo performances.

My interpretation of Wape theatrical clowning takes a different approach from that for sacral clowning; here we are not concerned with archaic, received ceremony but with inventive, ad hoc comic routines mirroring the concerns of the youths who perform them.[22] To my Western sensibilities, a number of the skits have a cynical edge of mocking cruelty that continued to mystify me throughout my fieldwork. Young Wape men, although they have a well-developed appreciation of the ridiculous, are generally soft-spoken and considerate companions to males and females alike; the society as a whole has little of the day-to-day sexual antagonism anthropologists so frequently record for Highland New Guinea societies. How then does one explain young men's sardonic pleasure in enacting skits that put women—especially mothers—in such an unfavorable light in terms of Wape cultural values?

Most of the plots in table 1 are about people; only the last one mocks nature, in the form of a cassowary. Plots one through six

TABLE 1
Plot Summaries of Niyel Carnival Comedy Skits

Plot	Village	Date
1. Two women mourn for men away at plantation	Otei	June 1970
	Otemki	January 1971
	Taute	October 1971
2. Man gives baby to woman, who feeds it rocks	Otei	June 1970
3. Woman cries that her baby is dying	Otemki	January 1971
4. Man angry that his two babies died because of wife's bad care	Otemki	January 1971
5. Pregnant woman squats then stands	Teloute	January 1967
6. Two women scraping sticks as if cleaning taro	Taute	October 1971
7. Fat man (European?) in coveralls	Otei	June 1970
8. Man makes bad sago for mother's brother	Otemki	January 1971
9. Man tries to shoot toy snake with bow and arrow	Taute	October 1971
10. Man making a garden falls down	Teloute	Janaury 1967
11. Man at plantation calls to his village	Teloute	January 1967
12. Man imitates a cassowary	Teloute	January 1967

involve the mocking of women, while plots seven through eleven mock men. What is different in the content of the two sets of gender plots is the tenor of the satire. The male mocking skits, with one important exception, are good-natured in the sense that they are more silly than malicious. The exception is a man making "bad sago" for his mother's brother. In this patrilineal society, the relationship between a mother's brother and a sister's son is one of ambivalence. While a mother's brother is thought of as nurturing and his home as a place of refuge, the relationship is one of recurrent economic exchanges that initially validate and then continually evaluate the status of that relationship. Young men often feel at a disadvantage because their mother's brother may impose magical sanctions if obligations toward him are not fulfilled. They also are the ones most likely to leave Wapeland to work on distant copra plantations as contract laborers, only to return home to have much of their new wealth syphoned away by a mother's brother's insistent demands. At least that is the way young men talk among themselves about their mother's brothers. A fantasy skit gifting a mother's brother with rotten sago is a safe but emotionally satisfying way to get even in a relationship frequently perceived as one-sided.[23]

I also want to call attention to one other male-oriented plot that I will refer to later. As a Wape fat man is an oxymoron, plot seven in Otei village featuring a man in bulging coveralls is undoubtedly poking fun at whites. Wape men sometimes joke about the unusual height and girth of Westerners, and the people of Otei, whose village lies just beyond Lumi airstrip, are frequent visitors to Lumi station where the majority of local expatriates (foreign missionaries, traders and government employees) live. But the satire, while mocking, is as gentle as most of their skits about Wape men.

Part of my interest in clowning is that I never have been comfortable observing circus clowns; my feelings about them are unresolved. While often fascinated with their irreverent and grotesque lampoons, the underlying sentiments often strike me as vulgar and mean-spirited, yet I find myself deeply attentive in the way I might be while watching an old news clip of the Fascist ranting of Hitler. In the end I always feel cognitively sullied and annoyed that I am so easily attracted—if only momentarily, of course—to actions that, on one level, I do not honor and, that, on another, I admire for their audacity. Therein lies the power of clowning: it is anticulture because it evinces no shame. The cultural parameters and restraints that bound ordinary behavior are vain-

Carnival Clowning in Wape Society

gloriously ignored, and suddenly, the observer's affective world is transformed. Most of us are both enthralled and repelled by the possibilities set up.

What, then, about the plots that mock women? Just as the plots that mock men are gently sardonic except for one, those that mock women are the obverse. Only one, plot six, is funny but compassionate. The others, in terms of Wape values, hold women up to humorous ridicule. The first four ridicule aspects of motherhood, and plots three and one, respectively, ridicule a women's grief at the death of her baby and at the absence of her husband working on a far plantation. In all of these plots there is a bitterness about mothers and wives that is not easily explained in broad cultural terms. But the prima facie evidence is uncontrovertable: the plots indicate that youths find mature women highly problematic.

While Wape men definitely consider themselves superior to women, in everyday life there is a minimum of chauvinistic posturing. Wape men generally value their wives—wife-beating is rare (Mitchell 1990a)—and sons appear to have good relations with their mothers. Or had I missed a crucial bit of ethnographic data about mothers and sons? Were these negative skits, like the one about the mother's brother, commenting on a kinship relation that is culturally conflicted? If so, it was not a pervasive problem that informants complained about (as they did about mother's brothers) or one that I had observed.[24] Or is it that the mother-bashing skits are a form of what Adler called "masculine protest" (Munroe 1955:376–77), in which untested youths are attempting to assert their dominance as males by ridiculing women. There is some credence to this approach if we look more closely at the social situation of Wape youths.

Until puberty, Wape boys live in the family home with their parents and siblings. As infants and toddlers, however, they are not tied as closely to their mothers as in some societies, because fathers, older siblings, and other relatives all take active roles in their upbringing. A father, especially, willingly carries a child, male or female, around the village while his wife is working sago in the forest. Still, this is a society with no initiation ceremonies that publicly signal the attainment of manhood. Like most American boys, Wape boys have to find their own way into manhood. One way of furthering that goal is to mark that which is considered female, for example, reproduction and emotional expressiveness, in a derisive way that elevates maleness. By theatrically deconstructing that which is considered intrinsic to females, maleness becomes a bold ploy that surmounts the love and care of women.

Carnival and Western Contact

Most carnival descriptions, as I have indicated, are not for egalitarian animistic societies like the Wape, but for stratified hierarchical Christian societies where status inversions are important features and a "fundamental transformation of conventional roles, proprieties, and hierarchies is celebrated" (Bernstein 1986:105).[25] Princes and prelates may be mockingly imitated by the proletariat in Christian societies, but the Wape exclude their colonial rulers from their carnival characters. Patrol officers, priests, nuns, ministers, doctors, and nurses, for example, occupy superordinate, sometimes contentious, power positions vis-à-vis villagers, but these relationships are not satirized in the clown skits. Only the fat man clown, if I am correct, seems related to the colonial experience and, with his overbearing size, might be interpreted as a generalized metaphor for the intrusive white man.

In many ways, there are two distinct worlds in Wapeland, that of the West and that of the Wape, and synchrony is minimal. Accommodations to the West have been many; for example, carnival celebrants mostly wear Western-type clothing, but these accommodations are basically superficial. Even the overlay of Western government is thin, and although it has challenged the structural integrity of Wape culture it has not transformed it. In respect to a syncretism between Christianity and the Niyel curing festival, there is none, although this is not true for the indigenous festivals of many other peoples of the world who have been missionized by Catholicism. Unlike Mexico or Guatemala, whose populations were brutalized and forcibly Christianized several hundred years ago, Wape contact with the West is recent, and while the work of the missionaries is relentless, it is not brutal. The Wape have a choice. Although the early missionaries tried to suppress the Niyel ritual cycle as "evil," blaming Satan "for enticing Christians back into the heathenism of their festivals" (McGregor 1982:96), the gatherings were lawful and the colonial government tended not to interfere.[26]

Had the expatriates among the Wape been perceived as flagrantly undermining of Wape society as the Songhay of Niger perceived the French (Stoller 1984), they too undoubtedly would be rendered similarly vulnerable as objects of satire and humorous ridicule. However, as Wape society continues to change and becomes more directly influenced by Western educational, health, and political institutions, the theatrical embryo inherent in Niyel clowning will probably extend its satirical interest from the kinship and

Carnival Clowning in Wape Society

gender experiences of the village to include those of an enhanced problematic world. But for most Wape today, participation in the traditional Niyel festival is not a consciously defiant gesture against outside influences, but a spiritually powerful way to celebrate their place in Wape society.

Laughing at Gender and Kinship

Jokes, as Douglas notes, "do not affirm the dominant values, but denigrate and devalue" (1968:369). The joking actions of subversive sacral and secular clowns disorganize the present, sometimes delightfully and sometimes, like a Charles Addams cartoon, ominously. Either way, subversive clowning is always an act that attacks prevailing cultural constructions. Its seductive appeal is in presenting a view of the *other*; a fleeting glimpse of life minus the contemporaneous lines of order.

While a graduate student I worked for a time on a psychiatric ward for disturbed children (Mitchell 1966). On St. Valentine's Day one of the boys I had disciplined approached me with a huge grin and a handmade valentine. The heart, roughly cut from chartreuse construction paper, was decorated with a defecating anus and a urinating penis. The penciled greeting said, "Fuck You." Instantaneously, my apprehension of valentines was transformed forever.

Not every joke succeeds as well in dissolving old meanings, but all, however feeble, expose the status quo by showing that it is subjective and arbitrary. There is another way. From this perspective, subversive clowning is a liberalizing social form. Challenging, provoking, sometimes threatening, it imposes an alternative view, carefully framed in place and time, of what is. Although the shock value of the clown's performance marks it affectively as discontinuous from the expected, it is an integral part of the continuous flow of human action, not something outside of it.

The Wape have no terms for gender or kinship, but they lexically distinguish between men and women and an assortment of relatives with dogmatic views about the nature and expectations of each category. In a society where kinship and gender are coterminous with social relations, they are culturally charged targets for parody and ridicule. So in the sacral and secular clowning of the Niyel carnival, kinship and gender are folded over, shamelessly played with, and the "moral imagination" (Beidelman 1986) is amused.

This ludic deconstruction of kinship and gender dissembles the cultural order inherent in, for example, ideas about in-laws, mother's brothers, wives, mothers, sisters, and men and women generally, but, as we have seen, it is only a cognitive game. Thrilling and frightening possibilities are momentarily set up, but the temporal boundaries of carnival are unyielding. In the same way that Dante's excursion into the Hell of an anti-Christ reflects the glory of a reigning God, the anticulture clowning of the Niyel carnival reflects the dominance of Wape culture. But, this too, is deceptive. Carnival's power to deconstruct and subvert the expected and the ordinary does not end with the tossing off of costumes. Through the individual imagination, carnival sustains the heretical. As a nascent reservoir for remembered images of difference that challenge contemporary practice, carnival has a praxis of its own.

NOTES

The data for this chapter are based on six performances of the Niyel ritual in six different villages over a fifteen-year period extending from 1967 to 1982 and including my observations and interviews in the following five villages: Otei (June 1970), Wilkili (August 1970), Otemki (January 1971), Taute (October 1971), and Yebil (October 1982), as well as on McGregor's (1982) report on Teloute village's Niyel festival (January 1967). My indebtedness to all involved is obvious. The research was supported by a grant (1 RO1 MH 18039) from the National Institute of Mental Health and a Faculty Research Grant from the University of Vermont and facilitated by help from the government of Papua New Guinea and the Lumi Sub District headquarters; the New Guinea Research Unit of the Australian National University; the Franciscan Catholic Mission; the Christian Missions in Many Lands; Taute village and surrounding communities; and my co-field-worker, Joyce Slayton Mitchell. For critical comments on drafts of this chapter I am grateful to the participants of the ASAO clowning sessions. For comments on the revised version, I wish to thank Thomas O. Beidelman, Rena Lederman, Annegrete Pollard, Annette B. Weiner, and the ASAO Monograph Series editorial board, Lamont Lindstrom, Joyce Linnekin, and Nancy McDowell.

1. For representations of carnival in Europe, see Goethe (1987), LeRoy Ladurie (1979), and Macrobius (1969); for the Caribbean, see Hill (1972), Manning (1978), and Nunley and Bettelheim (1988); and for the Americas, Edmonson (1956), DaMatta (1984), Kinser (1990), and Turner (1967).

2. In Olo, the Wape language, *niyel* (*ningu* pl.) is the name for fish. In its festival usage, however, it refers to fish spirits that cause sickness. In Tok Pisin, the lingua franca for the Wape and much of Papua New Guinea,

the festival is called "sing sing long dewel pis" which translates into English as "festival of the fish spirit." In this chapter I refer to it as the Niyel festival or carnival. For more ethnographic information on its organization, meaning, and distribution, see Mitchell (1987, 1988a, 1988b, 1990b, and 1991) and McGregor (1982).

3. The Wape do not have a generic term for these spirits. I gloss them as *demons*, as all have the power to bring indiscriminate harm. Other than the Niyel, the names of the others often vary with the village.

4. Eco notes that "comedy and carnival are not instances of real transgressions: on the contrary, they represent paramount examples of law reinforcement. They remind us of the existence of the rule" (1984:6). Zijderveld makes a similar point in relation to "ceremonial fools," noting that "if these fools do express any opposition, it is meant to contribute to and stabilize the existing composition of society!" (1982:145). Nelson's (1990:174) recent book takes a similar view. All of these writers take the position that humorous subversion is ultimately in the service of the reproduction of culture. A distinction should be made, however, between carnivalesque inversions whose intention is satirization and which, through time, may indeed be subversive, and those whose intention is one of sincere imitation. Regarding the latter, the carnival inversion displayed in New York City's "voguing" balls by mostly black and Latin gay men and lesbians documented in Jennie Livingston's film, *Paris Is Burning*, does fit the safety valve theory. According to Brown, the participants dress up as supermodels, film stars, executives, and military officers, not to satirize them, but to imitate them as perfectly as possible (1991:14).

5. The term *Wapeland* is not an official designation but used in my writing to refer to the geographic area inhabited by the Wape.

6. See Mitchell (1987) for an account of fieldwork with the Wape and an overview of the society. Also see Mitchell (1979, 1988a) for discussions of Wape egalitarianism and the exchange system and Mitchell (1973, 1988b, 1990b) for data on Wape health and curing.

7. Apte (1985) provides a summary of anthropological studies of humor, including the comedic performance of clowns. Although the terms *clown, fool, jester, buffoon* (Steward 1931), and *mummer* are often interchangeable in the literature, Alford and Alford (1981:160) distinguish among the *clown*, the *fool*, and the *jester*, although they admit that the three "sometimes overlap in the same individuals." The clown "intentionally creates humor with himself or herself as the target or butt." The jester "intentionally creates humor, but not with himself or herself as the target or butt" while the fool "is the unintentional butt or target of the laughter of others." However, I am less sanguine than they are in the belief that most "humor specialists . . . fit predominantly into one category."

8. In the anthropological literature on sacral clowning in preliterate societies the term most frequently used is *ritual clown*, for example, Handelman (1981), Hieb (1972b, 1979), Honigmann (1942), Makarius

(1970), and Werbner (1986). But I have not followed this usage, preferring to adopt a wider interpretation of ritual (cf. Leach 1966) that denotes ritual clowning as either sacral or secular. I then use the term *sacred clown* (or *sacral clown*) to distinguish a clown type whose performance is related to a form of sacred power, in contradistinction to the *secular clown* whose performance, although highly ritualized in terms of stylized repetition, is performing independent from a supernatural nexus. On secular ritual, also see Moore and Myerhoff (1977).

9. The Western calendar was adopted by the Wape after Western contact and the learning of Tok Pisin. In terms of periodicity, Olo, the indigenous language, does not distinguish between days or the moon's cycles. Before European contact, the Niyel carnival was planned to coincide with a full moon to illuminate the dance ground and facilitate visitors' movement through the forest. Today, the carnival is still held as near as possible to the full moon for the same reasons.

10. McGregor (1982:59–61), however, records that the final rituals in the festival he studied occurred in the afternoon because the dancing had not continued long enough and the ground was too muddy.

11. Informants told me that clowning always had been a part of the Niyel festival but could not give a reason why it occurred at this festival and none of the others.

12. The mask is composed of a tall narrow framework that rests on the carrier's shoulders and is steadied by both hands holding a short pole extended down in front of him. His head and upper body are shrouded in fibers, while the upper frame of the mask is crowned with plumes of feathers. Extending from the frame are small painted panels and batons of fur or feathers, which bounce and wave when the mask is carried.

13. This public presentation of the penis, perceived by the audience as both shameful and ludicrous, is reminiscent of Nachman's (1982) account of the Nissen grand sorcerer's exhibitionism to initiates, although the cultural framing of the two performances are radically different.

14. These exhibitionistic dances now are rarely seen, although many mature villagers have witnessed them. According to villagers they were banned as lewd by both the government and the missions with the threat that transgressors would be jailed. Babcock also reminds us how the "religious crimes code" of the United States Bureau of Indian Affairs in the 1920s was targeted in part toward the scatological and sexual play of Indian clowns (1984:113). It would, however, have taken more than a jail threat to end the custom of Wape exhibitionistic dancing. Illegal gambling, for example, is a favorite activity among Wape men (Mitchell 1988a). Wape contact with Western sensibilities in New Guinea towns and outstations have had a strong negative impact on Wape customs that violate their own as well as the West's view of propriety. The fact that the Niyel carnival is an occasional source of passive exotic entertainment to government and mission personnel living on remote stations, plus the Wapes' own ambivalence to exhibitionistic dancing, probably hastened its demise.

Carnival Clowning in Wape Society 161

15. This is similar to the effect the Iroquois False Face clowns have on their audience. Fenton reports that "The False Faces evoke guarded smiles at fine performances, but no belly laughs" (1987:451), although he also notes that their "total effect is both terrifying and extremely humorous" (1987:406). However, unlike the Wape father- and mother-in-law, the False Faces "play practical jokes on lazy people" (Wallace 1969:82). Also see Stoller's description of the *Hauka* clowns among the Songhay who are "supposed to be funny as well as horrifying" (1984:167).

16. For a discussion of nudity as costume in classical Greek society, see Bonfante (1989).

17. Douglas (1968:365), in an earlier and theoretically important paper on joking, makes essentially the same point. Observing that "a joke is a play upon form," she adds that joking "brings into relation disparate elements in such a way that one accepted pattern is challenged by the appearance of another which in some way was hidden in the first."

18. The anthropological interpretation of ritual, as I am pursuing it here, has been heavily criticized by Lewis, who, based on his fieldwork with the Gnau, who live not far from the Wape, argues that there must be "positive grounds before we assume that we need to look for a symbolism or expression that is not apparent or explicit in the minds of the actors or in the reasons that they give for what they do" because this "may lead us in unbound speculation to light on what we want to find" (1980:220). There are merits to aspects of Lewis's argument, especially if the alien analyst assumes that there is "a single right meaning intrinsic to the object or action," as he infers for some unnamed anthropologists, but this is rarely the case. Hermeneutics is about interpretations, not dogma. An interpretation is just that, an informed speculation about meaning that, unlike a well-constructed scientific experiment, can be neither proven or disproven. As long as the provenience of the interpretation is specified, it is a form of inquiry in which all—local or visitor—can participate.

19. For example, one pioneering missionary, Donald McGregor, who was fluent in the Olo language and had attended several Niyel festivals, studying one in detail, was surprised when I pointed out to him a cross-dressed man dancing in a festival.

20. At the Yebil 1982 Niyel carnival, I observed one incident of scatological clowning, something I had neither seen nor heard about. During the Saturday afternoon dancing in the village plaza, a great commotion was caused by an uncostumed man running aggressively around the area carrying a basket of human feces that he threw about seemingly indiscriminately. One woman, angered by the feces thrown on her house ladder, lectured him loudly as she cleaned up the mess, to the further amusement of the crowd. This incident is similar to the one described by Bailey (1924), when the clowns of Taos Pueblo accidentally hit an old lady with a flying apple, and emphasizes the ambivalence some observers have toward clown performances. The background data I obtained on the Yebil 1982 performance are both incomplete and contradictory.

21. Plots four and ten through twelve were observed by McGregor (1982) in Telote village.

22. I regret that I did not pursue in more detail the implications of secular clowning while in the field or, at the very least, interview some of the actors about their satirical performances to seek out the inspiration for their skits. For example, are some of the skits take-offs on actual events or are they all just ideas that amuse the actors because they show someone at a disadvantage?

23. When I suggested to complainants that a man who is a sister's son is usually a mother's brother, this did not change the felt legitimacy of their complaints as sister's sons. For a brief description of the mother's brother–sister's son exchange relationship, see Mitchell (1988a).

24. While I do have evidence in specific families about mother-son conflict, these incidents were considered unusual by others.

25. Jung (1956:195), in a short paper appended to Radin's classic study of the Winnebago trickster figure, also notes the reversal similarities between the trickster in different societies and the European medieval carnival.

26. In the late 1960s, the missions began to retreat from their wholesale condemnation of the Niyel carnival, although it remains a major problem to reconcile theology and praxis in their mission work.

REFERENCES

Alford, Finnegan, and Richard Alford
    1981   A Holo-Cultural Study of Humor. *Ethos* 9:149–64.

Apte, Mahadev L.
    1985   *Humor and Laughter: An Anthropological Approach*. Ithaca: Cornell University Press.

Babcock, Barbara
    1984   Arrange Me into Disorder: Fragments and Reflections on Ritual Clowning. In *Rite, Drama, Festival, Spectacle: Rehearsals Toward a Theory of Cultural Performance*, ed. John J. MacAloon, pp. 102–28. Philadelphia: Institute for the Study of Human Issues.

Bailey, F. M.
    1924   Some Plays and Dances of the Taos Indians. *Natural History* 24:85–95.

Bakhtin, Mikhail
    1968   *Rabelais and His World*. Trans. Helene Iswolsky. Cambridge: Harvard University Press.

Beidelman, T. O.
  1986 *Moral Imagination in Kaguru Modes of Thought.* Bloomington: Indiana University Press.
Bernstein, Michael Andre
  1986 When the Carnival Turns Bitter: Preliminary Reflections Upon the Abject Hero. In *Bakhtin: Essays and Dialogues of His Work*, ed. Gary Saul Morson, pp. 99–121. Chicago: University of Chicago Press.
Bishop, George Victor
  1976 *The World of Clowns.* Los Angeles: Brooke House.
Bonfante, Larissa
  1989 Nudity as a Costume in Classical Art. *American Journal of Archaeology* 93:543–70.
Bouissac, Paul A. R.
  1972 Clown Performances as Metasemiotic Texts. *Language Sciences* 19:1–7.
  1982 The Meaning of Nonsense (Structural Analysis of Clown Performances and Limericks) In *The Logic of Culture*, ed. I. Rossi. South Hadley, Mass.: Bergin & Garvey.
Brown, Joe
  1991 'Cinderellas' Flock to 'Voguing' Balls. *International Herald Tribune*, August 12.
DeMatta, Roberto
  1984 Carnival in Multiple Planes. In *Rite, Drama, Festival, Spectacle: Rehearsals Toward a Theory of Cultural Performance*, ed. John J. MacAloon, pp. 208–40. Philadelphia: Institute for the Study of Human Issues.
Douglas, Mary
  1968 The Social Control of Cognition: Some Factors in Joke Perception. *Man* 3:361–76.
Dozier, E. P.
  1961 Rio Grande Pueblos. In *Perspectives in American Indian Culture Change*, ed. E. H. Spicer, pp. 94–186. Chicago: University of Chicago Press.
Eco, Umberto
  1984 The Frames of Comic "Freedom." In *Carnival!*, ed. Thomas A. Sebeok, pp. 1–9. Berlin: Mouton Publishers.
Edmonson, Munro
  1956 New Orleans Carnival. *Caribbean Quarterly* 4:233–45.
Engibarov, Leonid G.
  1988 Self-Portrait of a Clown. *UNESCO Courier* (January):16–22.

Fenton, William N.
    1987   *The False Faces of the Iroquois*. Norman: University of Oklahoma Press.

Gell, Alfred
    1975   *Metamorphosis of the Cassowaries: Umeda Society, Language and Ritual*. London: The Athlone Press.

Goethe, Johann W. von
    1987   The Roman Carnival. In *Time Out of Time: Essays on the Festival*, ed. Alessandro Falassi, pp. 13–34. Albuquerque: University of New Mexico Press.

Handelman, Don
    1981   The Ritual Clown: Attributes and Affinities. *Anthropos* 76:321–70.

Handelman, Don, and Bruce Kapferer
    1972   Forms of Joking Activity: A Comparative Approach. *American Anthropologist* 74:484–517.

Hieb, Louis Albert
    1972   *The Hopi Ritual Clown: Life as It Should Not Be*. Ann Arbor: University Microfilms.
    1979   The Ritual Clown: Humor and Ethics. In *Forms of Play of Native American Indians*, ed. Edward Norbeck and Claire R. Farrer, pp. 171–88. St. Paul: West Publishing Co.

Hill, Erroll
    1972   *The Trinidad Carnival: Mandate for a National Theatre*. Austin: University of Texas Press.

Honigmann, John J.
    1942   An Interpretation of the Social-Psychological Functions of the Ritual Clown. *Journal of Personality* 10:220–26.

Irvine, Judith T.
    1979   Formality and Informality in Communicative Events. *American Anthropologists*, 81:773–90.

Jenkins, Ron
    1986   Clowns, Politics and Miracles: The Epic Satire of Dario Fo. *American Theatre* 3:10–16.

Jung, C. G.
    1956   On the Psychology of the Trickster Figure. In *The Trickster: A Study in American Indian Mythology*, ed. Paul Radin, pp. 195–211. New York: Greenwood Press.

Kinser, Samuel
    1990   Carnival, American Style: Mardi Gras at New Orleans and Mobile. Chicago: University of Chicago Press.

Laski, Vera
    1958   *Seeking Life*. Philadelphia: American Folklore Society, vol. 50.

Leach, E. R.
  1966 Ritualization in Man in Relation to Conceptual and Social Development. *Philosophical Transactions of the Royal Society of London,* 251:403–08.
LeRoy Ladurie, Emmanuel
  1979 *Carnival in Romans.* Trans. Mary Feeney. New York: George Braziller.
Lewis, Gilbert
  1980 *Day of Shining Red: An Essay on Understanding Ritual.* Cambridge: Cambridge University Press.
Little, W. Kenneth
  1986 Pitu's Doubt: Entree Clown Self-Fashioning in the Circus Tradition. *Drama Review* 30:51–64.
Makarius Laura
  1970 Ritual Clowns and Symbolic Behaviour. *Diogenes* 69:44–73.
Manning, Frank
  1978 Carnival in Antigua (Caribbean Sea): An Indigenous Festival in a Tourist Economy. *Anthropos* 73:199–207.
McGregor, Donald E.
  1982 *The Fish and the Cross.* 2nd ed. Goroko: Melanesian Institute for Pastoral and Socio-Economic Service.
Macrobius, Ambrosius A. T.
  1969 *The Saturnalia.* New York: Columbia University Press.
Makarius, Laura
  1970 Ritual Clowns and Symbolical Behavior. *Diogenes* 69:44–73.
Mitchell, William E.
  1966 The Baby Disturbers: Sexual Behavior in a Childhood Contra-culture. *Psychiatry* 29:367–77.
  1973 A New Weapon Stirs up Old Ghosts. *Natural History* 82:74–84.
  1979 On Keeping Equal: Polity and Reciprocity among the New Guinea Wape. *Anthropological Quarterly* 51:5–15.
  1987 *The Bamboo Fire: Fieldwork with the New Guinea Wape.* 2nd ed. Prospect Heights, Ill.: Waveland Press.
  1988a The Defeat of Hierarchy: Gambling as Exchange in a Sepik Society. *American Journal of Ethnology* 15:638–57.
  1988b Magical Curing. (Videofilm.) Prospect Heights, Ill.: Waveland Press.
  1990a Why Wape Men Don't Beat Their Wives: Some Correlates of Domestic Tranquility in a New Guinea Society. In *Domestic Violence in Oceania,* ed. Dorothy Ayers Counts. Honolulu: University of Hawaii Press.
  1990b Therapeutic Systems of the Taute Wape. In *Sepik Heritage:*

Tradition and Change in Papua New Guinea, ed. N. Lutkehaus et al., pp. 428–38. Durham: Carolina Academic Press.
 1991 *The Living, Dead and Dying: Music of the New Guinea Wape.* Smithsonian Institution Folkways Cassette Series 04269 (Orig. Folkways Record Album FE 4269, 1978).

Moore, Sally F. and Barbara G. Myerhoff, eds.
 1977 *Secular Ritual.* Amsterdam: Van Gorcum.

Munroe, Ruth L.
 1955 *Schools of Psychoanalytic Thought.* New York: The Dryden Press.

Nachman, Steven R.
 1982 Anti-Humor: Why the Grand Sorcerer Wags His Penis. *Ethos* 10:117–35.

Nelson, T. G. A.
 1990 *Comedy: An Introduction to Comedy in Literature, Drama and Cinema.* Oxford: Oxford University Press.

Nunley, John W., and Judith Bettelheim
 1988 *Caribbean Festival Arts.* Seattle: University of Washington Press.

Steward, Julian H.
 1931 The Ceremonial Buffoon of the American Indian. *Papers of the Michigan Academy of Science, Arts and Letters* 14:187–207.

Stoller, Paul
 1984 Horrific Comedy: Cultural Resistance and the Hauka Movement in Niger. *Ethos* 12:165–88.

Swabey, Marie Taylor Collins
 1961 *Comic Laughter.* New Haven: Yale University Press.

Turner, Victor
 1967 Carnival, Ritual, and Play in Rio de Janeiro. In *Time Out of Time: Essays on the Festival,* ed. Allessandro Falassi, pp. 76–90. Albuquerque: University of New Mexico Press.

Wallace, Anthony
 1969 *The Death and Rebirth of the Seneca.* New York: Alfred A. Knopf.

Wark, Lynette, and L. A. Malcom
 1969 Growth and Development of the Lumi Child in the Sepik District of New Guinea. *Medical Journal of Australia* 2:129–36.

Werbner, Pnina
 1986 The Virgin and the Clown: Ritual Elaboration in Pakistani Migrants' Weddings. *Man* 21:227–50.

Zijderveld, Anton C.
 1982 *Reality in a Looking-Glass: Rationality through an Analysis of Traditional Folly.* London: Routledge and Kegan Paul.

WHEN SHE REIGNS SUPREME: CLOWNING AND CULTURE IN ROTUMAN WEDDINGS

Vilsoni Hereniko

As a boy growing up on Rotuma, I took for granted that at weddings an old woman made a fool of herself and other people as well. Only recently did my interest in indigenous Pacific theater make me realize that clowning was more than just a funny old woman ordering the chiefs and the men to do her bidding. In fact, the clown's behavior during weddings is an integral part of the celebrations, and the wedding a microcosm of Rotuman culture. To study clowning in this social context is to gain insights, not only into the customs and values of Rotumans, but also into the reasons for the existence of clowning.[1]

In this essay I focus on the sacred clown who performs in traditional Rotuman weddings. I use the term *sacred* to mean religious, while the word *clown* refers to an individual whose antics cause overt signs of mirth or laughter among spectators. These data were gathered in December 1987 and January 1988, during research visits to Rotuma. I returned to the island again in December 1989 and observed two more weddings, where two different clowns performed. Though I draw comparisons with these two later weddings where appropriate, the case study presented here is of the 1987 wedding.[2]

According to Apte (1983:190), humor displays occur during rituals performed at the following times: at calendrical ceremonies to mark the change of seasons, such as harvesting activities or anniversaries of prophets and saints, and at rituals performed to mark important transitions in an individual's life—birth, initiation, puberty, and marriage.[3] An official clown is usually featured at calendrical ceremonies, whereas relatives and friends take the formal clown's place at rituals marking important transitions.

Ritual clowning has been observed in many parts of the world, including North America (e.g., Steward 1930, Bricker 1973), sub-Saharan Africa (e.g., Norbeck 1963; Evans-Pritchard 1929), and Southern India (e.g., Marriott 1968; Miller 1973). Werbner's article (1986) on Pakistani immigrants' wedding rites in Britain is one of the rare studies that deals with clowning in a wedding context. Nearer to Rotuma, Tanner (personal communication) witnessed female Fijian clowns performing in a gift-giving ceremony in a man's village (Savatu) years after he had been married. Women of the groom's clan, dressed in overalls and riding hobby horses, mock-attacked the bride's male relatives, who accepted the ambush in good humor. Later the clowns attended a ceremony on their own where they drank a ceremonial drink and performed "lewd" dances. Rutz (personal communication), another anthropologist who did fieldwork in Fiji in the 1960s, also witnessed women dressed as men at the birth of a chief's son performing "lewd" dances and mock copulation. Tanner's and Rutz's accounts suggest that sexual clowning occurs at occasions where fertility is a vital element.

Similarly, ceremonies related to agriculture are also often fertility related. In Fiji, male clowns enforced embargoes on the use of crops or lifted the taboos at the beginning of the first-fruit festivals (Clunie and Ligairi 1983). Tahitians also performed first-fruit festivals that included pantomimes, choral chanting, and erotic dancing intended to invoke the procreative forces of nature (Oliver 1974:93).

Role reversal—when those in authority are ridiculed—is also widely distributed in Oceania including Fiji (e.g., Diaper 1853, Wilkes 1845), Samoa (e.g., Shore 1978, Sloan 1941, Kneubuhl 1987), Tonga (Hau'ofa 1988, Bott 1982), Tokelau (e.g., Huntsman and Hooper 1975), Tahiti (e.g., Oliver 1974, Henry 1928, Ellis 1834), and Hawaii (Emerson 1965, Luomala 1984).

In terms of clowns and gender, the picture is somewhat mixed. According to Makarius (1970), clowns in North American Indian cultures are usually males invested with magical powers. This is similar to Samoa, where the lead comedian in a *fale aitu* (comic sketch) is always male (see Sinavaiana, this volume), and unlike Tokelau, where both male and female clowns play equally important roles in their version of the Samoan comic sketch, or the *arioi* society of Tahiti, which drew its members from both sexes.

Numerous theories have been offered to explain the functions of humor (see, for example, Mitchell, introduction, this volume, and Apte 1983: 204–05). Radcliffe-Brown (1940) proposes several functions of joking among kin and nonkin relationships, such as the release of tension and resulting avoidance of conflict; Lowie (1920)

Clowning and Culture in Rotuman Weddings

proposes that social control is the main function; Hammond (1964) asserts that humor provides emotional catharsis and indirect communication; and Murdock (1949) suggests that humor releases sexual impulses and aggression. According to Apte, studies of humor in religious contexts emphasize "the psychological benefits of humor by claiming that it satisfies the need for cathartic release of tension and of antisocial feelings and for vicarious gratification of sexual urges and other infantile desires usually repressed in normal social interactions" (1983:205).

Studies by Shore (1977, 1978), Kneubuhl (1987), and Sinavaiana (this volume) all concur that the comic sketches of Samoa serve as an informal avenue for resolving conflict, with less emphasis on vicarious gratification of sexual impulses. Huntsman and Hooper's 1975 study of clowning in Tokelau concludes by asserting that the performance of the female clowns is a conservative force that does not basically challenge the normal structure of male-dominated Tokelauan society.

This essay examines clowning on Rotuma to see how it relates to the various theories summarized above. Clowning is depicted as multivocal and serving many different functions, some overt and others covert. Though largely a conservative force, clowning has the potential to effect changes at the sociopsychological level. As practiced today, the Rotuman clown's functions are mainly secular; in the past, the evidence indicates she was a sacred clown that mediated between human beings and powerful forces in nature.

The Context

Rotuma is situated approximately 470 kilometers north of Fiji. Located at the crossroads of Micronesia, Melanesia, and Polynesia, Rotuman culture has been influenced by all three regions. About 12 kilometers long and at its widest 5 kilometers across, Rotuma has a population of approximately 2,500. The general scholarly consensus is that the original inhabitants came from either Melanesia or Micronesia, followed by Samoan and Tongan invasions about the beginning of the seventeenth century (e.g., Gardiner 1898; Churchward 1938; Eason 1951). Christianity was introduced in 1839, and in 1878 there were religious wars between the Catholics and the Methodists. Warfare culminated in cession to Britain in 1881; since then, Rotuma has been administered as part of Fiji, although its culture and language are different. About one-third of the inhabitants are Catholics; two-thirds are Methodists. Although the majority regard themselves as Christians, beliefs in the efficacy of traditional spirits or gods to punish transgressors of traditional norms still persist.

The Rotuman social system is based on the concept of related individuals who have a common ancestry. These individuals constitute a kin group, with a claim to rights in a particular piece of land. As Rotumans inherit privileges from both parents, each individual has eight kin groups, corresponding to the home territory of each of their great-grandparents.

Rotuma's chiefs, whose titles are inherited, wield little political influence today. At life-crisis ceremonies they may be seen seated in prominent positions; their role today is mainly ceremonial. A male chief heads each village or district on the island but rarely impinges on the day-to-day affairs of his subjects. Such was not the case in the past, when Rotuman society was much more hierarchical, and a king was overall ruler of the island.

Traditional Rotuman culture has always had a strict code of conduct regarding premarital sex for girls, as reflected in the emphasis on virginity for the bride. The arrival of Christianity with its own list of prohibitions further reinforced beliefs in the value of female chastity before marriage, obedience, respect toward parents and elders, politeness in interpersonal relationships, and hard work, among other well-known Christian virtues. As marriages in the past were arranged, it was common for couples not to have met until the wedding day. Today, most couples marry out of love; however, the gift exchanges and some rituals of old are still practiced.

Rotuma is still relatively isolated, although a wharf built in the 1970s and an airstrip opened in 1981 have made modern goods and equipment, as well as Western ideas, much more accessible. Copra used to be the main source of income, but since the early 1970s it has been surpassed by remittances from relatives living in Fiji, Australia, New Zealand, and the United States. Concrete houses, refrigerators, indoor toilets, motorbikes, and pickup trucks are now commonplace.[4]

This study of the Rotuman clown contains examples that are obviously "evolved traditional" (Kaeppler 1989:236). At best, it captures the state of the art of Rotuman clowning in the latter part of the 1980s and casts some light on an age-old institution that is now betwixt and between as it vies for a slot amid shifting values and rapid changes.

Clowning and Culture in Rotuman Weddings 171

A Case Study of a Clowning Performance

Unlike other parts of the Pacific, such as Tonga and Samoa, where clowning at weddings is usually by women who perform spontaneously, Rotumans have an invited clown whose role is formal. In theory, she is the supreme ruler of the wedding and all the associated rituals.

A woman past childbearing age and known for her abilities at clowning is formally approached weeks before the wedding by the bride's family, who solicits her services. But before she can agree, custom dictates that she seek permission from her district chief to take up this role. A formal clown is usually the best guarantee that wedding guests will be entertained, for although typically there is spontaneous clowning by close relatives of the bride and groom during the wedding celebrations, their humorous antics are episodic and brief. In this chapter I make occasional reference to spontaneous clowning by what I call *funny women;* my main focus, however, is on the invited clown, the *hän mane'äk su* (the woman who plays the wedding).

In the past, the main consideration for the choice of clown was skill; today, relation to the bride's parents is the main factor. Growing acquisitiveness among Rotumans motivates relatives of the bride to want to keep within their kin group the rewards of fine mats[5] and food that are customarily bestowed on the clown. Second, a close relative is easier to influence; she can be told frankly where the boundaries of license lie. If she oversteps the boundary of "privileged expression" (Shore 1977:311) — as defined by those who selected her — she can be denied the customary rewards without fear of retaliation.[6]

Figure 1 is a drawing of the typical physical setting for wedding celebrations on Rotuma. The seating arrangements symbolize the union of two kin groups through marriage. Paradoxically, the oppositional arrangement of kin groups also symbolizes the tensions inherent in marriage. On Rotuma, a person marries into another kin group and acquires new obligations along with a wife or husband.

The clown wore a bright red dress on this day and carried with her a three-foot stick. Red flowers adorned her hair, which was pulled away from her face and tied in a bun at the back. She also wore a yellow grass skirt around her waist, and where her grass skirt ended could be seen a white cotton material that she wore

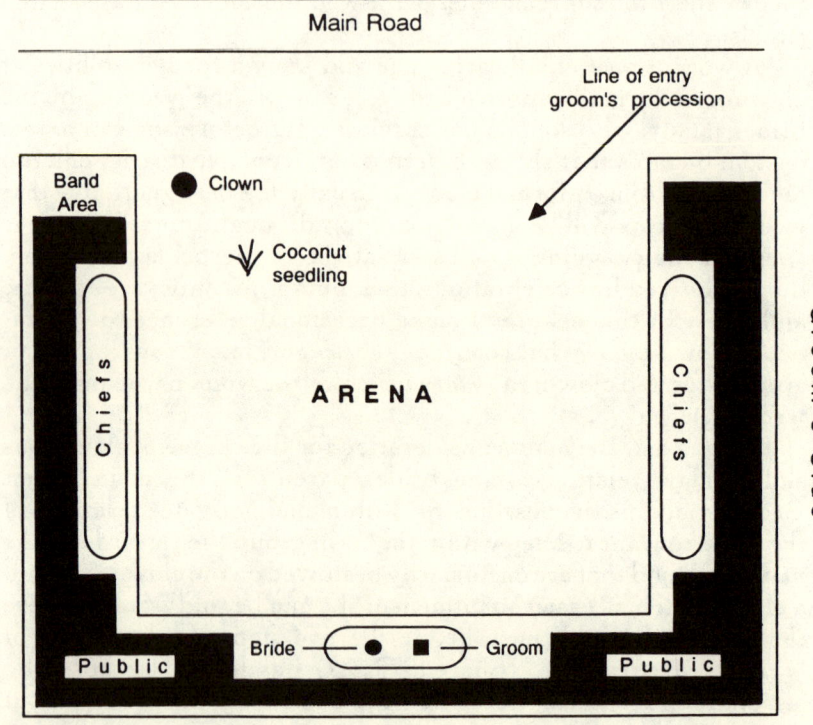

FIG. 1. Typical setting for Rotuman wedding celebration.

under her dress. She carried a fan, and occasionally she pulled out a handkerchief to wipe the perspiration from her face.

About 7:30 in the morning the bride, her relatives, and the chiefs of her district took their seats underneath and around the temporary shelter—built especially for the celebrations—to await the arrival of the groom's party scheduled for 9 o'clock. As people sat around waiting the band played some songs and the clown tried to stimulate some activity among the spectators. Occasionally she succeeded in forcing someone to dance with her in the arena.

The hired band for the wedding consisted of a group of men whose equipment included an electronic keyboard, several electric guitars, and loudspeakers. They played mainly contemporary and popular songs in the English language; as a concession to the assembled company, they occasionally sang a Rotuman song in a pop style. Youths and adults alike danced in disco style.

As soon as the groom's party appeared on the main road the singing and dancing ceased. The groom's procession squatted low on the ground as a mark of respect. At the front of the procession was the groom, his best man, and their "chaperone"—a woman skilled in Rotuman oratory—who was invited to request entry into the arena on the groom's behalf. Behind them were women carrying the fine mats followed by more women laden with mats of lesser importance and yards of colorful material.[7] The chiefs from the groom's side were next; at the rear were the men carrying the *kava* (piper methysticum) and baskets of food.

After a favorable response by an orator from the bride's side, the groom's party stood up and approached the center of the arena. The groom took his seat on top of the fine mats on which sat his bride, while the chiefs from the groom's district sat on the ground to the groom's right, to face the chiefs of the bride's side. Women relatives of the groom screened the temporary shelter with their colorful fabric—in the olden days fine mats would have been used—to signal the beginning of the play frame. The band played a lively tune, and the merrymaking began.

Between the period when the groom's party joined the bride's and the lunch hour, a number of rituals were performed, in the following order: the church wedding service, the symbolic cutting of hair for both bride and groom, a public display of fine mats to be used for sleeping purposes for the couple, the wrapping of fine mats around the bride and groom, and the carrying of the bride and groom from the bride's side of the arena to the groom's side.

The band played most of the time, sometimes even during rituals. Those who were not directly involved in the rituals danced or fooled around, led by the clown. Part of the clown's role was to undercut the seriousness of the rituals—and what they symbolize—by making the audience laugh.[8] Sometimes she hurried people or hurled mock insults at them. The bridal couple, however, was ignored; they were outside the clown's sphere of influence. As bride and groom, they were symbols of procreation on the wedding day— objects of veneration. Their time is spent sitting quietly on fine mats, waiting for rituals to be performed to them, and observing the unbridled antics of the clown and those she chooses to dance with or ridicule in public. Like ritual, with its prescribed procedures and solemnity, the restrained attitude of the couple contrasted starkly with the unbridled activity of the clown and her troupe of funny women. The festivities culminated in feasting at about 12:30 in the afternoon, after which the crowds started to disperse.

The Clown's Role

The clown is chief entertainer. It is her responsibility to ensure that the wedding guests have a good time, which means lots of laughter and dancing. After all, assessment of her success or failure as a clown depends on her ability to entertain the assembled crowd.

Although it is true that wedding guests are predisposed to merrymaking—particularly if the marriage has the blessing of both kin groups—considerable skill is still required to keep people entertained throughout the morning. The clown has to get it just right; she has to be funny without a hint of showing off.[9] Though her rule is supreme, she is expected to be able to laugh at herself. For example, when she shouted in English "Come on, music!" or said her name was "Princess Sakura," people laughed at her English, knowing that she could barely speak the white man's language.[10] She was indirectly poking fun at her lack of Western education by elevating her status through the use of a "superior" language. This added to the humor; everyone knew she was just an ordinary housewife from across the road.

The clown's success also depends on the cooperation of her audience. However, increasing contact with Fiji and the rest of the world means young people today care little for the significance of the clown's role, and even young chiefs or the district officer representing the Fiji government on the island may not feel as bound by custom as their predecessors. The clown therefore has to remain within the boundary of licensed behavior. The boundary, however, is imaginary and undefined; it is simply assumed that she, and everyone else, know where the limits are.

My recent observations of Rotuman weddings bear testimony to a growing uncertainty about the clown's role in present-day weddings. In one wedding the police band from Fiji provided the music. Many Fiji Rotumans attended, and one, in particular, was acting as the master of ceremonies and presuming to be the coordinator of the day's proceedings. In one instance he announced over the microphone that the next dance was "the couple's dance." When the music came on, the clown—who did not understand this custom—was the

Clowning and Culture in Rotuman Weddings

first to stand up with her partner. The emcee hurried over to the clown and told her to sit down. She obeyed. When interviewed later, she said her instinctive reaction was to tell the Fiji Rotuman that as clown she had supreme authority over him and everyone else. But because her usurper has a high position in the Fiji government, she felt obliged to submit. That the clown did not assert her rights is significant; this incident symbolizes her ambivalent position today and the power that urban Rotumans wield—deliberately or otherwise—over their rural compatriots.

Rotuman Values

Clowning is related to a society's values in an inverse way. For example, the Rotuman clown, by ostensibly subverting the important Rotuman values of behaving appropriately, containing one's sexuality, and maintaining social harmony, evokes laughter from the spectators. Paradoxically, the clown's violation of these values reinforces them at the same time. Furthermore, her behavior—and that of other funny women who join in the fun—provides another view of the structure of social relations, which invigorates and unhinges the foundations of the patriarchal view of society, albeit temporarily. Although it is true that clowning and comedy "remind us of the existence of the rule" (Eco 1984:6), they also remind us that such rules do not exist without popular support.

The following transgressions of important Rotuman values by the clown are presented in terms of the frequency with which she violated them.

Behaving Appropriately

The female clown causes amusement by behaving like a male. In a society where the chiefs are men, role reversal is particularly enjoyed. This wedding was no exception; during the celebration, the clown

- Ordered a group of girls to bring her a drink.
- Ordered some women to clap their hands, three others to pick three men to dance.
- Forced two men who had refused to dance earlier to stand up and dance.
- Ordered those dancing in the shade, including the district officer, to move out into the sunshine.

- Poked a man in the ribs and told him to dance.
- Admonished and swore at the band boys who said that she "smelled of shit."
- Scolded the band for stopping the singing too soon after she had picked a man to dance.
- Refused to agree to a suggestion that the chiefs be served the "ceremonial drink" before lunch.
- Refused to allow another woman to dance with the young man she was dancing with.
- Beat a dog that had wandered into the arena with her stick.
- Ran her stick across the corrugated iron ceiling and shouted at the top of her voice.
- Forced a white Australian man, who was videotaping, to dance.
- Hurried the band whenever it was slow to play.
- Ordered several people belonging to the same clan to dance.
- Threatened to beat up several people who refused to obey her orders to dance.
- Grabbed hold of a chief's waist and led him along.
- Said she was taking a chief home at the end of the wedding.
- Ordered two chiefs to stand in the hot sun.
- Ordered a drunken man to leave the arena.
- Commanded the crowd to address her as "Princess Sakura."

In all the above, the clown was in one way or another claiming her prerogative as supreme ruler of the wedding. During the period of liminality,[11] the world was turned upside down; the weak (women) became strong, and the strong (men) were obliged to submit.

In instances when the clown ordered other females to do her bidding, the spectators laughed because the clown's arrogant manner inverted the norm of polite behavior that Rotumans regard as proper and fitting in social interactions. Her rudeness and macho behavior (running her stick across the ceiling, for example) were incongruous with her gender and context. Her behavior, however, was reminiscent of what men do, particularly those who throw their weight around because of intoxication or arrogance. In fact, she was mocking the typical macho image and reflecting back to the men their own behavior.

The higher the status of the clown's target, the louder the laughter. In the case of the chiefs, the clown and the old women sitting close to her took great delight in getting their own back. Once or twice the clown was annoyed at the reluctance of some chiefs to obey her orders to dance, and women close by were quick to remind her of her powers and to offer advice. Their coaxing was a challenge that the clown always took up, and in one or two difficult

Clowning and Culture in Rotuman Weddings

cases, she even went down on her knees in mock deference. The reluctant chiefs obliged in the end. What was not achieved by force was won through exaggerated politeness. By humbling herself, the clown focused attention on the chiefs' stubbornness, if not arrogance. Her message was: "Look, I can force you to obey me, I can even hit you with my stick, but I won't. Instead, I'll go down on my knees to beg you, sir." By embarrassing her chief, in this inverted manner, she won. Of course it can never be proved that this was her intention; the point is that the clown's actions were open to different readings and therefore potent.

The clown was accompanied by several old women, secure in their roles as wives and mothers. A woman from the groom's side challenged men from the bride's side to a karate duel, and the taking up of this challenge by a man caused much hilarity.[12] The karate duel consisted of exaggerated arm-swinging movements and manly posturing. There was no actual body contact between man and woman despite the swinging arms and kicking feet. Contrary behavior was often the cause of humor.

Controlling Sexuality

Sexual explicitness in public is anathema to Rotumans because it draws attention to the individual. The clown and other funny women, however, violated taboos on provocative sexual behavior. Through gestures, rolling eyes, mock faints, and erotic idiom they improvised sexual innuendos that delighted the spectators. Watching the clown and her funny women provided vicarious gratification for the spectators. Even the chiefs joined in. The clown stimulated laughter by the following means:

- She said she was in love with the Australian video man.
- When the Australian stood up to dance, she grabbed his hand and pulled him around the arena, chased by a Rotuman man who pretended to be the clown's native lover. The clown grabbed the Australian's hand and both eloped to another part of the arena. She shouted as she ran: "I don't want a Rotuman man." At the end of the skit, she grabbed the white man's face and smacked a kiss on his lips, surprising everyone, if not herself.
- When her husband danced with a young girl, she acted jealous.
- When she saw her husband she announced, "I told him to stay at home today; I have no idea what he's doing here."
- After the clown had picked the same man to dance a second time, the man's wife shouted, "Why are you always picking my hus-

band? Are you in love with him?" The clown replied, "Your husband is bald. Who would want him?"
- She picked a young man to dance, rolled her eyes, then did a mock faint on the ground. She did the same with the Australian.
- She held a chief by the waist and directed his movements.

The most explicit sexual come-on was initiated by an aggressive funny woman. Grabbing a chief by the waist, she guided him over a lone coconut seedling that was in the arena so that its leaves brushed against the inside of their thighs as they strode giggling over it. "Making love to a coconut seedling" was replayed a few times; the audience loved it. Mock sexual activity delighted the audience, as though suggestive sexual activity brought out into the open what could only be entertained in the mind. What was usually taboo in public was now flaunted for everyone to witness.

Maintaining Social Harmony

To observers, the clown's behavior provokes conflict. Since the clown is from the bride's side, male relatives of the groom are often the butt of her humor. She sits next to the kin group of the bride, an indication of her alliance with them. In cases where she is a close relative, the clown is a biased mediator; the mock opposition appears therefore to favor the bride's kin. Yet, by inversion, her mock antagonism becomes a form of social control. The following actions of the clown were directed at the groom's party:

- She ordered the chiefs from the groom's side to dance or stand in the hot sun, but rarely did she order the chiefs from the bride's side.[13]
- When the young men from the groom's side were carrying the bride on their shoulders and it seemed the bride was going to fall, the clown shouted, "Why is it that all the men from the groom's side are weak and ugly!"
- Sometimes she shouted rude or threatening comments to the relatives of the groom. For example, when a funny woman from the groom's side went over to challenge a man from the bride's side to a karate duel, she shouted to her, "Hurry up, and choose your partner quickly!"
- She acted as though the funny women from the bride's side were her allies; not once did she criticize their behavior.

There are certain tensions that are common in any marriage. Because relatives of the couple can vent their frustrations, fears, and tensions in mock banter or anger during the marriage celebrations, potential sources of conflict are channeled creatively in socially acceptable ways. In a population of less than three thousand, most are related or at least acquainted with one another. As to be expected, a close-knit community places a high premium on harmonious relationships.[14] The process of diffusing tension through humor in a socially acceptable frame is therefore necessary.

The uncontrolled behavior of the clown and the funny women burlesques male authority and inverts its normal expression. Part of the humor arises from the juxtaposition of male and female characteristics in the clown and the funny women. Male strength and authority combined with female temperament results in chaos. As the clown and her troupe of funny women move around, forcing the chiefs and other men to dance or stand in the hot sun, hurling mock insults at one another, hitting a dog that yelps and runs across the arena, it becomes obvious that without restraint and control, life is impossible. By hurling mock insults at the opposing kin group and engaging in a mock karate duel with a male from the opposing kin, a negative picture of conflict—between males and females and between kin groups—is presented. Peace is valued all the more.

Potential conflict could be due to a number of factors. Sometimes the parents or relatives of the bride or groom may not agree with the choice of partner, the kind of wedding planned, or the venue. Parents of the bridal couple may be ambivalent about losing control over a loved one, whether the pair will get along, even where they will live. Because of the extensive work weaving the fine mats and preparing the wedding feast—which should be so plentiful that the guests may eat as much as they want and still take leftovers home—close relatives of the couple are easily upset by criticism, intended or imagined. Matters trivial to outsiders take on an incredible significance, as illustrated by the following incident.

Before midday the couple was taken to the church for a Christian service and ceremony. At the appropriate moment, the groom was asked to lift his bride's veil. This he did, but he did not kiss the bride. Further along in the church ceremony, the bride's father stood up to seek an explanation. "Is it because my daughter is black?" he asked. "I know some people say my daughter is as black as stone; if the groom loves my daughter, why didn't he kiss her?" Silence. Startled to hear such direct communication, the congregation recognized impending conflict. The seconds ticked away as the ominous question hung in the air, waiting for an answer. The groom's father stood up, looked around, and began: "Your daughter is beautiful. Of course my son loves her. I apologize. It is our fault. Perhaps it is ignorance of the ways of the white man that my son did not behave appropriately." Though brief, the groom's father's attempt at reparation was moving and his voice shaky. At the end of his apology, the groom's father bent down and kissed the bride. A hymn was sung and the ceremony continued. All seemed well again.[15]

Practices of the Past

Today the Rotuman clown's performance is secular, but it is likely that in the past her performance was sacred and linked to spirit powers. To explore this possibility I examine theories on the origins of theater elsewhere and other early ethnographic evidence.[16] The divine theory traces the origin of drama to a divine force or spirit. For example, Fijians of old believed that the composer of traditional dances was spiritually possessed by a *veli* (a rustic and contrary gnome), who gave the dances and songs to the composer that he, in turn, taught to the villagers (Clunie and Ligairi 1983:55).

The evolutionary approach claims that drama developed from the human need to control and influence the natural and unforseen forces around us. Through rituals and sacrifices, humans sought to dominate the elements or other powerful forces or, failing that, to harness their services. Those who propose this view refer to Asian cultures or to Aristotle's claim that the beginnings of classical tragedy were in the sacred dithyramb of the Dionysian sect (Echeruo 1981; Owemeyala 1972; Horn 1981).

Horn argues that because of human limitations as material beings, we are fearful of what we see as immaterial for it cannot be contained or dominated. Our impulse "is to concretize, to make the invisible visible, the infinite finite, and the superhuman human" (1981:183). As a result, many societies have generated multiple gods who control the elements of wind, sun, and rain or the mysterious forces that cause illness. As human beings desire communication with the gods, the supernatural becomes physicalized—in trees, rocks, birds, fishes, animals, or as other human beings. Rotumans, for example, believed in family gods in the form of sharks, turtles, and sacred rocks with humanlike shapes (MacGregor 1932). They also believed that when human beings were possessed, they became mediums whose utterances were direct communications from the spirits, not unlike the explanations offered by Sinavaiana (this volume) regarding Samoan clowning. Horn argues further that if a human being is believed to be a representative of the supernatural world, then he is a "person with unique knowledge and powers who leads and supervises the worship of and ritual communication with the unseen agencies" (1981:184).

It is probable that the Rotuman clown was formerly considered to be either a medium or representative of the spirits and not personally responsible for what she said or did. This helps to explain why the chiefs today (and other men and women as well) submit to her abusive and outrageous antics. Rotuma's most famous clown, who enthralled wedding guests with her performances during the 1960s, used to blacken her face. The blackened face (Rotumans refer to the *atua*, 'ghost,' as either black or red),[17] the symbolic elevation of the bride and groom on fine mats, and the fear of offending the spirits expressed by the clown who featured in the 1987 wedding are reasons supporting this speculation.

Gardiner mentions the use of a stick held above the head and moved rhythmically to and fro with the singing during prayers to a spirit in a Rotuman ceremony for a firstborn (1898:465). It is possible that the stick carried by the clown, even today, has a similar significance—as a symbol of procreation and hopes for many children. As a phallic symbol, the stick has not escaped the notice of modern day Rotumans, who sometimes use it as a hobby horse or a substitute penis when fooling around with the clown. Preoccupation with sexual imagery was suggestive behavior that was probably intended as communication with the spirits. Morenhout (cited in Oliver 1974:923–24) provides a similar explanation for Tahiti's *arioi* (strolling players) society's obsession with the sexual act.

A photograph of Rotuma's famous clown, Ioane (mentioned above), is instructive of the clown's dramatis persona. Along with her blackened face, she wore a man's shirt and short pants. Over her head was a cap, which looked like elastic pants; between her lips was a cigarette. As the clown's behavior displayed male characteristics, it follows that male attire was worn. Women clowns dressed as men are recorded for many societies elsewhere; in Oceania these include Fiji (Tanner 1990),[18] Tokelau (Huntsman and Hooper 1975: 427), and the Lusi-Kaliai who perform at ceremonies for the firstborn (Counts and Counts, this volume). But there are no hard and fast rules; rather, it is for each clown to improvise a persona.

Another practice of the past (Vaivao Fatiaki, personal communication) involved relatives of the groom arriving on the night before the wedding with food and implements and hiding these around the area of the bride's home. The bride's relatives then tried to discover where the goods had been hidden in order to steal or destroy whatever they could find. During this time, the clown had license to beat up people, particularly those from the groom's side. Her abusive nature—in this instance and during the wedding proper— earned her the name *hän re mane'äk su* (the woman who desecrates the wedding). Over the years this term became *hän mane'äk su* (the woman who plays the wedding). These different meanings indicate a shift in emphasis in the clown's role: from being essentially a religious icon in the past to a secular clown today.[19]

Conculsion

On Rotuma, the age-old institution of choosing a female clown called the *hän mane'äk su* to preside over wedding ceremonies still continues. The woman chosen is usually someone deeply knowledgeable about Rotuman culture. Though female, she takes on male characteristics, and chiefs and men who in everyday life outrank her must submit to her wishes.

Traditional Rotuman society has a strict code of conduct, upon which virtues of fundamental Christianity were later superimposed. Personal relationships are guided by ideals and values of social harmony, and polite behavior and sensitivity to other people are the hallmark of the ideal Rotuman personality. But Rotumans are human beings with unresolved tensions and frustrations that need expression; play is essential, therefore, for the well-being of Rotumans and for human beings everywhere. As Parman (1979:330) observes, we need dreams during the night and play during the day, "to prevent epilepsy, internal time-locking, madness, or other maladaptive aspects of synchrony."

But the wedding frame does more than provide a vent for the dissipation of pent-up feelings, for momentarily shaking off the constraints of culture and religion, and for exploring a world of considerable license. It offers a safe context for experimenting with exotic ways of behaving. To the foreign wedding guest, this frame of privileged expression is without rules.[20] But rules exist, even if they are etched only in the minds of those Rotumans steeped in their culture. As the clown moves around pointing her stick and ordering individuals to do her bidding, the scene she creates is one of inverted order—with the clown as chief—punctuated with moments of disorder. In entertaining the crowd, she inverts and subverts the rules of correct behavior. The chiefs and men are

Clowning and Culture in Rotuman Weddings 183

displaced from their elevated positions, and the customary hierarchical structure of social relations is dissolved. The stage is set for play; tensions between males and females, chiefs and commoners, and different kin groups are diffused, displaced, or resolved. Unlike real life, however, there is no physical combat between those pitted against each other, for laughter reigns supreme in the clown's world of make-believe.

But the clown does more than provoke laughter through mock insults, burlesque, exaggeration, use of irony, or deriding others or herself. Through humor she reinforces the values of Rotuman society: having a good time, polite and respectful behavior, restrained sexuality, and interpersonal harmony. By lampooning important persons and values, the clown reminds everyone who the chiefs are and what values make up the cornerstones of Rotuman society. Indeed, the Rotuman clown's use of humor endorses the general theories of social control and carthasis, indirect communication, and vicarious gratification of sexual impulses.

Rotuman clowning, however, does not merely maintain and reinforce the status quo. Chiefs and other men who have been subjected to a clown's destructive and authoritarian behavior at a wedding will have been invigorated by a view of the world where the women reign. It is plausible that such "shock therapy" (Babcock 1984:103) will challenge and perhaps modify, albeit undramatically and unnoticably, their view of women as the weaker sex or their own chauvinistic attitudes. As is the case with Tokelauans (Huntsman and Hooper 1975:428), the indirect communication from the women to the men is this: chaos will ensue if men do not temper their strength and authority with dignity and control.

The antics of the sacred clown and her funny women provide the community—in the same way that the cinema and theater do in industrialized societies—with plenty to talk and laugh about for a long while. The status of an old woman may even be elevated to that of star actor in the eyes of the community. On the other hand, another may be labeled a show-off, and even another useless, never to be asked again. Chiefs may even be criticized for being too proud or arrogant to join in the fun. In the case of the clown whose relatives refused to thank her at the end of the wedding, the experience will have given those involved an opportunity to assess their commitment to each other and to the values that are important to them. Clowning in Rotuman weddings is both a conservative and a progressive force.

If indeed the origin of clowning is in religious beliefs about fertility and the role of the spirits in procreation, then the clown was an integral part of ritual. As the representative of the supernatural world, she supervised the rituals that were enacted to invoke the gods to act. Assuming the persona of a spirit, she was neither male nor female, human nor divine, but a liminal being. Her laughter was the mocking laughter of the gods who ruled over mortals and whose power was manifested in bad luck, illness, inability to conceive, and thunder and hurricanes.

But why should humor be juxtaposed with serious ritual? Perhaps Cox (1969:70) has the answer when he tells us that laughter is "a higher form of consciousness, a way of confronting the higher realities on which the whole of existence rests." Perhaps it is only when ritual and humor are juxtaposed as "a double exposure on one plate" (Rodway 1962:113) that reflexivity can be fruitful. The answer may never be fully understood. As scholars, we have a tendency to categorize and theorize so that we end up with definite answers to puzzling questions; however, in matters where humor and ritual, or restraint and unbridled license, are juxtaposed, I am inclined to agree with Babcock, who writes: "The meaning is as transitional as it is transitory: in between, in the interplay; in the interconnections, the disjunctions; at the intersections, the crossroads; in the journey, not the arrival" (1984:108). It is the ambiguity in communication between clowns and the rest of society, between human beings and the supernatural, that makes sacred clowning so powerful and difficult to pin down. However, like our ancient predecessors who needed to dominate and control the powerful forces of nature, we scholars are caught in this elusive attempt to control and order our material, as if it is possible to capture multivocality in print.

The Rotuman clown, once so central to the efficacy of rituals associated with marriage and fertility, still lingers on. Instinctively, present-day Rotumans sense that laughter—as embodied in the clown—is important to their integrity as a people with a certain temperament and a cultural heritage. Yet, as my observations of recent weddings indicate, the clown's demise is imminent. Soon there will be the curtain call. Still, it is my hope that, come what may, the clown who makes a fool of herself and others at weddings will always remain a part of Rotuman life. As a traditional cultural icon in the frame of a wedding, the sacred clown embodies the wholeness and complexity of Rotuman culture—and what it means to be a Rotuman—in a way that rational analysis, or a scholarly paper, does not know.

Clowning and Culture in Rotuman Weddings

NOTES

I wish to acknowledge the help of Peter Miles and Aren Baoa of the University of the South Pacific who accompanied me to Rotuma to videotape the clown. Fieldwork on Rotuma was funded by research funds from the University of the South Pacific. My grateful thanks to the couples whose weddings I observed and of course to the clowns and their relatives.

For discussions related to this chapter, I am grateful to Alan Howard, Jan Rensel, Epeli Hauʻofa, Ron Witton, Ron Crocombe, Geoffrey White, John Charlot, Brian Macdonald-Milne, Kerry James, William Mitchell, and the ASAO members who shared their research at the 1989 Texas conference. An award by the Center for Pacific Islands Studies at the University of Hawaii and the Pacific Islands Development Programme of the East-West Center in 1990 allowed me the time to complete this chapter. I wish to record also my gratitude to my wife Pat and son Daniel for their patience during my absences on Rotuma and Hawaii.

1. See Berger (1976:15) who asserts that because humor is closely connected to the culture codes of society, to understand what makes people laugh is to gain insights into society's values.

2 This chapter is a preliminary investigation into the Rotuman clown and written while in the process of writing my dissertation on clowning in Polynesia. The interpretations here are tentative. A video recording of the wedding referred to in detail in the case study and another focusing specifically on the clown's performance are available on request from the Director, University of the South Pacific, Media Unit, P.O. Box 1168, Suva, Fiji.

3. Rotumans have no initiation rites; however, first births, deaths, and marriages are important transitions. Marriage celebrations are the most complex and elaborate.

4. Only a quarter of all Rotumans live on the island today. For social changes since 1960, see Rensel (1991).

5. Fine mats are indispensable for all religious ceremonies. According to MacGregor (1932), the weaving of fine mats was consecrated by the killing of a pig and clowning. Men and chiefs who passed by on the road were abused by an old female clown who treated them outrageously, so much so that a man ended up urinating in his trousers. As fine mats are used in marriages, feasts, and burials, their meanings are multiplex. In traditional weddings, their use pervades most rituals.

6. This was indeed the case in a wedding held in 1989. The bride's parents felt that the clown who presided at their daughter's wedding was unduly harsh on the wedding guests; they refused to thank her in the way of a fine mat and food, as required by custom.

7. The mats were woven by female relatives of the groom. There are at least four categories of mats with varying degrees of value, with the finest of greatest importance. The bride's relatives prepare mats and cooked food

also, but as they are on their home ground, their contributions are assembled beforehand. The colorful cotton material used for screening the temporary shelter was imported from Fiji.

8. It is beyond the scope of this chapter to discuss the meanings of the rituals. See Malo (1975) for an elaboration.

9. This is best summed up by Clarke, who writes in Crumrine (1969:14). See Werbner for another statement on the importance of a "sense of balance" in clowning (1986:243).

10. The clown called herself "Princess Sakura" to make her name sound exotic. Her real name is similar in pronunciation and spelling; this play on words is part of the humor.

11. See Turner (1984:26), who writes: "the performances characteristic of liminal phases and states often are more about the doffing of masks, the stripping of statuses, the renunciation of roles, the demolishing of structures."

12. A karate expert was very much in the news earlier in the year for claiming to be the king of the island. The funny woman was parodying this "king."

13. Female relatives of the groom are allowed to mock-challenge those from the bride's side.

14. See Howard (1970) for a detailed discussion of this important feature of life on Rotuma.

15. In the dancing that followed this ceremony, there was a deliberate attempt by the close relatives of the bride and groom to be seen to have reconciled their differences as evidenced by their dancing together.

16. See Brockett (1964:77–79) for other theories not mentioned in this study.

17. Red is the usual color of dress for Rotuman clowns today. The fine consecrated mats of the past used red feathers at the edges. Red is also associated with royalty in Polynesia, where chiefs on islands such as Hawaii were believed to have a divine origin.

18. For early accounts of what Fiji clowns wore at first-fruit festivals or at dances, see Clunie and Ligairi (1983:46–71) who draw from the various sources. For descriptions of what the Samoan clowns of old wore, see Sloan (1941:77, 107) and Grimshaw (1907:331–32). For the *arioi* society of Tahiti, see Ellis (1834:216); for Marquesas, see Angas (1866:332).

19. Vafo'ou Jiare, a respected folk historian, believes that the wedding clown was a fairly recent introduction because the behavior of the woman who plays the wedding is so antithetical to Rotuman values of propriety and decorum, particularly toward the chiefs. But Rotuman oral narratives in fact contain numerous accounts of antithetical Rotuman behavior, for example, male-like females leading rebellions against their chiefs, female tricksters outwitting cannibal giants, and female mediators negotiating between quarrelling chiefs. Furthermore, it is precisely in the

nature of the sacred clown to turn the world on its head, as evident in the literature on clowning the world over. It is Jiare's belief that the wedding clown was introduced from Tonga by the colonial chief Ma'afu, who is thought to have visited Rotuma with his daughter Sariro, who taught the Rotumans the custom of hiring a clown to preside at weddings. He bases his theory on a specific *tem ta* (poetic chant) that refers to a woman strutting in front of others and ordering the chiefs to do her bidding. There are, as I have indicated, a number of problems with Jiare's interpretation, not the least of which is that Tongans do not have a sacred clown who presides at weddings.

20. There are rules that are implicit; certain acts (murder, for example) are not permitted. Mitchell writes that clowning is always an act that annihilates the valued cultural constructions humans have evolved (this volume). In Oceania, the *arioi* society of Tahiti is one of the most extreme examples of this phenomenon. See Oliver (1974:913–14), Henry (1928: 237–41), Andersen (1969:435–51), and Ellis (1834) for more information on this fully fledged theater company that—according to Angas (1866: 296)—traveled around "spreading moral contagion." This team of strolling players practiced sexual freedom and infanticide. They ridiculed priests and others (Andersen 1969:438) and performed "acts of degradation" that, to describe —according to the missionary Ellis (1834:243)— would give the reader "pollution and pain."

REFERENCES

Apte, Mahadev L.
    1983   Humor Research, Methodology, and Theory in Anthropology. In *Handbook on Humor Research*, ed. Paul E. Mcghee and Jeffrey Goldstein, pp 183–211. New York: Springley-Verley.

Andersen, Johannes
    1969   *Myths and Legends of the Polynesians*. Rutland, Vt.: Charles E. Tuttle Company.

Angas, George French
    1866   *Polynesia: A Popular Description of the Islands of the Pacific*. London: Society for Promotion of Christian Knowledge.

Babcock, Barbara
    1984   Arrange Me Into Disorder: Fragments and Reflections on Ritual Clowning. In *Rite, Drama, Festival, Spectacle: Rehearsals Toward a Theory of Cultural Performance*, ed. John J. MacAloon, pp. 102–28. Philadelphia: Institute for the Study of Human Issues.

Berger, Arthur A.
    1976   Anatomy of the Joke. *Journal of Communication* 26(3):113–15.

Bott, Elizabeth
 1982 *Tongan Society at the Time of Captain Cook's Visits: Discussions with Her Majesty Queen Salote Tupou*. Wellington: Polynesian Society Incorporated.

Bricker, Victoria Reifler
 1973 *Ritual Humor in Highland Chiapas*. Austin: University of Texas Press.

Brockett, Oscar
 1964 *The Theatre: An Introduction*. New York: Holt, Rinehart and Winston.

Churchward, Clerk Maxwell
 1938 The History of Rotuma as Reflected in Its Language. *Oceania* 9:79–88.
 1940 Tales of a Lonely Island. *Oceania Monographs*, no. 4. Sydney: Australian National Research Council.

Clunie, Fergus, and Walesi Ligairi
 1983 Traditional Fijian Masks and Spirit Masquers. *Domodomo* 1:46–71. Suva: Fiji Museum.

Cox, Harvey
 1967 *The Feast of Fools*. Cambridge: Harvard University Press.

Crumrine, N. Ross
 1969 Capakoba, the Mayo Easter Ceremonial Impersonator: Explanations of Ritual Clowning. *Journal of Scientific Studies in Religion* 8:1–22.

Diaper, W.
 1853 *Jackson's Narrative from J. E. Erskine's Journal of a Cruise Among the Islands of the Western Pacific*. London: John Murray.

Eason, W. J. E.
 1951 *A Short History of Rotuma*. Suva: Government Printer.

Echeruo, M.
 1981 The Dramatic Limits of Igbo Ritual. In *Drama and Theatre in Nigeria: A Critical Source Book*, ed. Yemi Ogunbiyi, pp 136–48. Lagos and London: Nigeria Magazine Publications.

Eco, Umberto
 1984 The Frames of Comic "Freedom." In *Carnival*, ed. Thomas A. Sebeok, pp. 1–9. Berlin: Mouton Publishers.

Ellis, William
 1834 [1829] *Polynesian Researchers, During a Residence of Nearly Six Years in the South Sea Islands*, 2nd ed. London: Fisher, Son and Jackson.

Emerson, Nathaniel
 1965 *Unwritten Literature of Hawaii*. Rutland, Vt., and Tokyo: Charles E. Tuttle Company, Inc.

Evans-Pritchard, E. E.
    1929   Some Collective Expressions of Obscenity in Africa. *Journal of the Anthropological Institute of Great Britain and Ireland* 59:311–31.
Gardiner, Stanley
    1898   Natives of Rotuma. *Journal of Royal Anthropological Institute* 27:457–524.
Grimshaw, Beatrice
    1907   *In the Strange South Seas*. London: Hutchinson and Company.
Hammond, P.
    1964   Mossi Joking. *Ethnology* 3:259–67.
Handelman, Don
    1981   The Ritual-Clown: Attributes and Affinities. *Anthropos* 76: 321–70.
Hau'ofa, Epeli
    1988   Oral Traditions and Writing. Paper presented at the Commonwealth Institute, London.
Henry, Teuira
    1928   *Ancient Tahiti*. Bishop Museum Press Bulletin 48. Honolulu: Bishop Museum Press.
Horn, Andrew
    1981   Ritual, Drama and the Theatrical: The Case of Bori Spirit Mediumship. In *Drama and Theatre in Nigeria: A Critical Source Book*, ed. Yemi Ogunbiyi, pp. 181–202. Lagos and London: Nigeria Magazine Publications.
Howard, Alan
    1970   *Learning to be Rotuman*. New York: Columbia University Press.
Huntsman, Judith, and Antony Hooper
    1975   Male and Female in Tokelau. *Journal of Polynesian Society* 84:415–30.
Kaeppler, Adrienne
    1989   Art and Aesthetics. In *Developments in Polynesian Ethnology*, ed. Alan Howard and Robert Borofsky. Honolulu: University of Hawaii Press.
Kneubuhl, Victoria
    1987   Traditional Performance in Samoan Culture: Two Forms. *Asian Theatre Journal* 4:166–76.
Lowie, Robert
    1920   *Primitive Society*. New York: Horace Liveright.
Luomala, Katherine
    1984   *Hula: Ki'i: Hawaiian Puppetry*. Honolulu: The Institute for Polynesian Studies.

MacGregor, Gordon
  1932 Unpublished field notes. Honolulu: Bishop Museum.
Makarius, Laura
  1970 Ritual Clowns and Symbolical Behaviour. *Diogenes* 69:44–73.
Malo, Tiu
  1975 *Rotuman Marriage.* Suva: The South Pacific Social Sciences Association.
Marriott, M.
  1968 The Feast of Love. In *Krishna: Myths, Rites and Attitudes,* ed. M. Singer. Chicago: University of Chicago Press.
Miller, D. B.
  1973 Holi-Dulhendi: Licensed Rebellion in a North Indian Village. *South Asia* 3:15–22.
Murdock, George Peter
  1949 *Social Structure.* New York: Macmillan Company.
Norbeck, Edward
  1963 African Rituals of Conflict. *American Anthropologist* 65:1254–79.
Oliver, Douglas
  1974 *Ancient Tahitian Society.* 3 vols. Honolulu: University Press of Hawaii.
Owemeyala, Oyekan
  1972 Folklore and Yoruba Theatre. *Research in African Literatures* 2(2):121–24.
Parman, Susan
  1979 An Evolutionary Theory of Dreaming and Play. In *Forms of Play of North American Indians:* 1977 Proceedings of the American Ethnological Society, ed. Edward Norbeck and Claire R. Farrer, pp. 17–34. St. Paul: West Publishing Company.
Radcliffe-Brown, A. R.
  1940 On Joking Relationships. *Africa* 13(3):195–210.
Rensel, Janet
  1991 Housing and Social Relationships on Rotuma. In *Rotuma: Hanua Pumue, Precious Land.* Suva: Institute of Pacific Studies.
Rodway, Allan
  1962 Terms of Comedy. *Renaissance and Modern Studies* 6:102–24.
Rutz, Henry
  1990 Personal communicaton with Vilsoni Hereniko. ASAO meeting, Hawaii.
Shore, Bradd
  1977 A Samoan Theory of Action: Social Control and Social Order

in a Polynesian Paradox. Ph.D. dissertation, University of Chicago.

1978　Ghosts and Government: A Structural Analysis of Alternative Institutions for Conflict Management in Samoa. *Man* 13: 175–99.

Sloan, Donald
1941　*Polynesian Paradise: An Elaborated Travel Journal Based on Ethnological Facts*. London: Robert Hale Limited.

Tanner, Adrian
1990　Personal communication with Vilsoni Hereniko. ASAO meeting, Hawaii.

Turner, Victor
1984　Liminality and the Performance Genres. In *Rite, Drama, Festival, Spectacle: Rehearsals Toward a Theory of Cultural Performance*, ed. John J. MacAloon, pp. 19–40. Philadelphia: Institute for the Study of Human Issues.

Werbner, Pnina
1986　The Virgin and the Clown: Ritual Elaboration in Pakistani Migrants' Weddings. *Man* 21:227–50.

Wilkes, Charles
1845　*Narrative of the United States Exploring Expedition 1838–1842*, vol. 3 Philadelphia: Lea and Blanchard.

WHERE THE SPIRITS LAUGH LAST: COMIC THEATER IN SAMOA

Caroline Sinavaiana

AMONG SAMOANS, clowning often plays an integral role in public celebrations and other gatherings, such as weddings, dedications of new buildings, entertainments for visiting groups, and fund-raising events.[1] The forms of public clowning fall into two categories, which I designate as spontaneous, for performances that are nonscripted or nonrehearsed, and scripted, for performances that are planned or rehearsed.[2]

Spontaneous clowning is largely associated with dance forms. For example, at wedding celebrations it is not unusual for some of the older female guests to depart from their usual dignity and decorum by leaping to their feet to improvise a comical dance. Suggestive hip-wagging, rolling on the floor with legs kicked up in the air, and flipping up the backs of their skirts typify antics, which are received with shrieks of delight and laughter from the other guests, who may then be inspired to rise and join in the clowning.[3] In another example, that of traditional choral singing, the leader integrates physical clowning antics with his direction of the singers.

Scripted clowning, unlike the spontaneous form, represents a more formalized comic expression, with performers meeting well in advance of the occasion to prepare and rehearse their presentation. Although a presentation may include songs and comedy sketches, it is only the songs that can be characterized as scripted in the literal sense, since they are not only composed, but written down. Created for special occasions by various occupational or other groups, these songs often contain criticism leveled at specific government officials or employers. The comedy sketches, *fale aitu* (literally, house of spirits), on the other hand, are also composed but, unlike the songs, not written down.

A salient point to note at the outset is that scripted clowning,

Comic Theater in Samoa 193

that is, the songs and comedy sketches, provides the only public arena in Samoan society that traditionally allows for popular criticism of figures and institutions of authority. It is with such comedy sketches that this chapter primarily concerns itself. Six performances and their themes are considered as they correspond to the cultural context that informs their meaning and relevance for Samoans.

In the traditional cultural milieu of Samoa, where authority figures are accorded great respect and deference, particularly in public or formal arenas, these comedy sketches represent a dramatic departure from social conventions of propriety and decorum. In his exhaustive study of social controls in Samoan society, Shore (1977:332) argues persuasively for the idea that these sketches represent one among several avenues of "privileged expression," which serve to mediate conflict in relationships culturally determined toward complementarity.[4] Such relationships typically include those between titled and untitled persons, pastors and their congregations, parents and children, and teachers and students. One purpose of this chapter is to consider how the comedy sketch, as a cultural institution in Samoa, offers a socially sanctioned vehicle for overtly criticizing authority figures through the protective frame of theater.

In a larger sense, however, this study addresses the role of comedy sketches to test the conventions and expectations of society in general, to challenge the order and propriety—the constraints—of everyday life through comic satire and burlesque. Thus, while most of the following performances tend to focus on relationships of authority, one sketch addresses the dynamics of *feagaiga* (respect covenant) relationships like those existing between men and women, which Shore (1977:416) characterizes as traditionally marked by mutual control and harmony, rather than authority.[5] Here, social conventions regarding marital privacy are violated by lampooning a typical argument between husband and wife.

While the comedy sketches do address conflicts intrinsic to Samoan society, a great many ridicule Western figures and institutions of authority. Some of the most popular themes of these comic sketches include parodies of Western politics, potentates, religion, education, medicine, and popular culture. Examples of performances from these categories are discussed later as they provide a critical portrayal of the West, however veiled in caricature and play. Such fun house images of the West provide a rare clue to certain Samoan perceptions about neocolonial authority figures that are denied formal expression in any other fashion.[6] A secondary purpose of this chapter, then, is to suggest an indigenous critique of the West, as implied in several representative types of comic sketches.

In a neocolonial context like Samoa's, what can be gained by closer attention to her folk humor is a nonofficial, collective view of political authority that is uncensored by the normative courtesies of formal discourse. While traditional ethnographies have focused on description and analysis of various cultural practices, little has been done to locate Samoan aesthetic traditions, like folk comedy for example, in a geopolitical terrain of power relations with the West. What I hope to contribute to the discussion of Samoan society in general is a more indigenous perspective, which might contribute in some preliminary way toward the mapping of that liminal territory.

The Samoans

Samoa is a group of eleven volcanic islands, with a combined area of approximately 1,200 square miles, located in the southwestern Pacific. In Western Samoa, where much of this study was undertaken, most of the 168,000 people live in the coastal flatlands that gradually slope upward to a mountainous interior. The primary language is Samoan, a member of the Austonesian linguistic family, with English used secondarily for international purposes. While most Samoans identify themselves as Christian—the first European missionaries arrived in the late nineteenth century—there is still a widespread belief in spirit lore.

The basic social unit is the extended family, headed by a chief who represents clan interests at the village council, which arrives at decisions by consensus. As the dominant political institution at the village level, the council controls use of land and sea resources, levies fines and punishes crimes, settles disputes, and sees to the nomination, creation, and disposition of chiefly titles. Formal marriages customarily involve elaborate exchanges of goods, and descent is cognatic or nonunilineal. While chiefly titles are generally, but not exclusively, held by men, the female line exerts its political influence through a veto power over council decisions.

Following a period of European colonization from the late nineteenth century until the midtwentieth century, Western Samoa became politically independent in 1962. Today, a residual western model of civil organization still overlays the traditional polity. The parliamentary-style government is administered by a prime minister, with a separate head of state providing traditional ceremonial leadership. In the last thirty years, a tremendous outmigration of younger Samoans seeking paid jobs in New Zealand, Australia, American Samoa, and the United States has caused an essential shift in the country's economic base. Traditionally dependent for subsistence and export revenues on agricultural and fishing products, the country now counts remittances from overseas as a major part of its annual income. A thriving tourist industry represents another recent development in Samoa's attempts at economic diversification.

In the late nineteenth century, as the great Western powers vied for the acquisition of various island nations in the Pacific and elsewhere, Samoa was summarily divided, with the western islands taken by Germany and the eastern islands by America. The legacy of this colonial past is all too clearly operative in the neocolonial present, in which the eastern group, American Samoa, remains under the direct economic control of the United States, while the politically independent western islands continue to operate largely within an overarching economic structure created and maintained by their former New Zealand and European administrators.

The Comedy Sketch

Samoa's comedy sketches are satirical interludes that are scripted orally, rehearsed, and then performed in public with much improvisation by a small troupe of players who are generally men in their youth or early middle age. These village comics are trained and directed by the most accomplished comedian among them as rehearsals for the sketches proceed.[7] Plots are often marked by the humorous ridicule of authority figures, who are dramatically epitomized through the use of caricature and parody. In the plays, normative status roles are reversed: the high is made low and the world temporarily turned upside down, as characterized in carnival traditions elsewhere.[8]

A basic understanding of comedy sketches *(fale aitu)* requires some familiarity with the Samoan concept of *aitu* (ancestral spirit or ghost). In Samoan tradition, the ancestral spirit represents the particular type of deity believed to originate in a human incarnation. In modern times, this supernatural entity is widely believed to be the ghost of one's dead relative, who may reappear occasionally to cause trouble for living family members. When these ghosts do appear, they generally have specific requests for some corrective action to be taken on their behalf in the world of the living. Depending on their satisfaction with the quality of human responses to their requests, the ghost will then either disappear or continue to trouble the family with mysterious ailments, which may include possession.

In the comic sketch, the lead comedian is considered by the audience to be a ghost while in character during the sketch. For it is the ghost who delivers the punch lines that carry the social or political criticism home to the particular authority figure being lampooned. Such authority figures, for example, elders, parents, teachers, religious ministers, government officials, and political leaders, are often present in the audience and are expected by custom to take all this clowning in the spirit of fun.[9] Meanwhile, the comedian is not considered to be the author or true spokesperson of the criticism. Rather, it is the ghost who is speaking such thoughts through the *agency* of the clown. This supernatural sanction, then, theoretically relieves the actors of responsibility for what is said and done in the comedy.

One comic device in the sketches is a momentary stepping out of role by the clown to comment on the stage action as though a mere observer or to interact directly with the audience. Such a singular breaking of the dramatic frame serves ostensibly to distinguish between the actor's real-life identity from that of the stage persona, who is purportedly animated by a possessing ghost.[10] Another popular device apparently serving a similar purpose is for the comic to assume the persona of a transvestite or *fa'afafine* (literally, the way of a woman), especially when delivering punch lines. Here, the clown affects the effeminate posturing and a kind of seductive wheedling tone stereotypically associated with transvestites in Samoa.

Shore points out the corresponding nature of the two roles, ghost and transvestite, in their shared liminality and "cognitive ambiguity" (1978:178). Because each occupies a structural role that is betwixt and between those of normal human existence—the transvestite being neither male nor female, and the ghost neither human or spirit—they share a "license for privileged expression" unique in ordinary discourse (1978:178).

Other characteristic comic devices include extensive verbal play such as punning, mimicry, and double entendres, especially those of a sexual nature. Male virility, female virtue, and adultery, for example, are mocked in passing, with the occasional lewd gesture or posture used as a kind of comic punctuation.[11] In general, however, the comedies of today are reportedly less explicit sexually than those of past years, according to some older consultants who report childhood memories of scantily clad actors and more characteristic use of obscenity in word and gesture. Another favorite device in contemporary clowning is to confuse formal and informal languages to achieve hilarious violations of social protocols.

While comedians may be middle-aged men with a chiefly title of relatively humble rank, they tend more to be younger men of untitled status. In general, women do not assume the comedian's role in mixed company.[12] With the exception of one very famous comedian who makes his living by performing for the Samoan community of southern California, others generally work at the ordinary jobs expected of Samoan men, like farming, fishing, or less frequently, teaching. Training in the comedy sketch occurs as a kind of informal apprenticeship in which interested adolescents are given small parts to perform under the direction of the most senior comedian. One's degree of skill or accomplishment is measured by how many different characters and voices can be convincingly projected in a single performance. The sketches are composed and directed by the lead comedian, who may also conduct the singing and dancing portions of the show as well.

Comedy sketches are generally performed at night and outdoors, weather permitting. Customarily, the central village green provides the performance arena; in inclement weather, festivities are shifted to the village meeting house or some other communal building. Audience and actors generally face each other across an open space of variable distance, depending on the particular sketch and performance venue. Virtually all of my consultants reported that performances tend to occur much more frequently in the rural villages than in those closer to town. Except for the annual comedy competition during Independence Day festivities, performances are less frequent in Apia, the capital town.[13] At the present time, television crews from American Samoa and radio broadcasters from Western Samoa regularly tape these annual performances for airing during the year to a large enthusiastic audience.

Productions of skits, especially at the village level, are casually mounted with little use of costume, makeup, or props. Customary dress prevails, with actors wearing ordinary attire consisting of sarong and shirt. Often, the only performer in costume is the lead comedian, who affects some form of female costume, either Samoan or European. For example, he may wear the ceremonial headdress and leaf skirt of the Samoan princess or the brightly flowered dress imported from the West and favored by many Samoan women.

Again, the dramatic emphasis rests on physical and verbal mimicry of stereotypical characters, rather than on stage setting or other extraneous devices.

Comedy sketches usually take place as part of a larger entertainment or *koneseti* (concert) performed by one or more village associations, such as the church, school, or chiefs' council, usually for the purpose of fund-raising. The concert or benefit typically consists of singing and dancing, with a comedy skit being performed every four or five numbers. Except for the comedian(s) who may be hired if none is available in the village, all performers are members of the sponsoring organization. During and after each dance number or comedy sketch, members of the performers' extended families come forward with donations, thereby publicly demonstrating support for their relatives on stage. If larger sums of money are needed for some village project, the entire troupe may travel to other villages, islands, or today, even to other countries.

Plots of Comedy Sketches

Comic plots tend to fall into two general categories, with the cast of characters being drawn either from kin or nonkin groups. The kin-related plots commonly treat such themes as marriage or courtship tensions, jealousy between spouses or lovers, and problematic relations between parents and children. Non-kin-related plots tend to operate more in the political realm, that is, outside the family, with such common themes as exploitive or inept pastors and government officials, as well as various nonindigenous cultural institutions such as Western medicine and education. However, as in literary and dramatic works elsewhere, the key element of plot in all comic sketches is the resolution of some tension or conflict between major characters.

In the following performance summaries, the overarching theme concerns the dynamics of hierarchical relationships. The first two sketches center on Western institutions of medicine and religion, respectively. For purposes of discussion, I have assigned working titles to each sketch.

Performance One: "The Operation"[14]

This comedy sketch was part of an elaborate production of music, comedy, and drama that was performed by a large troupe of secondary school students from Western Samoa in 1973. They had brought their show to American Samoa in order to help raise money for the construction of a traditional meetinghouse intended for use in their cultural studies program. Because their production had been filmed by a television crew from Pago Pago, I was able to secure a copy of the tape from the archives there.

By village standards of comedy production this sketch was quite lavishly cast, costumed, and equipped with sophisticated props. The troupe of student entertainers obviously spared no effort in mounting their fund-raising variety show. A large cast included the doctors, the patient and his mother, several of the patient's family members, one nurse (played by the only female actor), and several orderlies or medical assistants. The main characters are the assisting doctor and the patient's mother, who engage in a running battle of words and blows, each supported by their respective teams of medical assistants and family members. The mother was played by a student around seventeen years old, known for his gifts as a stage clown. Dressed in a long flowery gown, he spoke in high-pitched tones and whining cadences, which quickly escalated into strident yowls and verbal attacks on the medical team. Her foil, the assisting doctor, was portrayed as a loud-mouthed, abrasive brute who appeared to act as an alter ego for the surgeon, who worked silently and firmly to get the job done despite the antic mother and her feisty entourage.

The performance tells of a questionable surgical procedure performed on a hapless boy, mysteriously afflicted, who is brought into the hospital by his mother. It seems that he is suffering from the night shakes, which are so severe that they cause his mother to start shaking by association. As the boy lies on the operating table in relative quietude, disturbed only by the constant shaking of his legs and feet, the doctor performs a diagnosis. Clad in mask, gown, and gloves, the doctor proclaims that "the urinary bladder has turned over—looks like the left side is bigger and swelling because of eating stale food—see how the patient's breath is like rotten ripe bananas."

When the doctor lifts a large wooden mallet in preparation for administering the "anesthetic," the boy makes a futile leap for freedom and is quickly strong-armed back to the operating table. The mother shouts: "Don't any one of you come to our house again—the government is wasting money on these guys," as her arms are pinned back by the orderlies. Once the boy is unconscious on the table, the family launches an attack on the medical team in an attempt to free the boy. Here the operation halts so that the medical assistants can forcibly subdue the family after a heroic resistance marked by much fighting and screeching.

Now the operation can proceed apace: the incision is made with a carpenter's saw, and intestinelike "organs" (actually, a longish string of large link sausages) are extracted with large pliers, to the accompaniment of anguished shrieks from the horrified family. The irate mother shouts insults impugning the skill and legitimacy of the medical team and, again, is repeatedly subdued by hospital orderlies.

> Oh, my God—my boy! . . . Oh no! Why the saw? See, he's opening up the boy's stomach—just like an animal's! Oh, I'm out of breath! . . . Why do you continue to plunge that pair of pliers inside? Oh, the baldhead! How come he became a doctor? You baldhead! Oh no, he's taking everything out!! Oh, what is left inside for him to live on??

Again the family is subdued, allowing the surgeon to proceed with the operation, which he does in silence with cool professional precision. The mother's running commentary of the proceedings provides the verbal text for the sketch, as she alternately exclaims, groans, complains, and vilifies the doctors. Finally, the offending "organ" (actually a large cluster of paper cups tied with string) is removed from the boy's abdomen and held aloft triumphantly by the surgeon.

In this performance, comic techniques of exaggeration, irony, and reversal combine to achieve the burlesque of a medical operation. The caricature of the operation as a brutalizing process for all involved, including the patient, his family, and the medical team, clearly reflects a genuine anxiety that Samoans sometimes articulate about certain Western medical practices. At one level, the morbid humor arises from a stark contrast with Samoan healing practices, which are characteristically marked by gentleness, the laying on of hands through therapeutic massage, and the inclusion of extended family members in the healing process itself. By contrast, the masks, gowns, and gloves of the Western medical professionals, along with their arrogant demeanor, serve both to distance and distinguish them dramatically from the patient's family, portrayed as unruly, uncouth specimens. In effect, patient and family are thus relegated to the status of passive agents, helpless observers rather than essential participants in the healing process.

The comic tension is further heightened by the ironic contrast between actions by the medical team that are brutally inhumane, on the one hand, and the professional context of a Western hospital that purports to heal the sick in an efficient, antiseptic manner, on the other. Instead of healing, the doctors create new orders of suffering. To the Samoan sensibility, such violation of one's social context is highly problematic, given the singular cultural value placed on fulfilling one's avowed role in a given situation as gracefully as possible. As Shore writes, "the violation of context, or the misappropriation of behavior to context in real life are Samoan conceptions of social disorder and contradiction" (1977:333). The comic energy of this skit, then, lies at least partially in the unresolved tension between Samoan cultural expectations of the healer's role and its unnatural desecration by Western medical practitioners.

Another satirical technique at work here is reversal, with the normally high-status roles of doctor and nurse being portrayed as demeaning and brutalizing. A subtext of neocolonial politics is also evident in the critical attitudes being expressed toward the Western cultural institution of medicine. As Western professionals represent an institutionalized matrix of colonial authority that is the political legacy of all Samoa, the mocking of their skill and technological superiority within the comic frame turns that political advantage on its head, albeit fleetingly, by making them look ridiculous. Thus, the theme of hierarchy is here played upon in terms of an authority base that is extrinsic to traditional Samoan culture.

Performance Two: "The Sermon"

The following sketch features a now-professional comedian named Petelo who is the most well-known and highly respected comic actor in all Samoa. His is the first name invariably mentioned in any discussion of the form, and his technique has set the aesthetic standard for both uncanny characterization and sophisticated verbal play. Where other comics might rely more on the use of broad physical gesture and slapstick, Petelo's forte is the nuance of language, intonation, expression, and subtle body movement. His ability to mimic a wide range of human and animal characters is so greatly admired by Samoan audiences that his promised appearance in a show is enough to guarantee a rousing success.[15] Among Petelo's best-known characterizations is that of the bumbling, greedy pastor whose defining trait is expressed by his ludicrous attempts to wheedle more donations from his parishioners through a variety of rhetorical shenanigans with the Gospel. The following summary was taken from a performance filmed around 1975 at station KVZK-TV in American Samoa.

In this skit, the main character is an elder minister who is assisted by two younger clerics. The entire segment consists of a mock reading of the Gospel, the elder pastor alternating with his deacon, accompanied by a running commentary of wacky exegesis.[16] The characters pretend to hold a book in front of them, as if solemnly reading from the Bible.

First, the congregation is exhorted to perform a series of contradictory actions ostensibly based on scriptural precedent. For example, "In those days when Bartholomew was making his home on the mountain of Calvary, he preached unto them to continue to sit tight, for those who sit tight will break their backs in two while those standing will turn into stone statues." Later, "Bartholomew" is quoted thus, "He who gives up his fortune will not get eternal life—amen—and they who give away their belongings will be sorry!" And later still, "He who holds on tight to his belongings will find the way to everlasting stupidity and his fingers will bend at the joints!"

Interspersed with such nuggets of inconsistency are pointed reminders to the congregation about the perils of selfishness and laziness. "And they continued to sit tight and stand up straight, and not a single person made an offering!" There is much laughter here, as the audience is expected, as usual, to make donations during a live performance, but no one yet had done so. Later, more relevant passages are "read": "And they refused to make any offerings unto the altar, because they are tired; they've contracted the infectious disease of laziness."

A subtext of this version has the "children of Deuteronomy" following the instructions for baptism by jumping into the "water for eternal life." Those that land in deep water, according to the elder pastor, begin thrashing toward dry land in a manner not unlike fleas hopping. By way of illustration, he then launches into a series of minute shuffling hops as he continues his disquisition, eyes steadily locked into the gaze of his presumably restless flock. Extending his explication of flealike jumping into the larger context of movement itself as an activity fraught with endless possibility, the pastor's own tiny hops now begin to resemble a kind of twitching dance step. By now, he is gesticulating dramatically and inappropriately to drive home his concluding points, which are somehow meant to affirm the inevitability of inertia: "He who stands will continue to stand, and he who sits will continue to do so forever!"

The figure being satirized here is that of the elder pastor, whose addled reading of the Scripture and nonsensical exhortations to his congregation make him a ludicrous figure of fun, rather than the august and honored personage of real life. Here, the comedian masterfully parodies the oratorical flourishes and nuances of the true-to-life sermon; that is, the style is correct, only the content is half gibberish. The laughable inconsistencies of his sermon and absentminded fumbling with biblical texts point up the foibles of his advanced age and his insistence on remaining overlong in the limelight. Such satire of a figure who in real life could expect to receive great respect by virtue of his social rank represents a dramatic reversal from cultural norms in which both pastors *and* elders occupy positions of high status.

In addition to foolhardy senility, pastoral greed is satirized in the minister's insistent efforts to browbeat his congregation into making donations. As a stock motif in the clown shows, such constant demand for contributions apparently strikes a familiar and appreciative chord with audiences. Over the last several years, a number of other Samoans have complained to me about the needless construction of ever-larger churches, despite the fact that original structures continue adequately to serve existing congregations. Several consultants have suggested competition among ministers for grander churches as the motivation for such never-ending financial appeals.

In this sketch, the comedian cleverly plays on this motif by his thinly veiled requests for donations from the real audience. Such shameless entreaty represents a departure from social convention, in which explicit supplication for payment is highly inappropriate. While the audience, by custom, may be expected to contribute donations during the performance, the bold articulation of that expectation explicitly constitutes bad manners and, thus, a departure from the ordinary canons of decorum and propriety. However, within the frame of the story, that is, of a biblical people being noted for their stinginess and laziness, the comedian has cleverly embedded his outrageous request for funds within the conceit of the sketch.

In the figures of pastor and doctor in the foregoing skits, we have portrayals of relatively recent arrivals to the Samoan cultural scene. Since the arrival of Christian missionaries in the 1830s, followed by a clamoring host of Western imperialists later in the century, Samoan society has been compelled to absorb such late arrivals as representatives of a new order of cultural authority. While traditionally the roles of pastor and doctor were more or less represented in the figures of shaman and healer, those particular social roles were virtually devoid of any kind of temporal authority.

Thus, the considerable political power obviously wielded by Western doctors and churchmen constitutes a structural anomaly in an indigenous Samoan political context. What such skits portray, among other things, is the problem of power being abused when misappropriated from the bicultural confusion of colonialism. As in all colonial situations, Samoa's indigenous political structure has been essentially altered and reorganized to accommodate an extrinsic and dominating culture. Here again, the comedy sketch offers a rare public opportunity to criticize those who exercise real and daunting social power.

Performance Three: "The Foolish Old Father"

As distinct from the previous sketches, which address the dynamics of hierarchical relationships in a public context, the two following performances turn inward to the more private context of family relationships. Here, social dynamics unfold more delicately, perhaps, as relationships turn not only on questions of authority and power, but also on bonds of mutual respect and cooperation.

The performance I call "The Foolish Old Father" was presented in a small village on the northeast coast of Upolu island in September 1988. The occasion was a fund-raising concert put on by the young men's association of the village. Most of the evening, as usual, was given to songs and dances, with a comedy sketch performed after every fourth or fifth number.

This sketch features three characters all played by one young comic in his early twenties. It opens with a young woman named Susie being approached by a suitor, an aggressive older man well-named Two-by-four *(Lua i le fa)* who sports noisy pretensions based on his self-inflated prestige as a hearse driver. (Hearses and hydraulic lifts for coffins are a recent arrival in Samoa and represent wealth and status.) As Two-by-four, the comedian affects a kind of restless, impatient swagger and bossy, impudent tone of voice. "Please go tell your father that I came for his chicken." Immediately taking a dislike to the arrogant stranger, Susie, with a distinctly feminine lilt in her voice, directs him to wait under the breadfruit tree while she goes to call her father. Moving under the tree, Two-by-four notices that he is standing in a crust of chicken droppings and challenges Susie about this. She coyly replies that she told him *not* to stand there, because the chickens sleep above in the tree. (When addressing the suitor Susie speaks in a polite idiom, even as she directs him to wait on the manure heap. Thus, her insult is even more exquisite. Since she is the "chicken" he has asked for, the offal he stands in symbolizes her low esteem for his charms.)

Addressing her father about the stranger, Susie speaks deferentially and with a kind of arm-swinging innocence: "Papa! Papa! There's man outside, as old as you." The old man has a distinctly crumpled demeanor and answers in thickened, slurred mumbles: "This is good! Come, my daughter, I think we have finally found what we have been looking for—in this man. I hear this guy drives Sefo's pickup; he delivers dead people around. This means if I die he can take my body for a ride to the new market and back. Come, let's go see him!" After a brief meeting with the would-be suitor, Susie's father quickly gives his blessing to the courtship based on the potential status *he* will accrue from being a deceased passenger in the much-admired hearse.

The last scene finds Susie bemoaning her fate as Two-by-four has already started to boss her around. She wails and protests, confronting him with his duplicity. While he makes implausible excuses, she accuses him of being nothing better than a liar and an empty-bottle collector.

The three characters are differentiated by the actor by means of changing voice, speech mannerism, posture, gesture, and attitude. As the suitor, the actor moves about with large movements in a kind of restless, impatient swagger, whereas Susie's movements are much more restrained and circumscribed, and the old man appears to remain virtually stationery. Such a solo performance of all three roles by a single comic was a tour de force in the evening's concert. His ease in shifting quickly and smoothly from one persona to another is a sign of virtuosity in the comedy sketch, according to all the consultants interviewed. The facility to adapt gracefully to a variety of dramatic roles, as illustrated here, corresponds to a high cultural value placed on social versatility in the ever-shifting course of one's daily life.

In this sketch, the object of ridicule is clearly Susie's father, who is portrayed as a senile, decrepit figure, doddering foolishly at the very edge of death. His patent self-interest moves him to act in a cavalier manner by giving his daughter away, as it were, to the aspiring con artist. Such a momentous decision made in unseemly haste would appear truly ridiculous to the Samoan sensibility, which is deeply rooted in a tradition of careful consideration, discussion, and consensual agreement among extended family members for such important matters as marriage arrangements.

Furthermore, his actions betray a lack of *alofa* (loving respect), which is the basic quality that is supposed to mark relations between parents and children. Ideally, that relationship is one of complementarity in which the father can expect to receive honor and respect in exchange for the care and protection of his daughter. Such heedless disposition of Susie's marriage represents a violation of his responsibilities to ensure her well-being as his child. By acting so selfishly and impetuously at her expense, he thus becomes a ludicrous figure, easily ridiculed by others.

Such dramatic mocking of the foolish old father, like that of the elder pastor in the last skit, depicts a reversal of normative status roles, which dictate that respect and deference by accorded to anyone who is elderly. In addition to the status of advanced age, however, both characters occupy social positions, as parent and minister, that command deference in their own right. As Shore points out, "the most popular objects of comic ridicule on the Samoan stage are those who combine several statuses normally commanding deference and respect" (1977:332). The moral here for both father and pastor is that violation of their social roles invites ridicule and mockery.

The theme of hierarchical relations is evident in all three foregoing sketches, however variously expressed in their respective social arenas, from family to Western hospital and church. In each instance, the authority figure—the foolish old father, the sadistic surgeon, the acquisitive pastor—is portrayed as abusing his position of control over others. Such abuse theoretically constitutes a violation of the complementary bond that is supposed to mark hierarchical relations. However, because complementarity is the cultural expectation here, there is no prescribed avenue for the expression of conflict or its mediation.[17] Hence, the girl cannot openly defy her father's actions; the patient's mother is powerless to truly challenge the doctor's sovereignty; and no one would think of openly criticizing the pastor, all because the traditions of Samoan culture do not allow such open violation of the complementary bonds between persons.

The plots of comedy sketches in which themes other than those of hierarchical relations are prominent tend to cluster around cross-gender, non-kin-based interactions. Typically, these sketches address the kinds of interpersonal tensions commonly found in marriage and courtship. In the following sketch, for example, we have a Samoan version of a classic marital argument.

Performance Four: "Jealousy"

This performance was presented in 1987 as an entry in the comedy sketch contest at the Independence Day celebrations in Western Samoa. The two characters, husband and wife, are played by well-known professional comedians in their early forties. The comic playing the wife's role wears a loose, flowered dress and somehow manages to project femininity despite his obviously male physique, mustache, and prominent tattoo. He speaks in a high-pitched voice occasionally engages in flirtatious exchanges with the audience by wagging his hips or waving coyly. The husband, on the other hand, is dressed in conventional formal male attire consisting of a tailored sarong and white shirt and speaks in a natural tone of voice. The skit takes place on a large stage that is bare except for the two microphones used by the comedians. While the husband remains stationary for the most part, the wife moves about pacing or gesturing to emphasize her points in the argument.

She opens conversationally with a word of introduction to the audience: "The scene you are about to see concerns last night and the secrets that often result in the breakdown of marriages." She complains to her husband about his heavy drinking and accuses him of having an affair with another man's wife. She addresses him primarily in English, a highly unusual departure from the ordinary in comedy sketches. He answers in Samoan, with the complaint that he's an uneducated man and therefore she should speak only in Samoan. She persists in speaking in English, and the argument continues.

She complains about his double standard: "The man always womanizing, and the woman sits tight. Yes, she just sits tight. The woman stays home and is nice. You see, and once she moves—then what? Make murder?" The husband then threatens to kill her if she dares to have an affair herself, further declaring that being jealous is "what men do." She then confronts him with a strange dress that she has discovered in their bedroom, whereupon he immediately falls to his knees and begs her forgiveness.

The humor here lies as much in hyperbole as in satire, with laughter greeting the wife's rapid-fire scolding.[18] The other element that consistently inspires laughter is the anomalous use of English by the wife. As comedy sketches are generally conducted in Samoan, like any intimate conversation between Samoans, the departure from linguistic convention here is noteworthy. The wife's persistent use of English serves to distance her psychologically from her husband, with the effect of alienating and demoralizing him, as he implies when he tells her to speak Samoan. In another performance of the same sketch, recorded on commercial audiotape, the husband puts it more explicitly: "let's speak Samoan, and everything will be fine." Again, he makes the association between lack of education and lack of English proficiency (as well as threatens to blacken his wife's eye) *because* he is an "uneducated" man.

Such dramatic attention to the wife's anomalous use of English in addressing her husband suggests some rather complex tensions being expressed in the arena of marital discourse. On the interpersonal level, the wife employs English as a kind of verbal weapon in order to establish some territory of advantage for herself on their emotional battleground. In the verbal context of their discourse, she can thus gain the upper hand by exercising a linguistic prerogative lying outside her husband's ken. In effect, she inverts the emotional advantage in their relationship in her favor; now *he* is the one left feeling diminished for a change. Here the comic reversal in emotional leverage accounts in part for the humorous appreciation of the audience.

Another source of comic energy lies in the ambivalent nature of the marriage relationship in terms of the complementarity that is supposed to inform it. Since married couples are culturally bound to lend each other mutual respect and aid, there are no formal avenues outside of divorce for managing conflict when it does arise. What this skit humorously depicts, however, is what can happen when conflicts occur in a complementary relationship. In a sense, both husband and wife violate their intimate bond by introducing extrinsic elements—another sexual partner, another language—into their marital discourse against the express wishes of the other. Again, comic tension results from the violation of a prescribed social norm, in this instance, mutual cooperation in marriage.

In this sketch the theme of hierarchical conflict plays a far less prominent and clear-cut role than in the first three performances, which focused on relationships of authority as found in the contexts of doctor-patient, pastor-congregation, and parent-child bonds. While the reversal of emotional authority transpiring between husband and wife suggests a rather fluid or situational hierarchy, perhaps the more dominant cultural issue raised is that regarding the proper functioning of complementarity in its unranked mode. Such an emphasis on social bonds based on mutual respect and assistance like those customarily governing relationships between men and women is, in fact, characteristic of the category of comedy sketches involving themes of courtship and marriage.

The Comedy Sketch and Western Contact

The prominent role of the English language in the last example and two others to follow may provide a useful vehicle for discussing Western cultural influences on Samoan culture as expressed through the comedy sketch. The wife's inappropriate use of English with her husband is, quite rightly, perceived by him as threatening to his status as an educated man. Even after he asks her to speak in Samoan, she persists in using English, thus driving home her allegedly superior advantage in an intellectual realm. In one sense, he is appealing to tradition and custom, as though to say, "If only you would speak *our* language, everything could be solved between us." She continues, however, to defer linguistically to an outside authority, as represented by the English language, which serves to align her (however implicitly) with the dominant political force of the West, while neatly sidestepping the matter of direct communication in a personal context. In a culture where clear communication is highly valued at every social level, this purposeful obfuscation on her part is very bizarre indeed. In fact, it represents a reversal from the linguistic norms of Samoan, which tend toward repetition and paraphrasing in the interest of clarity.

Such use of English as a validating force that emanates from a cultural source extrinsic to Samoa is further evident in at least two other comedy sketches recently performed in Samoa and New Zealand, respectively. According to one consultant on Upolu island, a sketch I will call "The Interview" takes place in a personnel office where the main character, a young man who speaks only Samoan, sits for a job interview and inappropriately parrots stock English phrases. The conversation proceeds in the following vein:

> *Interviewer:* Good morning.
> *Young man:* I'm very well, thank you.
> *Interviewer:* What is your name?
> *Young man:* No thanks, I'm fine.

In another comedy sketch that was performed at a Samoan community hall in New Zealand by a fund-raising group visiting from Samoa, a similar story unfolds. In "Plenty of Money," a group of students are being drilled in English pronunciation. Among the phrases they are learning are "plenty of money," and "yes, I did it," and "thank you." After school, when some of the male students stop on the street to help someone who has been robbed and beaten, they are accosted by policemen who demand an explanation.

Police: Did you rob this man.
Boys: Yes, I did it.
Police: Why did you do this?
Boys: Plenty of money.
Police: Get in the wagon. We're taking you to the station.
Boys: Thank you.

In both of the above sketches a violation of linguistic context is a primary source of much comic tension and laughter. Unlike the first four skits, however, the object of ridicule is neither an authority figure nor a complementary partner. It is not the policeman or the employer being satirized. Instead, the butt of the joke is a person or group distinctly disadvantaged in the situation. In other words, the implied criticism is turned inwardly to a collective self rather than outwardly to some authority or cooperative partner, as is more commonly the case in comedy sketches. This unusual shifting of the satirical spotlight from authority to subordinate figure represents a formal anomaly in the comedy sketch, which bears further study.[19] For now, however, I would suggest one possible line of interpretation suggested by Samoa's neocolonial experience.

As the two skits imply an equivalency between knowledge of English and personal validation if not power, an insufficient amount of knowledge proves embarrassing at best and disastrous at worst. In the three sketches featuring the English language as a central motif, including the jealous wife piece, the characters' relationship with English is problematic in the sense that their personal worth has somehow mysteriously become contingent upon acquiring the language of the colonizing culture. The language itself, then, comes to symbolize the tensions of cultural adaptation, particularly in the colonial context, where indigenous people have no essential choice in the matter.

What then, is the relevance of comedy sketches to such difficult questions of cultural politics? In the overweening cultural context of Samoa, which mitigates against any overt criticism of authority, the comedy sketch can function as a kind of psychological escape valve for resentments against individuals and institutions of authority. In the neocolonial milieu, it can also serve to dispel the mystique of foreign authority figures in a way that makes access to a cultural other more feasible than would otherwise be the case.[20] Like clowning traditions in many cultures, the comedy sketch can provide a sociopsychological catharsis of collective tensions in a fashion both entertaining and delightful rather than threatening and disruptive.

Conclusions

Turner (1984) writes of cultural performances like ritual, carnival, and theater as acting to comment, criticize, and celebrate various dimensions of human relatedness. Both Turner's notion of such "multi-vocality" in social drama and Bakhtin's (1981) parallel concept of the essentially polyphonic nature of all verbal discourse nicely illuminate some of the rich aesthetic textures to be found in the comedy sketch.

Clearly a reflexive form of expression, traditional Samoan comedy uses a wide range of humorous devices like parody, satire, and slapstick to effect a dramatic reversal or inversion of normative status roles in society. Other comic conventions include a central persona that affects certain distinguishing characteristics of ghost and transvestite, two figures sharing a liminal status in Samoan culture. Their structurally ambiguous nature endows both with a license for privileged expression, with which social norms of decorum and propriety can be humorously violated. Through such symbolic violations of social convention, the comedy sketch can serve to liberate us, however momentarily, from the quotidian cares and constraints of orthodox society.[21]

The comedies characteristically dramatize conflicts arising in complementary relationships, where there are generally no formal avenues for mediating such tensions. The most common targets for satire are those authority figures normally commanding deference and respect, like political leaders, pastors, parents, and teachers. Or, in fewer examples, they might also be respect covenant partners, like men and women, whose relationships are culturally prescribed to be harmonious and cooperative.

The exceptional sketch that targets a disadvantaged figure for ridicule is noteworthy in its departure from the aforementioned comedic tendency to satirize either authority figures or complementary peers. More detailed consideration of this and other significant variations in the form of the clown show might well suggest some corresponding cultural anomaly not readily expressed or apparent otherwise.

In Samoa's neocolonial context, the comedy sketch implies an indigenous critique of various forms of Western culture. Performances observed and recorded over the last twenty years commonly lampoon Western education, religion, medicine, politics and politicians, and popular culture. Conversely, such an implicit critique of a cultural other also suggests a process of cultural revitalization, in which customary values, for example those found in traditional medicine, religion, and language use, are tacitly acknowledged and reinforced by way of contrast. More systematic study of the dynamics of culture contact as reflected in the comedies would provide a unique contribution to Samoa's social and cultural history. One likely venue for such investigations are the sizable Samoan communities abroad, in the United States and New Zealand, for example, where comedy sketches are as popular as they are back home.

In his reflections on the richly liminal nature of cultural performance, Turner comments on the constructive role of ambivalence in regard to the canons of social convention. For Turner, the importance of dramatic genres like theater, carnival, and ritual is that they offer us a stage where

> ambiguity reigns: people and public policies may be judged skeptically in relation to deep values; the vices, follies, stupidities, and abuses of contemporary holders of high political, economic, or religious status may be satirized, ridiculed or contemned (sic) in terms of axiomatic values, or these personages may be rebuked for gross failures in common sense (1984:22).

As Samoa navigates the fragile bridge "betwixt and between" the cultural epochs of ancient Polynesia and the modern West, we will continue to rely on our clowns to keep us both amused and alert to the serpentine currents below.

NOTES

The data for this chapter are based on six performances of *fale aitu* (traditional comedies) in six different villages over a 15-year period from 1973 to 1988, including personal observations and interviews in the following six villages: Pago Pago (March, April 1988, February 1989), Apia (May, July, August 1988), Poutasi (June, July 1988), Lalomauga (September 1988), Sasa'ai (June 1984, October–December 1988), Pua-

Comic Theater in Samoa

pua (November 1988). The research was supported by grants from the East-West Center and the Ford Foundation and facilitated by logistical support from the National University of Samoa and the Department of Rural and Economic Development (Ofisa o le Pulenu'u) of Western Samoa, the Folk Arts Program of the American Samoa Council for Arts, Culture, and Humanities, and residents of the aforementioned villages on the islands of Upolu, Savai'i, and Tutuila. For important discussions on the nature of traditional clowning in Samoa, I am especially grateful to Professor Bradd Shore and High Talking Chief Savea Foma'i Sapolu. For assistance with translations and helpful discussions regarding various possibilities for interpretation, I thank Lauano Ati Ilaoa.

1. As the nature and practice, if not frequency, of comic sketches are basically identical in Western and American Samoa, in this chapter I use the terms *Samoa* and *Samoans* to underline the prevailing cultural-ethnic identification that long predates the divisive, colonially imposed categories.

2. In addition to the public clowning forms discussed in this chapter, there is much nonpublic clowning in Samoa as well. I am grateful to Tialuga Sunia Seloti (personal communication) for the distinction between stage and cafeteria clowns, the latter tending to entertain others in communal working situations—like planting or weeding in the garden, for example. These informal clowns tend to improvise comic routines involving their co-workers and the task at hand and are appreciated for helping to make the work light.

3. At the 1988 dedication of a traditional Samoan building for the national teachers' association, the usual group songs and dances were punctuated with improvised clowning dances and skits. Virtually all women, these spontaneous clowns ranged from middle age to their early sixties, with the elders being more inventive and well received by the audience. At one time there were ten or more women from different village groups improvising a comic dance contest that extemporaneously evolved into a skit after one dancer began using a fallen tree branch as a telescope to "spy" on the other dancers.

4. Shore describes the role of comedy sketches as "covertly regulatory institutions" of social control (1978:177). With the exception of Shore's ethnographic studies of Samoa, there is scant mention of clowning practices and traditions by other anthropologists.

5. As such, Shore (1978:175–76) elaborates on Bateson's (1936:175–77) notions of complementarity and symmetricality by introducing the cross-cutting categories of ranked and unranked relations. In the latter case (Shore 185–87), relations are seen to be "structurally 'parallel' in some important sense, but logically or functionally complementary," for example, as marking bonds between brother and sister or high chief and orator.

6. For purposes of this discussion, I use the term *neocolonial* to denote the condition of informal colonialism as it exists in different versions in

American Samoa and Western Samoa. In American Samoa, the term *U.S. territory* is the official (euphemistic) designation for what is, in effect, a colony of the United States. While provisions for traditional governance systems were made as part of the original Deed of Cession, the prevailing frame of reference and political authority remains that of U.S. law. In Western Samoa, nearly thirty years of political independence have done little to alter the economic (and thus, it could be argued, political) hegemony of New Zealand and other Commonwealth nations. In recent years, such pervasive Western influence has been exacerbated for all Samoa by widespread exposure to American television and advertising via broadcasting from the American Samoa TV station, as well as increased availability of imported commodities, including Western foods, clothing, and electronic equipment of all kinds. Cash remittances in American dollars from Western Samoans employed in American Samoa, Hawaii, California, and elsewhere in the United States contribute to this trend. For helpful discussions about the prevailing forms of informal colonialism in Samoa, I am grateful to Iosefa Maiava, an astute political analyst and social commentator.

7. In Samoan, a widespread term for this comic actor is *fai fale aitu*, (the [one] who does/makes the comedy sketch). In English, most Samoans use the word *comedian*. In this chapter I use the terms *comic, clown,* and *comedian* interchangeably.

8. Comedy sketches are extremely popular with many Samoans and generally the highlight of any performance event. While filming performances at the 1988 Independence Day festivities, I met another Samoan who was filming comedy sketches for his relatives in Los Angeles.

9. Chiefs may also be targets of ridicule, although far less often than other authority figures, according to my consultants. While I could find no published or recorded performances of this kind, several consultants report having seen sketches targeting either a minister and chief together or the political machinations of candidates vying for chief's title.

A highly knowledgeable consultant reports seeing a performance several years ago in which a village pastor was being lampooned so skillfully and accurately that the pastor himself laughed hard enough to fall from his chair in the audience. He apparently required some medical assistance, and later the comedian was fined for succeeding at his art rather too well. This is the only such instance of formal retaliation against an actor that I encountered in my interviews and secondary research.

10. Kapferer describes a similar "role-distancing" (in Goffman's 1961 phrase) in his fascinating study of Sinhalese rituals of exorcism. Here, the "exorcist-dancers overelaborate their performance" by comically exaggerating gestures that cause errors like tripping, falling, and dropping torches, thus breaking the flow of the dance and its correspondingly demonic spell through laughter (1984:197–98). See Erving Goffman (1961:85–152) for his important essay on "role-distance."

11. Bakhtin writes that one important function of the medieval clown was to "degrade" the high gesture of ceremony and ritual to the more mundane realm of sexuality and other "lower" bodily functions (1968:20).

12. According to several female consultants, women do perform as comedians in comic sketches, but only in the context of an all-female audience. They remarked on the high degree of skill of women clowns, at the same time concurring with male consultants in the idea that women should not perform in mixed company given the frequent instances of sexual joking by both male and female clowns. Nevertheless, I did interview and film one woman whose claim to be the only female performing comedy sketches publicly to mixed audiences was borne out by other consultants and my own observation. When she does perform, however, it is always in an assisting role rather than as lead comedian.

13. Secondary schools in Apia often include student-produced comedies in their year-end or other special celebrations. Two consultants now in their early thirties also recalled frequent performances that were improvised as part of recreational school assemblies.

14. Kneubuhl, the noted Samoan playwright, recalls first seeing this sketch performed in the 1940s in Pago Pago by American sailors stationed in American Samoa during World War II (1988).

15. Like other accomplished comedians, Petelo is very much in demand by church groups and other organizations to direct and perform the comic portions of their fund-raising shows. One consultant reports that Petelo was persuaded several years ago to move abroad at the request of several church groups in the Los Angeles area, home to one the largest populations of Samoans outside Samoa. He has apparently acquired an agent and made at least one videotape of his performances.

16. According to Bakhtin, such "sacred parody" of sermons delivered in the vernacular, in addition to prayers, carols, and saints' legends, was part of the stock repertoire of the medieval comic theater (1968:14–15). See also Prell's 1988 report of "sacred parody" in a contemporary Jewish religious service.

17. In "symmetrical" relations, on the other hand, as Shore (1978: 185) has adapted Batesons' (1936:177) notion of "symmetricality," conflict is the cultural expectation and thus can be formally mediated by customary legal or judiciary sanctions. For example, two chiefs of equal rank or two villages might exemplify this type of relationship.

18. In regard to the mimetic and didactic potential of the comedies, one consultant, who is a popular "stage" clown in his small village, comments on the value of such parodies to demonstrate to the audience some of the absurdities and pitfalls of conjugal arguments.

19. For an exploration of such anomalous themes in *fale aitu* as symptomatic of "internalized" colonialism, see my 1992 study, *Traditional Comic Theater in Samoa: A Holographic View*. In chapter 5, "Neo-colonial Postscript: The Dismantled Self," and chapter 6 on "re-constructing a

cultural self," I discuss this issue in the context of neo- and post-colonial critiques by writers such as Frantz Fanon (1967, 1968); Aime Cesaire (1972); O. Mannioni (1964); A. Memmi (1965); and Gloria Anzaldua (1987).

20. In Sinavaiana (1992), chapter 7, "Historical Variations and the Art of Cultural Change," and chapter 8, "Backtalk from the Margins," I discuss the transformative potential of *fale aitu* as a traditional artform with an implicit project of resistance. For important work which foregrounds the agency of colonized peoples in resisting oppression, see Homi K. Bhabha (1986); Eugene Genovese (1972); Keith Basso (1979); Jill Sweet (1990); James C. Scott (1985); Michel de Certeau (1984); and Richard Terdiman (1985). For other groundbreaking work which explores the emergence of marginalized voices into the centrist discourse of cultural politics, see Trinh T. Minh-ha (1990); Cornel West (1990); Anthony Kwame Appiah (1988); Bell Hooks (1990); and Kobena Mercer (1990).

21. Bakhtin's discussion of the liberating aspects of the "carnival grotesque" in medieval European comedies could as well apply to comedy sketches among Samoans (1968:34).

REFERENCES

Appiah, Kwame Anthony
    1988   Topologies of Nativism. *Yale Journal of Criticism.* Fall 1988, vol. 2, no. 1.

Anzaldua, Gloria
    1987   *Borderlands/La Frontera: The New Mestiza.* San Francisco: Spinsters/Aunt Lute.

Bakhtin, Mikhail
    1968   *Rabelais and His World.* Trans. Helene Iswolsky. Cambridge: Harvard University Press.
    1981   *The Dialogic Imagination,* ed. Michael Holquist. Austin: University of Texas Press.

Basso, Keith H.
    1979   *Portraits of the Whiteman: Linguistic Play and Cultural Symbols among the Western Apache.* Cambridge: Cambridge University Press.

Bateson, Gregory
    1936   *Naven.* Cambridge: Cambridge University Press.

Bhabha, Homi K.
    1986   Signs Taken for Wonders. In *"Race," Writing and Difference,* ed. Henry Louis Gates, Jr. Chicago: University of Chicago Press.

Certeau, Michel de
    1984   *The Practice of Everyday Life*. Trans. Steven F. Rendall. Berkeley and Los Angeles: University of California Press.
Cesaire, Aime
    1972   *Discourse on Colonialism*. Trans. Joan Pinkham. New York: Monthly Review Press.
Fanon, Frantz
    1967   *Black Skin, White Masks*. Trans. Charles L. Markmann. New York: Grove Press.
    1968   *The Wretched of the Earth*. New York: Grove Press.
Genovese, Eugene
    1976   *Roll, Jordan, Roll: The World The Slaves Made*. New York: Vintage.
Goffman, Erving
    1961   Role Distance. In *Encounters: Two Studies in the Sociology of Interaction*. Indianapolis: Bobbs-Merrill.
Hooks, Bell
    1990   Marginality as Site of Resistance. In *Out There: Marginalization and Contemporary Cultures*. ed. R. Ferguson, M. Gever, T. Minh-ha, and C. West. New York: The New Museum of Contemporary Art, and Cambridge: MIT Press.
Kapferer, Bruce
    1984   The Ritual Process and the Problem of Reflexivity in Sinhalese Demon Exorcisms. In *Rite, Drama, Festival, Spectacle: Rehearsals Toward a Theory of Cultural Performance*, ed. John J. MacAloon, pp. 186–205. Philadelphia: Institute for the Study of Human Issues.
Kneubuhl, John
    1988   Personal communication with Caroline Sinavaiana. Taputimu, American Samoa. June 30, 1988.
Mannioni, O.
    1962   *Prospero and Caliban: The Psychology of Colonization*. New York: Praeger.
Memmi, Albert
    1965   *The Colonizer and the Colonized*. New York: Orien.
Mercer, Kobena
    1990   Travelling Theory: The Cultural Politics of Race and Representation. Interview by Lorraine Kenny. *Afterimage*, September.
Minh-ha, Trinh T.
    1990   Cotton and Iron. In *Out There: Marginalization and Contemporary Cultures*, ed. R. Ferguson, M. Gever, T. Minh-ha, and C.

West. New York: The New Museum of Contemporary Art, and Cambridge: MIT Press.

Prell, Riv-Ellen
 1988 Laughter That Hurts: Ritual Humor and Ritual Change in an American Jewish Community. In *Between Two Worlds: Ethnographic Essays on American Jewry*, ed. Jack Kugelmass, pp. 192–221. Cornell: Cornell University Press.

Scott, James C.
 1985 *Weapons of the Weak: Everyday Forms of Peasant Resistance.* New Haven: Yale University Press.

Seloti, Tialuga Sunia
 1989 Personal communication with Caroline Sinavaiana. Mapusaga, American Samoa. September 29, 1989.

Shore, Bradd
 1978 Ghosts and Government: A Structural Analysis of Alternative Institutions for Conflict Management in Samoa. *Man* (N.S.) 13:175–99.
 1977 A Samoan Theory of Action: Social Control and Social Order in a Polynesian Paradox. Ph.D. diss., University of Chicago.

Sinavaiana, Caroline
 1992 *Traditional Comic Theater in Samoa: A Holographic View.* Ph.D. diss., University of Hawaii.

Sweet, Jill D.
 1989 Burlesquing "The Other" in Pueblo Performance. *Annals of Tourism Research* 16:62–75.

Terdiman, Richard
 1985 *Discourse/Counter-Discourse: The Theory and Practice of Symbolic Resistance in Nineteenth-Century France.* Ithaca: Cornell University Press.

Turner, Victor
 1984 Liminality and the Performative Genres. In *Rite, Drama, Festival, Spectacle: Rehearsals Toward a Theory of Cultural Performance*, ed. John J. MacAloon, pp. 19–40. Philadelphia: Institute for the Study of Human Issues.

West, Cornel
 1990 The New Cultural Politics of Difference. In *Out There: Marginalization and Contemporary Cultures*, ed. R. Ferguson, M. Gever, T. Minh-ha, and C. West. New York: The New Museum of Contemporary Art, and Cambridge: MIT Press.

Notes on Contributors
Index

Notes on Contributors

KATHLEEN BARLOW is Visiting Assistant Professor in Anthropology at Macalester College, St. Paul, Minnesota. Publications based on her fieldwork with the Murik in Papua New Guinea include papers on female initiation, the dynamics of sibling relationships, male and female symbolism, and the role of women in trade. Presently she is collaborating on a study of regional exchange on the north coast of Papua New Guinea, with her focus on women's ritual and art.

DAVID R. COUNTS is Professor and Chair of Anthropology at McMaster University, Hamilton, Ontario, Canada, where he has taught since 1968. His research interests with the Lusi-Kaliai of New Britain, Papua New Guinea, include linguistics, social and economic change, and aging and dying. He is co-editor with Dorothy Counts of *Aging and Its Transformations: Moving Toward Death in Pacific Societies*, an earlier volume in this series.

DOROTHY A. COUNTS is Professor and Chair of Anthropology at the University of Waterloo, Waterloo, Ontario, Canada, where she has taught since 1968. Her publications on the Lusi-Kaliai include studies of folklore *(Tales of Laupu)*, female suicide, and domestic violence. She is co-editor of the recent volume, *Sanctions and Sanctuary: Cultural Perspectives on the Beating of Wives*. With David Counts, she is presently making a study of retired nomadic RVers in North America.

VILSONI HERENIKO is Assistant Professor in Pacific Literature, Center for Pacific Islands Studies, University of Hawaii at Manoa, Honolulu, Hawaii. One of the Pacific Islands' best-known young playwrights, he was born on Rotuman Island in Fiji and recently received his doctorate from the University of the South Pacific. His revised dissertation on the Rotuman clown is forthcoming from the University of Hawaii Press.

MARTHA MACINTYRE is a Senior Lecturer in the Sociology Department at La Trobe University, Bundoora, Victoria, Australia. Her field work on the small island of Tubetube, Milne Bay Province, Papua New Guinea, includes articles on kinship, gender, and exchange. She is also author of *The Kula: A Bibliography* and co-editor of *Family and Gender in the Pacific: Domestic Contradiction and the Colonial Impact.*

WILLIAM E. MITCHELL is Professor of Anthropology at the University of Vermont, Burlington. His early research was among New York City Chinese and Jewish families while his Pacific fieldwork has taken him to the Iatmul, Lujere, and Wape of Papua New Guinea's Sepik River Basin. His Pacific publications include studies of exchange, witchcraft, and therapeutic systems as well as an account of his Wape fieldwork, *The Bamboo Fire,* and the video film, *Magical Curing.* Most recently he coedited *Sepik Heritage: Transition and Heritage in Papua New Guinea* and is currently preparing a monograph on the seminomadic Lujere of the upper Sepik.

MARK S. MOSKO is Associate Professor and Chair of Anthropology at Hartwick College, Oneonta, New York. His most recent fieldwork with the North Mekeo, Central Province, Papua New Guinea, was in 1990. Included among his Mekeo publications are articles on kinship, religion, and social history, and a book, *Quadripartite Structures: Categories, Relations and Homologies in Bush Mekeo Culture.* His current research interests center on a comparison of personhood and agency in Melanesia and Polynesia and the problem of hierarchy in the Austronesian sphere.

CAROLINE SINAVAIANA is a founder of and Director and Resource Consultant in Intercultural Communications for the Pacific-Asia Institute for the Arts and Human Sciences, Pago Pago, American Samoa. Born in Samoa, she is currently involved in a variety of community-based projects in Samoa, Hawaii, and California as diverse as environmental management, art therapy, and traditional folk arts. Her dissertation for her recent doctorate in the Department of American Studies, University of Hawaii, is "House of the Spirits: A Social/Cultural History of Comic Theater in Samoa."

Index

Agency, 143, 196
Aggression, and joking relationships, 68
Alford, Finnegan, 40–41*n22*
Anthropology, 145; and clowning, vii–viii, 4, 34–35; and humor, 6–7, 9–10, 39*n7*, 39*n8*, 88, 104, 168–69; and rituals, 29–30, 161*n18*, 167–68
Antu Kikira (Lusi-Kaliai parody of outsiders), 95–96, 103*n8*
Apte, Mahadev L., 6, 167, 169; on gender, 33, 62; on humor and culture, 20, 39*n7*; on joking relationships vs. ritual clowning, 31, 104–05, 115, 123–24
Archetypes, and parody, 99
Aristotle, 13
Armin, Robert, 16
Audiences: and Lusi-Kaliai clowning, 93, 99; and Rotuman wedding clowns, 174; and Samoan comic sketches, 196, 203
Authority: figures and Samoan comic sketches, 195–96, 203–04, 206, 210–12, 214*n9*; of Rotuman clowns, 174–75
Avoidance relationships, 59, 82*n1*, 150

Babcock, Barbara, 160*n14*, 184
Bachelard, Gaston, 44*n50*
Bailey, F. M., 161–62*n20*
Bakhtin, Mikhail, 43*n46*, 146, 211, 215*n11*, 215*n16*
Barba, Eugenio, 10–11
Bateson, Gregory, 3, 60, 84*n15*, 213*n5*, 215*n17*, 216*n21*
Baudelaire, 38*n6*
Berger, Arthur A., 185*n1*
Bergson, Henri, 22
Bligh, Captain William, 21–22
Bruner, Edward M., 10
Burlesque, 138, 200; and *ipani* eating, 108–09, 113; as a technique, viii, 193

Carnival, 145–47, 156, 216*n21*
Chambers, Erve, 39–40*n16*
Charivaris, 23, 139–40
Chesterfield, Lord, 5, 13
Children: Lusi-Kaliai, 92–93, 95–96; Murik, 67, 68, 69, 70, 84*n14*
Church, the: and clowning, 17, 20, 201–03. *See also* Missionaries; Religion
Clarke, William C., 42*n32*
Clowning, viii, 19, 27–28, 82*n2*; as cultural conservation or subversion, 8–9, 19–20, 23, 24–25, 31, 37, 43*n45*, 43*n46*, 59, 78–79, 133–34, 143, 146–47, 157, 159*n4*, 169, 175, 183; informal, 28–29, 93, 192, 213*n2*, 213*n3*; limitations on, 67, 171, 174, 187*n20*; political implications of, viii, 4–5, 19–20, 22–25, 35, 43*n45*, 201, 210–12; ritual, 3, 20–21, 29–31, 37, 61, 90–93, 98–100, 138–40, 159–60*n8*, 161*n18*; ritual, vs. joking relationships, 31, 104–05, 115, 123–24; sacred, 4, 29–31, 148–51, 167–87; theatrical, 32–33, 152–55; types of, 4, 28, 82*n3*

223

Colonialism, 20, 203–04, 207–12, 213–14n6
Comedy sketches. *See* Skits
Communication, clowning as, 30
Compensation: for informal clowning, 68, 69; for kinship obligations, 65, 73, 110, 114, 126n8; for ritual clowning, 77–78, 93, 126n9, 133–34, 139–40, 151, 171, 185n61; for Samoan comic sketches, 198, 203
Competition, among Murik, 64–65
Conflicts: displacement of, by clowning, 59, 65, 178–80, 193; and Samoan comic sketches, 198, 206, 208, 211–12, 215n17
Connerton, Paul, 43n46
Contradictions, 30, 79, 141; of age and gender hierarchies, 62, 65; role, 60, 123, 134; as a technique, 19, 200–01, 202
Costume: and Lusi-Kaliai clowning, 91, 93–94, 102n3; nakedness as, 150; of Rotuman invited clown, 171–72, 181, 186n17, 186n18; and Samoan comic sketches, 197
Cox, Harvey, 184
Criticism, viii, 19–20, 143; and Samoan comic sketches, 192–93, 196, 211–12
Cultural reproduction: clowning as, 24, 37, 159n4; mortuary feasting as, 31, 105, 114, 120–21, 123, 124
Culture, and humor, ix, 13, 26–27
Curing festivals, 32, 146–62

Dance: Murik, 63, 74–77; Rotuman, 172–78, 186n15; Samoan, 192; Wape, 147, 148–51, 160–61n13
Darwin, Charles, 11, 38n4
Davis, Natalie Z., 23
Death and mourning, 30–31, 58; of the Murik, 74–79, 81; of the North Mekeo, 31, 104–26; on Tubetube, 131–34
Deconception, by North Mekeo mortuary feast, 108–09, 121–23
Desires, human, 61, 79–81
Dickson, W. J., 8
Doran, John, 42n34, 42n38
Double entendre, of Murik women, 71
Douglas, Mary, 60–61, 66, 73, 78, 79, 134, 157, 161n17
Dyad vs. group interaction, 31, 82n2, 104, 114–15, 123

Eco, Umberto, 159n4
Edman, Irwin, 40n18
Eggan, Fred, 59
Ekman, P., 11
Embarrassment, and laughter, 41n23
Emotions, study of, 10–12, 40n19
Erasmus, 38n2
Europeans, 16–18; mocking of, 95–96, 133; and Samoan comic sketches, 193–94, 201, 203–04, 207–10, 212; and Wape carnival, 156–57
Evans-Pritchard, E. E., 104
Exaggeration, as a technique, 19, 68, 141, 200, 214n10

Fale aitu (Samoan comedy sketches), 192–216
Fear, and laughter, 14, 41n27
Feinberg, Leonard, 41n26
Fertility ceremonies, 21, 110, 168, 181, 183–84
Fiji. *See* Rotuma
Firstborn ceremonies, 89, 92–93, 94, 181
Folklore, 8, 88–89
Food and feeding, 63, 64, 84n16; and *ipani* eating, 104–26; and the Murik, 71, 75–77; and the Tubetube, 133–34, 142
Fools, 140; historically, 15–19, 20, 41–42n30
Foucault, Michel, 41–42n30
Freud, Sigmund, 7–8, 14, 59

Gardiner, Stanley, 181
Geertz, Clifford, 59, 60, 79
Gell, Alfred, 21, 43n41, 83n7
Gender, 94, 155; of clowns and jokers, 17, 33–34, 35, 90–91, 142, 168, 197, 215n12
Gender roles, 59; of the Lusi-Kaliai, 99; of the Murik, 77, 80; of the North Mekeo, 125n7; reversal of, 93–94, 147, 175–76, 179, 182–83; of

Index

Samoans, 193, 194; of the Wape, 151, 153–54, 157–58; and work, 110, 112, 135, 142
Gender status, 58, 61–63, 65, 82n1, 82–83n6
Genitals, and clowning, 21–22, 67, 102n3, 149–50, 160–61n13
Ghosts. *See* Spirits
Gluckman, Max, 43n45, 59
Goody, Jack R., 68
Greediness, and *ipani* eating, 111–13, 117–18
Groos, K., 10

Hammond, P., 169
Hän mane 'äk su (Rotuman invited clown), 171–87
Handelman, Don, ix, 24, 30, 44n51
Hau'ofa, Epeli, 11–12, 22, 125n5
Hazlitt, William, 27, 41n22
Hertz, Robert, 107
Hierarchy, 43n46, 60, 61, 62; Murik, 65, 78, 80; Rotuman, 182–83; Samoan, 201, 206. *See also* Status
Hobbes, Thomas, 13
Hooper, Antony, 169
Horn, Andrew, 180–81
Hospitality: Lusi-Kaliai, 92; Murik, 71–72, 75–77, 84n18; North Mekeo, 108, 111–13, 117–18; Rotuman, 174, 179; Tubetube, 133–34, 142
Humiliation. *See* Ridicule
Humor, 5, 7, 10, 12–13, 26, 37–38n1, 40n20, 40n21, 40–41n22, 44n48; and culture, ix, 25–27; function of, 168–69; study of, 6–10, 12–15; on Tubetube, 140–41
Huntsman, Judith, 169

Iatmuls, 3
Incongruity, 41n28; and theory of laughter, 14
Indonesia, 43n42
Initiation, Murik, 70, 73–74, 81
Instruction, 23–24; and joking relationships, 31, 60, 66, 68, 71–72; and *mwara* kin, 65, 73
Inversion, 44n50; as a comic technique, 17, 19, 178–79, 182; of hierarchies, 43n46, 145, 211

Ioane (Rotuman clown), 181
Ipani eating, 104–26
Irony, as a technique, 200

Jiare, Vafo'ou, 186–87n19
Joking relationships, 31; Murik, 59, 65–84; vs. ritual clowning, 31, 104–05, 115, 123–24
Jourbet, Laurent, 13
Jung, Carl G., 162n25

Kant, Immanuel, 14
Kapferer, Bruce, 10–11, 24, 44n51, 214n10
Kern, Edith, 38n6
Kierkegaard, Søren, 14
Kinship, 59, 106; and joking relationships, 31, 58, 60, 65–84, 104; mocking of, 150–51, 157–58, 198, 206; obligations of, 99–100, 114, 153–54; rearrangement of, in mortuary feast, 58, 108, 117–18, 120–23; tensions of 171, 178–79, 186n15
Kiyo (shaming ceremony), 138–40
Kneubuhl, John, 215n14
Kneubuhl, Victoria, 169

Laughter, 5, 38n3, 38n4, 38n6; functions of, 13–15, 43–44n47, 84n20, 143
Lawick-Goodall, Jane van, 38n4
Leach, E. R., 29
Levy, Robert I., 23
Lewis, Gilbert, 161n18
"License to joke," 24, 31, 152
Lowie, Robert, 37, 104, 168–69
Lusi-Kaliai, the, 88–103
Lutz, Catherine, 11

MacAloon, John J., 10–11
MacGregor, Gordon, 185n5
Magic, 20, 36–37
Makarius, Laura, 77, 168
Malefijt, A. M. deW., 66
Malinowski, Bronislaw, 6
Marriage, 74; and exchange of North Mekeo, 106–07, 120–23; Lusi-Kaliai parody of, 96–98; tensions of, 99, 178–79, 206–09; and weddings, 91, 167–87

Martin, Lilian J., 37–38*n1*
Masks, 146, 148–49, 160*n12*
Mayo, Elton, 8
McGhee, Paul E., 43*n44*
McGregor, Donald E., 160*n10*, 161*n19*
McNamara, Brooks, 10
Mead, Margaret, 83*n7*
Melanesia, viii, 12, 43*n42*, 62, 145
Men: and joking on Tubetube, 140, 142. *See also* Gender; Gender roles; Gender status
Metacommunication, 60, 61, 79
Missionaries, 21–22, 132, 203; and the Wape, 156, 160–61*n13*, 162*n26*
Modesty. *See* Nakedness
Morenhout, 181
Morreall, John, 14–15
Mortuary ceremonies. *See* Death and mourning
Mother, role of: and the Murik, 63, 69, 80; and the Wape, 155
Mother Folly, 17, 38*n2*
Mourning. *See* Death and mourning
Munro, D. H., 13
Murdock, George Peter, 169
Murik, the, 30–31, 58–84
Mwara kin, 65–84

Nachman, Steven R., 160*n13*
Nakedness, 31, 67, 69–70, 102*n3*, 149–50, 160–61*n13*
Neediness, and the Murik, 61, 69, 77, 80
Nelson, T.G.A., 159*n4*
Niyel festivals, 32, 146–62
North Mekeo, the, 29–30, 104–26
Nudity. *See* Nakedness

O'Connor, John, 42*n35*
Order and disorder, 36–37, 38*n6*, 44*n54*; and clown as critic, 19, 37, 61, 182; and incongruity and humor, 5–6, 26, 41*n28*
Ortner, Sherry B., 62
Outsiders, mocking of, 91, 95–98, 133, 137, 154, 193–94

Papua New Guinea, 21, 43*n42*. *See also* Lusi-Kaliai, the; Murik, the; North Mekeo, the

Parman, Susan, 182
Parsons, Elsie Clews, 33
Pascal, Blaise, 22–23
Performance, viii, 10–11, 60
Petelo, 201, 215*n15*
Philosophy, and humor, 7, 12–13
Piddington, Ralph, 6, 39*n8*
Plato, 13, 22
Play, study of, 10
Plessner, Helmuth, 38*n6*
Politics of clowning. *See* Clowning, political implications of
Polynesia, viii, 18, 21, 33, 43*n42*, 62
Postmodernism, 9–10, 35–36, 40*n18*, 44*n52*
Power, 22–24, 100–01; and women, 70–71, 74, 82–83*n6*, 143, 147. *See also* Hierarchy; Status
Prescott, William H., 42*n37*
Protection: by Lusi-Kaliai kin, 99–100, 102*n4*; by *mwara* kin, 71–72, 73–74, 84*n17*
Psychoanalysis, and humor, 7
Psychology, and humor, 8

Radcliffe-Brown, A. R., 7, 59, 104, 168
Relief theory, of laughter, 14
Religion; 36–37. *See also* Church, the; Missionaries
Reproduction, cultural. *See* Cultural reproduction
Respect relationships, 59, 82*n1*, 115, 135; and Samoan comic sketches, 193, 204–06, 208
Ridicule, 99; and power differentials, 98, 195; as social criticism, 22–24, 138–40, 193–94
Rites of passage, 58. *See also* Death and mourning; Firstborn ceremonies; Initiation, Murik; Marriage, and weddings
Ritual clowning. *See* Clowning, ritual
Roasts, 23
Roethlisberger, F. J., 8
Role reversal, 23, 143, 168, 175–76, 195, 200–01, 206, 211
Roles. *See* Gender roles; Hierarchy; Role reversal
Rosaldo, Michelle, 62

Index

Rotuma, 31, 167–87
Rutz, Henry, 168

Samoa, 21, 32–33, 43$n42$, 192–216
Santayana, 41$n28$
Satire, 153–54, 193, 202–03
Savarese, Nicola, 10–11
Scaletta, Naomi M., 92
Schechner, Richard, 10–11
Scheff, T. J., 84$n20$
Schopenhauer, Arthur, 14, 37–38$n1$
Science, 36–37
Secret societies, 61, 83–84$n13$; Lusi-Kaliai, 94, 102–03$n7$; Murik, 66–67, 70, 73–74, 76
Self-presentation, 67
Seloti, Tialuga Sunia, 213$n2$
Sexuality, 59, 149, 177–78, 196–97; and the Murik, 69–71, 76–77, 80; and the Tubetube, 135–37, 142
Shaming ceremony *(kiyo)*, 138–40
Shore, Bradd, 21, 169, 193, 196, 201, 213$n4$, 213$n5$, 215$n17$
Siegel, Lee, ix
Skits, 21, 32, 137–38; during Niyel festival, 32, 152–55, 162$n22$; and Samoan comedy sketches, 192–216
Social organization, 64, 90, 106–07 147–48, 170, 194
Sociology, and humor, 8–9
Songs, 192
Sorrell, Walter, 9
Speech, clowning vs. joking, viii, 37–38$n1$, 82$n2$
Spencer, George Herbert, 14
Spirits, 77, 89; and license of clowns, 31, 195–96; and the Lusi-Kaliai, 92–93, 94, 95–96; and Rotuman weddings, 180–82, 183–84; and the Wape, 149, 159$n3$
Status, 17–18, 21, 29, 60, 61–63; and the Murik, 61, 65, 79–81, 82–83$n6$; and Rotuman wedding clowning, 176–77; and Samoan comic sketches, 195, 197, 206; and the Tubetube, 134, 139–40, 142
Steward, Julian, 3, 104
Strathern, Marilyn, 126$n18$
Superiority theory, 13–14, 22

Sweet, Jill D., 22
Swortzell, Lowell, 42$n34$, 42$n39$

Taboos, and humor, 40–41$n22$
Tahiti, 21, 23, 43$n42$
Talawasi (Tubetube jests), 130–38, 141–43
Tanner, Adrian, 168
Tensions, 84$n20$, 99–100; relieved through clowning, 59, 178–79, 183, 201, 210–12
Tonga, 22
Towsen, John H., 33, 42$n34$, 42$n39$
Transvestism, 23, 151, 181, 196; and Lusi-Kaliai, 90–91, 102$n3$
Tubetube, 28, 30, 130–43
Turner, George, 18
Turner, Victor, 10–11, 43$n46$, 59, 78, 186$n11$, 211, 212
Tyler, Stephen A., 9, 40$n17$

Values, cultural. *See* Clowning, as cultural conservation

Wape, the, 3–4, 31, 32, 42$n31$, 146–62
Weddings. *See* Marriage, and weddings
Welsford, Enid, 15, 18, 42$n38$
Werbner, Pnina, 168
Werbner, Richard P., 43$n41$
Westerners. *See* Europeans
White, Geoffrey M., 11
Wierzbicka, Anna, 11
Wife beating, 72, 99–100
Wikan, Unni, 40$n19$
Wilde, Alan, 44$n33$
Willeford, William, 42$n34$
Women: Lusi-Kaliai, 99; Murik, 58, 61–63, 80; Rotuman, 167–87; Tubetube, 130–37, 139–40, 142–43. *See also* Gender; Gender roles; Gender status
Work, 59, 135; and *ipani* eating, 109–14, 117, 125$n7$

Xiaotong, 23, 25

Zijderveld, Anton C., 20, 39$n15$, 41–42$n30$, 159$n4$